NO HUNGER IN PARADISE

The Players. The Journey. The Dream.

MICHAEL
CALVIN

NO HUNGER IN PARADISE

The Players. The Journey. The Dream.

CENTURY

1 3 5 7 9 10 8 6 4 2

Century
20 Vauxhall Bridge Road
London SW1V 2SA

Century is part of the Penguin Random House group of companies whose addresses can be found at global.penguinrandomhouse.com.

Song lyrics on page 106 – 'Many of Horror' written by Simon Neil/Biffy Clyro

First published by Century in 2017

www.penguin.co.uk

A CIP catalogue record for this book is available from the British Library.

ISBN 9781780896304

Typeset in 12.5/17 pt Minion by Jouve (UK), Milton Keynes
Printed and bound by Clays Ltd, St Ives plc

Penguin Random House is committed to a sustainable future for our business, our readers and our planet. This book is made from Forest Stewardship Council® certified paper.

For Lynn. The best youth coach I have worked with.

Contents

Acknowledgements

One of the enduring privileges of sportswriting is the access to greatness it allows. Household names become familiar figures and, occasionally, firm friends, but generally professional protocol demands a certain distance. I have breached unwritten rules by asking for an autograph only twice in more than thirty years. The first was given, with a salesman's smoothness, by a childhood hero, Pelé. The second was given, with customary grace, by Nelson Mandela.

I was in South Africa, preparing to cover a historic Rugby World Cup, when he made a memorable speech at the launch of his children's charity in Pretoria on May 8, 1995. It crystallised his compassion, dignity and foresight, and began with the observation that 'there can be no keener revelation of a society's soul than the way in which it treats its children'.

Those famous words lived with me through the

hundreds of hours of interviews I conducted for this book, each of which was transcribed by Caroline Flatley, who, as ever, was an invaluable sounding board during the writing process. I met many good people, burdened by the knowledge that, with shining exceptions, football does not treat its children kindly.

I hope this book will be a catalyst for a debate about how the game can better fulfil its duty of care. I know this may be unfashionable in an age of institutionalised mendacity, alternative facts and fake news, but I have faith in my trade to concentrate minds and challenge consciences.

The recent sexual abuse scandal confirms that what we still refer to as Fleet Street contains writers who will continue to do justice to such an important subject. Arresting work has already been done by Daniel Taylor, Ian Herbert, Henry Winter, Paul Hayward, Matt Lawton, Oliver Holt, John Cross, Oliver Kay, Matt Hughes, Matt Dickinson and others.

Developmental football also has important advocates in the sphere of social media. Sites like YouthHawk, Youth Academies and Scouts In Attendance provide an enlightening overview. Individuals like Aidan Roberts (England Youth), Philip Rolfe (Chelsea Youth) and the pairing of Gavin Cooper and Andrew Waldon (MCFC Reserves & Academy) offer insightful, exhaustive coverage.

I am hugely grateful to all those who agreed to speak to me, on and off the record, during my research. We might not always agree, but I thank Dan Johnson, of the Premier

League, for his rigour and professionalism. I am in the debt of Scott Field, Amanda Docherty, Andy Walker and James Webb, FA employees past and present.

At club level I valued the assistance and advice of Vicky Kloss, Simon Heggie, Alex Rowan, Phil Townsend, Dan Tolhurst, Simon Felstein, Matt Cecil, Paul McCarthy and Bruce Talbot. Tim Rich, Sally Wheatman, Tom Hopkinson and George Caulkin helped me along the way. Dominic Fifield alerted me to the importance of the affirming work being done at the Afewee Training Centre where Peter Armstrong was wonderfully supportive. To get a flavour of Steadman Scott's character and accomplishments, I would recommend *Uncle Steadman*, the 2013 film, directed by Stuart Everitt for Marmalade Productions. To gain further insight into systematic challenges, I would recommend the writing of Matt Whitehouse and Martin Calladine.

My name may be on the cover, but I have a great team behind me. I thank Ben Brusey, Selina Walker and Susan Sandon at Century for their faith and support. Huw Armstrong, Charlotte Bush, Gemma Bareham, Aslan Byrne, Chris Turner, Pippa Wright, Amelia Evans, Rebecca Ikin, Fergus Edmondson, Joanna Taylor, Josh Ireland and Glenn O'Neill, my design guru, have helped enormously. I must thank Razi Mireskandari for his legal insight and Rory Scarfe, my literary agent, for his sagacity.

I'd like to think fatherhood has informed aspects of this book, so I had better give my children, Nicholas,

Aaron, William and Lydia, and my granddaughter, Marielli, the credit they doubtlessly feel they deserve. The canonisation of my wife Lynn, who puts up with my restlessness and distraction during the writing process, can only be a matter of time.

Michael Calvin, February 2017

Preface

When Doves Cry

They are middle-aged men now, trapped in time. Just as the victims of Pompeii were mummified in their death throes, they were engulfed by a pyroclastic flow of fear, shame and self-loathing. Their courage, in confronting the abuse to which they were subjected as children chasing football's dream, is cathartic, but their vulnerability endures in adulthood.

Watching them unburden themselves, tears flowing down faces embalmed by sustained suppression of dark secrets, is a challenge to the concept of a civilised society and to modern sport's deceitful projection of innocence. Their tales of molestation and manipulation stir the conscience, since they conform to a pattern and merely hint at the scale of the scandal.

Football's victims – Andy Woodward, Steve Walters, Chris Unsworth, Jason Dunford, Paul Stewart, David

White, Gary Johnson, Matthew Monaghan and David Eatock, to give due respect to some of the pioneers who waived their right to anonymity – triggered an existential crisis in a game that has sagged beneath the weight of its duty of care.

In years to come Operation Hydrant will resonate alongside Heysel and Hillsborough as shorthand for institutional neglect and the propensity of those in authority to look the other way. At the last count, police were investigating 248 clubs, 184 suspects, 526 victims; there will be others, suffering in the shadows, unwilling to burden their families with the sins of their oppressors.

Research for this book began more than eighteen months before the *Guardian*'s Daniel Taylor followed the finest traditions of his craft in November 2016 and exposed the issue through a searing interview with Woodward, the former journeyman footballer ensnared by convicted paedophile Barry Bennell at Crewe Alexandra, the first of his six clubs.

It is not my intention to dwell on the subject of sexual abuse, since it will continue to be laid bare by more forensic journalists and more knowledgeable specialists than me. But their work chimes with mine, because it seeks to peel back the layers of an industry that can be cavalier with the truth and complacent about the susceptibility of children to the fantasies it creates, and the power it confers.

Youth football has a frontier spirit, since its coaches,

by definition, mould young minds and coax coherence from immature bodies. That is a huge responsibility, an enormous subject. There are few more compelling day-dreams in modern society than overcoming the odds and becoming a professional footballer.

The process incorporates unconditional love and unwise devotion, unacceptable influence and unforgivable cynicism. It has significance beyond the fundamental question of why some players make it, and others fall away into a chasm of apathy or regret. Excesses excused by football's prominence say as much about us, as parents, participants or supporters, as they do about the game itself.

Football's response to cataclysmic revelations of what appears to be a sub-culture of paedophilia has been little different to other institutions confronted by evidence of abhorrent behaviour, such as the Church or the BBC. Selective transparency reveals aspects of organisational culture that those in positions of influence would prefer to remain hidden.

Grandees blustered and blundered. Their advisers sought to scramble towards the moral high ground. An initial instinct for self-protection took hold because in a compensation-conscious society the prospect of football facing a PPI-style financial reckoning chilled administrators, in both clubs and governing bodies, to the marrow.

The Football Association sought to reassure parents

and the wider public just before Christmas 2016 by revealing that 99 per cent of its 7,814 grassroots clubs, encompassing 62,238 teams, had responded to a deadline to renew their safeguarding policies. Those that had not done so were suspended until further notice.

The Premier League stressed in a statement that similarly protective principles and practices have been enshrined in its academy structures. Clubs had followed the highest child-protection standards, being obliged to employ a full-time head of safeguarding, an academy safeguarding officer and a community safeguarding officer, all overseen by a specific board member.

Centres of Excellence operated by Football League clubs are wedded to the same safeguarding policy, which involves constant training and in-house education. The Professional Footballers' Association was rather less precise in outlining the nature of its response, with chief executive Gordon Taylor suggesting there were 'approximately forty' counsellors available to 50,000 current or former players.

Faltering action had greater impact than fine words. There was shameful initial reluctance to offer formal backing to the Offside Trust, an independent charitable organisation established by Woodward and four fellow victims of abuse to support individuals and families who have suffered similarly. It was neither too early nor too raw a topic for a gesture of appropriate benevolence and contrition.

The insistence of Martin Glenn, the FA's chief executive, that there had been no cover-up, was thrown into sharp relief by Chelsea's apologetic admittance of a £50,000 payment to former player Gary Johnson, to ensure his silence about his molestation by Eddie Heath, the club's chief scout in the seventies. Heath, who died of a heart attack more than twenty years ago, was also involved with junior teams in east London.

The timing of the confidentiality agreement, 2013, and its conditions, so stringent that until the club relented all parties involved were not allowed to acknowledge its existence, was startling, yet the culture it represented was familiar. Football abhors loose talk, even as it abides loose money or loose morals.

Other clubs in Chelsea's exposed position would certainly have considered the same solution. Nothing has changed, intrinsically, since an interim FA report into child protection in 2004, revealed by the *Independent*'s Ian Herbert, observed that 'closure and secrecy were perceived to be habitual' in a game that was 'reluctant to engage with professional expertise'.

Funding was pulled two years into what was intended to be a five-year investigation. One witness statement, which spoke of professional football as 'an aggressive, masculine environment in which bad language, threatening behaviour and verbal abuse features highly', concurs with my experience. So, too, does anecdotal evidence that complainants, generally parents seeking a response from politicians and football administrators, were ignored, patronised or directed elsewhere.

One case, unearthed during my research for this book, has been passed on by those involved, to be investigated by Operation Fremont, which is considering contemporary abuse alongside Operation Hydrant's investigation into historic offences. It concerns a coach claimed to have been seen behaving inappropriately when under-13 players were in a shower. An official complaint, registered by a fellow coach, was dismissed by a Premier League club following what parents believe to have been an insubstantial investigation.

The complainant, whose letter I have seen, left the club, together with the welfare officer who was his first point of contact. Both men are held in the highest esteem by their peers, and have given statements to detectives, but are circumspect about publicly acknowledging their role because they have a teaching background. The suspect currently works as a first team coach in the professional game.

I seek to balance the bad with the good, to offer insight into the people and philosophies shaping the future of English football. The journey begins, and ends, in the sink estates of south London, where sport supplements an admirable struggle to nullify nihilistic gangs. It features absurdly premature wealth and demonstrates the devastation wrought by economic and ethical poverty.

All human life is there, to quote that evocative old-fashioned tabloid masthead. There are names to remember, misjudgements to forget. I visited pristine training complexes, park pitches, international arenas, non-league grounds and hermetically sealed Premier League palaces; all, in their nuanced ways, failed to sanitise the fear and insecurity generated by the distortion of the power of opportunity.

Parents raged at their impotence. Boys seemed old before their time, and still radiated the vulnerability of infants. Coaches quietly questioned their consciences. There are good people at work, pursuing enlightened strategies, but too many shadows are cast over what should be a sun-dappled landscape by venality, opportunism and insensitive micromanagement.

A senior coach speaks of a 9-year-old at a Premier League club being paid £24,000 a year through his parents. A member of the England under-15 squad is understood to have been offered a two-year professional contract worth £45,000 a week. Entire families may be supported through a black economy driven by illicit incentives that include houses, cars and cash, but victims of an overheated system, shaped by political expedience and casual cruelty, are not hard to find.

The 6-year-old rejected because he has 'picked up bad habits'. The 8-year-old with a price on his head in what amounts to a meat market. The 9-year-olds called into a squad meeting at the training ground, who only realise they have no future at a Premier League club when they are told to leave the room after seeing the survivors being given next season's kits.

The aspiring scholars at another Premier League club who, in an era in which the intensity of youth training is blamed for the average age of players requiring hip surgery falling to 27, are informed by a cost-cutting chief executive they can only undergo scans if their parents have private medical insurance, or are willing to pick up the bill.

The father of a 12-year-old who feels compelled to keep a log of all conversations with an academy coach he is convinced is 'exploiting my child by toying with his mind'. The parent who sees a son suffer sustained bullying by an under-13 coach who bawls and belittles, while dispensing tickets for first-team matches to the favoured few.

The 15-year-old goalkeeper who sustains a double fracture of the jaw in training and is given two paracetamol tablets and the promise of a compensatory one-year contract extension, which is quickly and quietly reneged upon. Another goalkeeper, recruited at the age of 5, who learns he has been released at 16 through the club's website, which misspells his name.

The academy manager so constrained by the system he feels he has no official outlet to register his disgust that his most promising player has been lured to a bigger club by an informal offer of £250,000 in cash, accepted immediately after an FA Youth Cup tie by a father who has no compunction in using his son as collateral.

The reputable independent agent so powerless to prevent emerging players being poached that he sees international prospects spirited away by rivals who use duplicitous parents or close relatives as co-conspirators. The colleague confronted by the father of a so-called wonderkid, fresh from a solitary season in Northern Europe, demanding a personal payment of 5 million euros to approve a transfer to an English club.

This is a world of fear and loathing, where unprincipled agents stalk pre-teen players on social media, and circulate in training grounds, surreptitiously offering boys cinema tickets as tainted tokens of their esteem. Some have been smuggled through security checks in cars driven by complicit parents. To quote a principled specialist in youth recruitment, who is appalled by the scramble to secure players as young as 6 on pre-agreement contracts, 'everyone wants a new toy'.

Do not judge harshly those who speak in these pages on condition of anonymity. There are careers to sustain, nearest and dearest to protect. Such voices deserve to be heard, if only to balance the sophistry and self-promotion of an industry that commoditises childhood without deigning to acknowledge the cost.

The world has seen grown men weep. It rarely hears the primal scream of a boy, told he is a failure. This is what it sounds like, when doves cry.

1

Poverty Driven Children

'What's your dream, son?'

Steadman Scott is sitting astride a silver-grey FitBALL in a glass-walled alcove beside the entrance to the gymnasium at Brixton Recreation Centre. He is wearing a navy T-shirt that speaks of 'making the impossible possible'. His voice is tender and his brown eyes are wide, yet an unblinking stare hints at underlying hardness.

The boy is 6 years old. He bites his lower lip and lowers his head. He is wearing a pristine white Real Madrid kit, socks pulled fashionably over his knees. His delicate features, long loosely curled black hair and olive skin testify to his mixed heritage. He has an Australian mother; his father, a member of an Arabic Berber tribe from Chad, leans forward and mimes encouragement.

'Be a footballer . . .'

The words are mumbled, compressed, barely audible.

Scott smiles, shifts a black beanie hat so that it sits behind his ears, and extends his right hand so that it rests on the boy's shoulder. His gaze is unwavering. The boy does not flinch, but there is a tremor of alarm in his eyes until he sees his beaming father.

He finds the confidence to face his new teacher: 'If you haven't got that dream, son, you're going to have to walk right out that door, and never come back. If you want to stay here you have to prove yourself. You must be strong. It will be tough. I will be harsh on you. But I smell a footballer. Come with me.'

They walk around the fifth-floor landing to a sports hall. Heavy double-doors open to reveal around fifty boys, doing possession drills in three groups. Scott is drawn towards the beginners, and a boy whose tongue protrudes from the corner of his mouth as he concentrates on controlling a ball at walking speed.

The coach kneels, takes his pupil's right foot in both hands, and murmurs, 'Knee over the ball, light touch.' He rises, takes a pace backwards: 'Yes, yes. That's it. Put that in your mind. Don't rush it. Don't get lazy, now.' Suddenly, he swivels on his heels, and barks, 'I'm watching you, too,' at a more advanced group, who are weaving through blue cones without due care and attention.

Order is instantly imposed. He is looking for indications of mental strength, physical dexterity and technical skill. Bullying is punishable by exclusion, but aggression has its place within clearly defined limits. Scott knows that those who are unable or unwilling to defend themselves drown in the piranha pool of the professional game.

This is a prep school, run on old-school lines. Discipline is enforced rigorously. Training is designed to instil a love of the ball; its intention is to stimulate the imagination, thrill the senses. Conventional tactical education, the straightjacket of team shapes and systems, is left to the professional clubs, who salivate at the raw material assembled in unheralded surroundings.

'Bear in mind where these boys come from. First of all, I want them to know this is their time to shine, to be the star. If you want me to go mad, pass the ball, risk the ball, and I'll go crazy. Cherish the ball. Take three touches, two touches. Now I know you've got the ability. I'll teach you one v. one, going past people and defending. My job is to coach you how to play football, not give you a position.

'These kids don't get the chance to learn on grass. They act differently here to when they are out on the streets. Their parents don't exist. They feel safe, because only their dream exists. They know they must follow the rules, my rules. I will shout. I will test their spirit. I am their godfather. This is about preparing their bodies, and their minds, for what is to come.'

He spots more boisterousness out of the corner of his eye and raises his voice: 'You are a blackboard with nothing written on it,' he announces, oblivious to the confusion generated by the analogy. 'This is work. If you are here for fun you are in the wrong place. This is for a reason. We will teach you to hold yourself properly and conduct yourself right when you go to your professional clubs.'

Other supplicants are waiting. A mother pushes two sons towards him. They stand out in a sea of replica kit, since they are dressed in hand-me-down pullovers, grey shorts and black plimsolls. The younger boy is rejected gently, because he is no more than 4, but his brother is told to report the following week. The nominal session fee, £2, will be waived, as it is for so many others from visibly straitened backgrounds.

This is Afewee, the volunteer-driven community club created out of social chaos by Scott and his friend Tony Goldring in 1997. It has produced twenty professional footballers, and more than forty of their boys are among the 12,500 currently in the academy system. One player is spoken of in awe. Clyne. The surname is sufficient.

Scott spotted him, aged 8. He was small, quick and fierce, yet unusually quiet and self-contained. He played cage football until darkness descended and the walkways of Brixton's interconnected estates were reclaimed by heroin addicts, dealers, and opportunistic knife-wielding muggers as young as 11.

The story of Nathaniel Clyne – told by the tattoo on his left arm, where the inscription 'Baller from birth' accompanies an image of him as a toddler clutching a football – is modern fantasy made flesh. As a multi-millionaire, and a senior England international, the Liverpool defender is the ultimate survivor. He embodies aspiration and inspiration.

He was brought up just off Somerleyton Road, in a block of flats colloquially known as 'Gun City' or 'Murderzone' because of its adolescent enforcers. It was controlled by the Poverty Driven Children, a notorious gang challenged by mutational alliances such as Guns and Shanks, Tell No One, Siraq, Untouchables and All 'Bout Money.

They operated with impunity out of offices initially designated for caretakers, and forced vulnerable families out of their homes, which became a network of crack dens. Addicts would also shoot up behind trees, close to a foul-smelling underground car park into which only the foolhardy or the desperate ventured. Squatters moved in before the block was officially open: a front-page article in the *Guardian* used it to illustrate John Major's denunciation of 'grey, sullen wastelands, robbing people of self-respect'.

Scott saw the good amidst the bad: 'I saw a young man, very sharp, very disciplined, very good on the ball. Clyne had a bigger brother, Theo. Now Theo was very, very good. More skilful, but he was thinking he was all fancy. He had an attitude problem. Clyne, he didn't argue. He just got on with it. I asked him where his mother was.

'When she came I spoke to her about taking him here, upstairs in the Rec. I'd take him in, train him, work on his mentality, and eventually send him to Arsenal. He came from a gang place, but she was a good lady. Very strict. She cared. She understood. She saw our youth killing themselves with drugs, knives and guns. We spoke about hope, the dream. The rest is history.'

Her son scored six goals on trial as a winger at the age of 10, but Arsenal rejected him because he was supposedly too small. Spurs were similarly blinkered, yet Scott reassured Nathaniel there were ninety other clubs searching for someone like him. Clyne excelled at Crystal Palace, made his Premier League debut for Southampton, and was sold to Liverpool for £12.5 million in July 2015.

The system seizes on him as a status symbol, a source of self-justification, but he remains a statistical anomaly. Less than one half of one per cent of boys who enter the academy structure at the age of 9 will make a first-team appearance. More than three quarters are jettisoned between the ages of 13 and 16.

The odds get no less intimidating the further a boy progresses. Almost 98 per cent of boys given a scholarship at 16 are no longer in the top five tiers of the domestic game at the age of 18. A recent study revealed only 8 out of 400 players given a professional Premier League contract at 18 remained at the highest level by the time of their twenty-second birthday. Since only 180 of the 1.5 million boys who play organised youth football in England at any one time become Premier League pros, the success rate is 0.012 per cent.

Margins are fine and critical decisions are occasionally taken arbitrarily. They are influenced by political nuance, naked self-interest and nervousness stimulated by suspicion. If natural talent was the determining factor, Andre Blackman, an Afewee contemporary of Clyne who was eagerly signed by Arsenal as a teenager, would be playing in the Premier League.

Instead in May 2016, at the age of 25, he was attempting to reinvent himself at MAS Fez in the Moroccan Botola league. His athleticism and sense of adventure from left back made him a favourite of the Fatal Tigers, one of North Africa's biggest supporters' groups, but exile at the thirteenth club of a bewilderingly indisciplined career was not without its challenges.

'I come in at half-time and suddenly I'm alone,' he explained, with a telling sense of bewilderment. 'The rest of the team goes into another room to pray. They're like magicians on the ball, but without a brain. They go for goal, work an opening, and can't stop themselves doubling back to try to beat their man again.

'The football is technical and they want me to stay for another eighteen months, but I'm not sure. The manager got sacked at the end of March and we're in danger of going down. To be honest, I'll have a look around when I get back to England in June. Not heard anything, have you? My agent will sort the rest.'

Blackman's struggle, and Clyne's success, has special resonance in an area defined by deprivation and social contraction. There are more shootings in the borough of Lambeth than in any other part of London. Life expectancy amongst males is five years lower than the capital's average. The crime rate on the estates is double the mean, the robbery rate triple. Almost two thirds of children come from single-parent families.

Yet Brixton remains a vibrant community, despite the social schizophrenia of gentrification over the past five years, which has inflated rents and led to simmering tension. Football has wider significance, collective importance expressed through the interdependence of four of the principal figures in Afewee, which, loosely translated from Jamaican patois, means 'It is for we'.

Scott, the figurehead, is 60, but when engaged, channelling private passions and enduring frustrations, he appears at least a decade younger. He is a commanding character, who manages to minimise and disguise the handicap of having only 40 per cent mobility – the legacy of a chronic back injury sustained during unsupervised weightlifting sessions when he was in prison.

'Young boys trying to impress each other, squatting, lifting big weights with no instruction, no technique,' he explained quietly. 'When I leave Her Majesty's confinement I was coaching and had a bag of footballs slung over my shoulder. Suddenly, something clicked. I collapsed and couldn't move for six months. I thought my life was over.'

When he is not at the Rec, he can usually be found lying on the floor of his flat, less than half a mile away, to ease constant pain. When he is there, nodding sagely and bowing respectfully to those who seek his confidence or advice, he is in his element. He mistrusts those developers who have designs on the centre, opened in 1994 as a consequence of Lord Scarman's condemnation of a lack of local leisure facilities.

'This is my temple. This is my church. This building gave me life. This building create I. This building is history. As a Brixtonian for fifty years, I don't call this the Recreation Centre. I call it the Re-Creation Centre, because it was meant to re-create my generation, and future generations. It is for the community. It is for us.

'Our mission is to put belief, passion, hard work and discipline into our youngsters. When I was first around here there was nobody to motivate us. Imagine yourself as a ten-year-old with a speech impediment, newly arrived from rural Jamaica. In the sixties, black people didn't have an identity, didn't have a voice. You were invisible because of the colour of your skin.

'My memory of an English education is of sitting at the back of classes. I was scared people would laugh at me. There was one teacher, who sit down with me and take time, so I can break down the word and pronounce it. This lady showed me passion, patience, discipline. She made an impact so big that the principle of Afewee was based on her classroom. We try to inspire.

'Our youngsters are in gangs. Why have they gone astray? Why did my generation go astray? As a young man in the seventies I couldn't find no job to give me self-esteem. There was no black people working in no Barclay Bank, no black people in no government office. Guys like us, who came for a better life, had only sus laws, stop and search.

'Just imagine, late at night, if you are out of your community. You have to hide from police, racist white guys. This environment led to riots in 1981, 1985, 1995. We chose not to follow our fathers, the Windrush Generation. We weren't content to be content. We decide to have dreams. We embark on the street. The system criminalised my generation, turned us into rebels.'

Societal revenge was swift. To use Scott's plaintive phrase, 'the judge slaps me in the face'. He was sentenced to six years for a drugs offence he continues to dispute. It proved to be a pivotal experience; he studied counselling theory and summoned the inner strength to survive personal trauma.

'My life outside fell apart. After eighteen months my wife wanted a divorce. I said yes, I can't afford to argue. If you want to do it, do it. You can't cry or do crazy things when you are inside because it will only get you a longer sentence. You have to take a deep breath and cope with it.

'I am sitting in my cell and I look deep into myself. What was my strength when I was walking the streets? I was a qualified football coach, weight trainer, swimming teacher. What was my passion? Helping young boys. I tell myself: "Stop chasing money. The grave is coming near. What is the purpose of your life?"

'When we've passed away people will talk about what we have done. This is about how you treat your fellow human being and your community. I can talk about how I love my community because I do this for free. If you show a kid love and respect, attempt to understand his world instead of leaving him to his own devices, he will not rob or kill your kids.'

Peter Armstrong, secretary of Afewee Training Centre, also assists their boxing programme, established under head coach Bobby Miltiadous in response to the 2011 riots. An openly gay former university teacher, who set up an HIV charity following his diagnosis with the condition in 1991, he provides administrative rigour and philosophical support.

'For Steadman, Afewee works at that level of helping to ensure equality within the community, and particularly Brixton. It was his experience that such equality was so lacking it led to chaos, which led to legislation. This is not just a football organisation, because its success leads indirectly to social progress.

'Kids can learn ball skills quite quickly. But will they have the attitude to practise and practise? Will they be able to deal with Steadman's shouting, the badgering, the repetitive drills and the commitment to come here three times a week? It is those sorts of qualities which will make them successful in life.

'People talk about teaching kids confidence, self-esteem, belief in their dream. I don't think that can be taught. It is instilled into the kid by exposing him or her to an environment which allows the development of those competences. A good coach does that, and that is all the justification you need for promoting sport.

'You don't have to march the kids into the classroom to teach them life skills. Nobody can teach wisdom, patience, tranquillity or serenity, because those higher-level competences are innate, but our kids are gaining experience of self-mastery on and off the pitch.'

Tony Goldring, the principal football coach, first met Scott at a course for the unemployed in 1990. They are similar in terms of background, since he admits, 'I turned into a bit of a bad lad,' due to a lack of positive role models. His under-8 team, London champions in the 2015–16 season, were unbeaten in twenty-nine matches, but he recognises results are of marginal significance, compared to the pastoral nature of his work:

'Football has the capacity to teach children to be confident, proud, never to settle for second best. They are encouraged to excel, inspire. We have had our struggles, but if a programme like ours didn't exist there would be more crime. Dysfunctional families would drift. Let's not kid ourselves. There are massive problems. There is still a huge divide between haves and have-nots.

'We attempt to embrace everyone. It is a bigger responsibility, but part of our job is to develop the emotions and qualities which help to produce a better citizen, who is better equipped for life. Never forget these boys and girls are the fathers and mothers of the future. By embedding discipline and promoting self-worth, we are helping the community to help itself.'

Jay Jay Lodge is Afewee's emissary to a darker world. He uses his 'Spare Everyone' initiative, designed to offer freedom of movement across gang boundaries, to secure safe passage for the boys. A large, loose-limbed man with an easy laugh, he has the zeal of the convert and a backstory that justifies his observation that 'I hold a lot of weight around here'.

He was sufficiently promising, as a defensive or left-sided midfield player, to be signed by Crystal Palace at 14, and trained with the Jamaican national team when he briefly returned to his native island. His moment of clarity came in Brixton prison, where he was serving time for hospitalising three men who attacked him. He could see his flat through the small, barred window of his cell, and resolved to change.

'I got involved with a whole load of street stuff, fast money and the rest of it. I was selling. I was a name. If you've got to have a fight or a tear-up, that's how it goes, but I'm not trying to kill no one. I was never a bully. I just wanted to live nice and do whatever I had to do. That's how I threw away my football dreams.

'I'm trying to show these kids you don't have to do that. Football is about hope, but some are already on the roads, selling drugs, walking with knives. They have no future, because if you have no focus the streets will get the better of you. Sell weed, sell coke, sell heroin. These are the easy ways, but they lead to a dead end.

'When you are in prison, sitting down with a ten- or fifteen-year rack, jail is very, very hard. Some people are just not cut out for it. They become the victims, made to do naked star jumps because they pretended they had a gangster lifestyle. They're inside with real people, who don't give a fuck. That's when you realise you are not the bad man you thought you were.

'If I am totally honest most of my family are gang-affiliated. My cousin was shot fifteen times two weeks ago. He's still alive. So when people come to me with tales of the glorious life, wanting to be a drug dealer, I give them real-life examples of what is still happening out there. I tell them, "It is up to you. Come to our side of the road and do some productive things."

'This is people's lives we are talking about. This is not a game. We have watched people die, people get stabbed, but we have also watched people make something of themselves. Footballers, at a certain level, have a real power in the community. They probably don't realise what the youth are looking for from them.

'Afewee is something that is heartfelt, for and from the community. Start with Steadman, and you know how to handle yourself at those big clubs. When they are shouting at you in the dressing room it will not faze you. Our boys know how to speak to a man. They have presence, conduct themselves in a certain manner. They won't be standing there with their shirts hanging out.'

As if on cue, he broke off to welcome Nathan Mavila and Leo Chambers, two neo-pros from West Ham who had returned to the Rec to pay their respects. They were sleek, attentive, engaged, at ease with the excitable boys they had agreed to train that evening. Each, at 20, had reached a critical phase of his career.

Their dilemma was instructive and over-familiar to anyone associated with English football: a new contract was unlikely that summer, since academy products are easily disposable. Some are kept on as 'bodies' to service anaemic under-21 or under-23 teams; most are allowed to wither on the vine, since homegrown players are deemed to lack the lustre of ready-made foreign signings.

Mavila, a left back, was doing sufficiently well on loan at Wealdstone in the Conference South to attract interest from Serie B clubs in Italy. 'Steadman basically made me,' he said. 'He talked about being a winner. He told me to be the one everyone remembers, the one who gets signed, the one who makes their family proud.'

Chambers, a technically accomplished defender in the mould of Rio Ferdinand, and a former England schoolboys captain, was on loan at Colchester United in League One, following a year out with a persistent leg injury. 'I came here from the streets,' he said. 'I'd never played an organised game, never had a training session. Steadman taught me how to hang with the ball, how to move. He was brilliant.'

Jay Jay rocked back on his white plastic seat: 'Much love, brothers,' he said, as they headed upstairs to meet their mentor. 'Good boys,' he added approvingly, before heading to his next outreach assignment at the Evelyn Grace Academy, a highly regarded local school where he had that morning confiscated knives from boys aged between 11 and 14.

Josh Bohui, the school's star pupil, could be found some 200 yards away, past the One Love Cafe, with its inscription from Scott's hero, the Jamaican orator Marcus Garvey: 'Be as proud of your race today as our fathers were in days of yore, we have a beautiful history and we shall create another in the future that will astonish the world.'

The England under-17 winger, at the time one of Brentford's best prospects, was on a small artificial pitch in a replica stadium at Pop Brixton, a centre for start-ups, small businesses and community organisations. He was demonstrating the Afewee Way in a one-on-one session with another alumnus, England women's under-19 forward Rinsola Babajide.

They were spellbinding, operating in the head space where football meets flamenco. Their session was a fusion of agility and attitude, skill and street smarts, grace and guile. It contained elements of urban basketball, surging athleticism, subtlety at speed, showmanship. They had game, and they knew it.

Afewee takes pride in developing strong female role models. Karin Muya rejected a professional contract with Chelsea Ladies to take up a scholarship at Notre Dame in the US. Keishana Kelly, a childhood friend of the Clyne family, was personally selected by David Beckham to coach at his Los Angeles academy. She returns to her roots to work at the Rec when two young children and teaching commitments permit.

Babajide is the future. Though she is working with athletics coach Gorgui Thiam to develop physical strength, her style is intrinsically artistic. She speaks of 'creativity and freedom', of 'being there, mentally'. There is something affectingly ethereal about her description of 'football taking my mind off everything else', and of 'disappearing into myself'.

I would cherish the memory of her spontaneity, their joy, since it was all too easy to be ambushed by more unsavoury realities. Those closest to Vontae Daley-Campbell, an England under-16 international nurtured by Scott and taken to Arsenal at the age of 9 by Goldring, tried to restrict the circulation of his contact details, but were unable to prevent an agent calling him with the curt order: 'Get your uncle to answer his fucking phone.'

At 28, his uncle, Nathan, is another Afewee product. He earned a degree in sports coaching and development at Southampton University after being released by Wycombe Wanderers at 16, and was playing semi-professionally for Grays Athletic, a supporter-owned club in the Ryman Premier League.

His role is to protect his nephew and shepherd his sister, Vontae's mother Anna Marie, through a scrum of opportunists and fair-weather friends. His guidance is paternal, informed by personal experience of football's harshness and an intimate knowledge of the boy's background and personality. He blocked incessant calls from the abusive agent, one of twelve who contacted him within a week of his nephew's England debut, because he simply didn't trust him.

'Steadman gave us both somewhere to escape to, instead of being on the streets, where it is so easy to take the wrong pathway. He also gave us some kind of structure. He made you do what you were meant to do. There were rules that could not be broken. That influence spills over into the rest of your life, your schooling, when you are making that dangerous transition into the real world.

'I try to be on the level with Vontae. I was not perfect. I tell him not to repeat my mistakes. I can see what is happening around him. A young footballer gets so much attention. People are contacting him directly through social media. It is rife. They talk positively because that is what they think he wants to hear. They are just trying to get his buy-in.

'He is a product if we are being honest. He is only fifteen but at the end of the day, for representatives or sponsors, it is about money. I try to filter all the interest; it is amazing how many people want him because of word of mouth. When they admit they've never even seen him play they are ticked off the list.

'I'm proud of Vontae, because he is taking a lot of it on board and he is realising he has to do extra if he wants to be a pro, but I am also trying to educate my sister, because people will take advantage where they can. It is cut-throat. If they can find a way to sway her they will do so.'

Vontae, a physically imposing full back, is watchful and reserved, yet makes a point of kissing his mother on the way to the dressing room after each match. Such unabashed expression of love defies the emotionally constricted reputation of so many young footballers; the screensaver on his smartphone, a portrait with his mother taken at a tournament in Italy, confirms the depth and interdependency of their relationship.

Anna Marie is 36, grandmother of two baby girls. She

has three children; Vontae is her only son. They have a striking resemblance, since each has a wide, warm face. He has inherited her speed, as she had hopes of becoming a 200-metre runner before she fell pregnant. Her protective instincts are as strong now as they were when he was 10, when she moved the family from Brixton to Clapham 'because I could see the gangs getting to him'.

She has a strong social conscience, and works voluntarily with the homeless and the vulnerable at the Ace of Clubs centre, where she is known simply as 'The Footballer's Mum'. The charitable community-based operation offers shelter, food, clothing, washing facilities, welfare and employment advice to up to 100 people a night.

That figure has doubled in the past year, as the human cost of a politically driven austerity programme becomes apparent. More audacious visitors follow Anna around local supermarkets, where she often spends £20 of her own money on biscuits for the centre, and offer to carry her bags in return for something to eat: 'Some of them have not eaten for days. I don't scorn them, like some do on the streets. They can get a full meal for fifty pence or a pound, but if they haven't got the money I give it to them anyway. What's the harm in that? In return you get their gratitude and respect.'

Despite early educational difficulties, Vontae is studying for thirteen GCSEs at the London Nautical School with the help of a club-appointed tutor. His has not been an easy journey since he was a relatively late developer in a football sense and went through a socially awkward phase in which he had to learn to control his temper. Anna's pride is tangible.

'Vontae has lived an up-and-down life. There have been times when he has had a battering, when he has had to grow up quicker than he wanted to, but in a way I am happy that he has had his tough moments. At first, at Arsenal, he couldn't bond. No one talked to him. It is horrible seeing your son struggle like that, but at thirteen things started to turn. Fourteen was the year of the Big Bang. The other players could see how good he was, how powerful he was. He was The Beast. Suddenly, he became the one they all looked up to.

'If any of my children have a dream I tell them to go for it. I will do everything I can to help. I tell them to have respect for themselves, because without that, how are they going to respect others? Manners go a long way. I'd love Vontae to eventually be in the first team but sometimes just words are enough. "I love you, Mum" means so much. I have never let him down. I have always been with him, no matter how hard it has been. I wanted to make sure I am the first one he turns to whenever he needs anything.'

The irony of maternal influence being a vital factor in such a macho environment had struck me in that sports hall in Brixton, when my eye had been taken by a lad excelling in a game against boys three or four years his senior. 'I've never seen a seven-year-old like him,' confided Goldring, who had evidently sensed the intensity of my interest. 'He has all the attributes to be a superstar, and his mum knows the politics of what is happening.'

The name of Ezra Tika-Lemba had already featured in countless Chinese whispers. His mother, Lorianne, wanted to give him the broadest possible experience, so he played for Arsenal, Chelsea, West Ham and Fulham. Liverpool, Manchester City, Tottenham and Crystal Palace were equally ardent suitors. He was physically strong, nimble and blessed with an instinctive appreciation of space, but that was an adult, one-dimensional, professional judgement.

It was only when he snuggled into his mother's shoulder, as we sat on a low bench in the corner of the hall, that the child emerged. He had worked a hole in his new socks, by picking at a loose thread, and complained his boots, size four and a half, were too tight. Tiredness had chipped away at his natural chirpiness. Lorianne, who juggles two zero-hour-contract jobs with football commitments, smiled indulgently, and reflected on 'the goofball' who loved to sing, dance and play the guitar.

'When they come off the pitch, and you see them out of their football kit, you realise, "Oh my God, they are babies,"' she said. 'The pitch is a stage that makes them seem five years older than they are. You have to be very careful in terms of the pressure you put on them, remembering they are children. It has to be an enjoyable environment but I let Ezra know it can be serious.

'Most newborn babies are chubby and soft. I swear to God Ezra was born with a six-pack. I said to my mum, "I think I've given birth to Superman. I'm just waiting for his special powers to kick in." He wasn't one of those children who has had a ball since he was baby. He didn't understand the game, he kinda learned it here. This is his home, really.

'This is where you learn to be a champion, to challenge, to drive. Steadman and Tony will whip him into shape. This is about growing young men, responsible and thoughtful men who work well under pressure. I know football is cut-throat, male-oriented. A few people are already whispering to me about agents, but I cannot think of giving up any of my responsibilities as a parent. I am Ezra's advocate, his spokesperson, but first of all I am his mum.'

Ezra had signed a two-year contract to play for Chelsea earlier that day, five days before his eighth birthday. He posed for photographs with Goldring in a No. 9 Chelsea shirt, worn back to front, over a fawn suit. As journeys go, his will be as hazardous as that of a newly born sea turtle, struggling across the sand towards the sanctuary of the ocean.

2

The Missionary's Position

The Fulham coaches distilled the threat, defined the tactics and dictated the tempo at which they expected their team to play. It was a tough European tournament, featuring Paris Saint-Germain, Monaco, Marseilles, Inter Milan, Bayern Munich, Anderlecht and Feyenoord, but it was deemed to be winnable.

Their performance-planning was impeccable, their professionalism admirable. The missing ingredient, perspective, was supplied on the first night away in France, during a routine bed check. Two of the players had a teddy bear on their pillow. A third slept in a nappy. They were, after all, 9 years old.

Nick Levett remembered the significance of that lesson the following December, when he organised a ninety-minute training session based on the principles of counter-attacking. The response from his squad was so loose as to be incoherent. The lethargy and confusion only made sense when he learned that one boy had been informed Father Christmas did not exist by a teammate just before the session began.

'A ten-year-old kid is not half a twenty-year-old. It doesn't work like that. Children are not mini-adults. They're very, very different. We use all these football words, worry as much as we want about winning and all the adult stuff, and we forget that they are kids. Father Christmas made my Xs and Os and all the important football stuff that I was ready to instil irrelevant. Absolutely irrelevant.'

As the FA's Talent Identification Manager, with specific focus on the recruitment of players from the ages of 5 to 11, Levett has a missionary's mindset. He has a responsibility to challenge, an instinct to innovate, a duty to dilute the ignorance and arrogance that seep down from the professional game to junior football.

He sees the extremes, 10-year-olds released by text message and teenagers prevented from playing for up to eighteen months while clubs haggle over their market value. He seeks to educate those clubs who reject a boy for a sudden lack of physical co-ordination when a simple conversation with his mother would have elicited the information he had grown an inch in three weeks.

'That lad was released at fourteen, after being told he was in line for another two years. He had no idea what his legs were doing. He began misplacing simple passes. His self-esteem was shattered. His mates were telling him he was rubbish. The reason was simple, but no one gave him a break.'

Levett understands his principal role is to 'ignite the fire' that enables a child to fall in love with a simple ball-game. He is a systemic version of Brixton's Steadman Scott, since his sessions include variations of one v. ones, two v. twos and three v. threes, designed to foster natural movement and reward technical skill. As Albert Einstein insisted, 'Logic will get you from A to Z; imagination will get you everywhere.'

Fun is all too often regarded as a four-letter word in academy football. Levett seeks to capture the imagination; one deceptively informal drill asks boys to envisage being chased by pirates around a desert island. The ball is their treasure; if they lose control, they will be vulnerable to their pursuers, and the sharks lurking in the surf.

Boys are encouraged to pretend to be characters they see in films, or in e-games played on their phones. One possession drill is based on the antics of Lightning McQueen, the slot car from the Pixar *Cars* franchise. 'You have to understand the child in front of you,' Levett insisted. 'You need a different skill set, an empathetic coach.'

That is a hard sell when one head of recruitment at a Premier League academy continues to insist, against all logic and experience, that it is possible to identify a professional footballer at the age of 5. A creative philosophy exposes the narrow-mindedness of his club, which insists boys are pigeonholed into specific positions from the age of 6.

Football's hierarchical structure dictates that coaches in the so-called foundation phase, up to 11 years old, are paid, on average, five times less than those at under-18 or under-21 level. Their wage scale starts at £18,000 a year. Such inequality is overlooked by clubs, who become accustomed to using their economic and emotional power as a blunt instrument.

'Typically the professional game will trawl for what they deem talent to be, at whatever age they see fit. They take what they want from the grassroots game, with very little feeling or empathy towards the kids who are left behind. They might go into an under-7s or under-8s team, take three kids, and all of a sudden the rest can't play because there aren't enough to make a team.

'Professional clubs aren't bothered about that. Then, however many years later, they discard one, two, or all three of the kids they have taken, often in a way that shows very little duty of care. Some English clubs, like QPR, are great in investing proactively in the grassroots, but, generally, it is certainly not a two-way relationship. Most just cherry-pick and hope something turns up.'

Dutch clubs, by contrast, have a holistic approach. AZ Alkmaar, typically, are in partnership with 120 grassroots clubs. They offer coaching seminars, website links, and advice from sports science staff on the principle that the broader the base, the bigger the opportunity. Money is not an issue at the highest level in England; entitlement and expedience are twin curses. The sense of social identity that inspires Athletic Bilbao, for instance, to invest 1.2 million euros in a three-year integration programme with 140 local clubs is an alien notion for the majority of sides in the UK. Even QPR's relatively enlightened approach only involves the donation of £50,000 to four partnership clubs.

Levett is a chinos man in a tracksuit, an earnest, technocratic type more generally found utilising thinking-time on the beanbags at Google's UK headquarters than in draughty school halls, preaching football philosophy to the converted. He coached part-time at Fulham for six years, but has a wide background, spanning primary school teaching, sports development initiatives, and experience in women's and disability football.

'I look back now and think, nah, I was never a coach. I was a technical instructor or a football organiser. It was from working with educators like Derek Bradley at Fulham and Pete Sturgess at the FA that I began to realise that coaching is about developing people.

'In my second year at Fulham I had a very challenging group. There were a few big characters, tough kids, inner-city London kids. I spent a lot of time working on them as individuals, conflict resolution stuff, so they would get better at working with others. I'd challenge them, "How are you going to manage it when someone has a different opinion to you about a tactic?" and deliberately put them into situations where I knew there would be issues.

'My intention was to encourage, support and develop their thinking skills, but I got pulled in by two of the full-time members of staff, for doing too much "social stuff" and not enough "football stuff", in their opinion. Four years later, it was the worst group in the club for bullying and racial tension, because they spent too much time on football and didn't deal with the people.

'I had a kid, in a younger age group, who was the best in his group. A couple of years later, when he had left me, I sat in a coaches' meeting when they were talking about him. They were letting him get away with things because he was still the best. That was bollocks, the complete opposite of what they should have been doing. There are boundaries and structures that everybody has to conform with, because it's a team, and the impact of not managing that causes all sorts of issues.'

Signs of psychological stress are easy to miss. Levett was struck by an Instagram post by a 14-year-old whose progress had been halted by injury. It was a cartoon image, of a boy surrounded by material rewards, cash, a car and a phone, and people shouting at him. The implications were inescapable: it was a pictorial representation of unsustainable pressure.

'The fear, for that kid, is of suddenly not being a potential footballer. The psychological impact of that is huge. So what support is there for those kids? Who picks up those pieces? In many cases the answer is nobody, and that's where we are failing our kids. We've got more resources than we've ever had in the game, and I think that, as adults, we should be embarrassed we let such things happen.'

The principles are sound, but are they applied on the ground? Part of the process of discovery involved a tortuous five-hour drive around a gridlocked M25 to Hinchingbrooke, an idiosyncratic state school set in the grounds of what was once Oliver Cromwell's family home in Huntingdon. His audience, over three hours in the Performing Arts Centre, consisted of seventy local coaches and youth recruitment officers.

Familiarity lent them a certain comfort, and they conformed to type. Some wore training tops emblazoned with their initials, the symbol of the clipboard warrior. Others failed to engage consistently, evidently seeing the evening as a box-ticking exercise in their pursuit of an enhanced coaching badge.

Sprinkled amidst the buzz phrases of personal development – extroverts are 'solar-powered', introverts are 'battery-powered', and poor coaches have 'a knowledge shield' which deflects innovation – was an invitation to think differently. How many were willing to embrace Levett's core message that psychological and social skills are of equal importance to technical and physical attributes in the modern game?

'Creative kids don't like to conform,' he told them. 'They have a need for originality, but are released from clubs by coaches who have different value systems and beliefs. You can't make a kid adapt to your view of the world. How do you know who the learners are? Search out the kid who is curious. He will practise on his own without you. If they rely on you they are not going to be distinctive. Your job is to make yourself redundant.'

He spoke of coaching as an intuitive process, in which the clues to a young player's driving forces and definitive characteristics are subtle, but strangely obvious in retrospect. Creativity cannot be constrained by time; the Dyson vacuum cleaner, for example, is the product of 5,000 prototypes, tested over fifteen years. Information in youth football may border on the banal, but the picture it helps to develop can be sharp and significant.

Which boy carries his bag to training, instead of delegating the duty to his dad? What is the player's mood, especially if he comes from a broken home? How does he relate to the parent who ferried him to the session? Does the parent stay, and take an interest in his progress? Who has furthest to travel? Is anyone having problems at school? What are the underlying reasons for a lack of concentration and commitment?

Such questions were given focus by the practical

session, staged in fine rain on a warm, misty evening. Delegates were asked to critique a twenty-minute seven-a-side match between two local under-9 teams on an undersized 4G pitch. In a re-creation of an old scout's trick, they were ordered to pick one boy, and concentrate on him entirely for the duration of the game before reporting back.

Like many observers, I chose Josh, the youngest and smallest boy, who played conveniently close to the touchline along which most of us stood. He was skilful, given time and space, but when he evaded a covering defender with a neat, quick turn he was scythed down by two bigger boys. He lingered on the ground for fully thirty seconds, picking pieces of rubber crumb from his mouth before being brusquely substituted.

Delegates described obvious traits and reached predictable conclusions in Levett's debrief. They reflected principally on Josh's lack of communication, which signalled a lack of confidence, but failed to notice the aftermath of his replacement. He was ignored by the two young coaches who oversaw his team, and spent the rest of the match sitting on his haunches with his head in his hands.

The lack of emotional intelligence in such treatment, and the wider failure of Levett's group to recognise the potential damage to the child's morale, was telling. Had any of the delegates summoned the curiosity to speak to the coaches, or the parents waiting behind the mesh fencing, they might have learned that Josh was a new player, in an unfamiliar environment. His inferior blue team was a composite group, unstructured compared to the cohesive nature of the winning yellow team, who had played together for several seasons.

The lack of deeper insight put into perspective Levett's attempt to invite his audience inside the mind of that 7-year-old: 'At that age a boy makes his decision to pass the ball on trust. He is asking himself, "Can I kick it that far? If I do will I be accepted by my team-mates?" He has to manipulate the ball, retain his balance, control his limbs. He has to change direction, show speed and flexibility. Are we too quick to say what he can't do, and write him off?'

Football has largely moved on from the absurd Lilliputian spectacle of 10-year-olds playing eleven-a-side matches on full-size pitches. But if the imposition of a senior structure on youth football is being addressed during the early years there are still too many issues, created by unreconstructed attitudes and unrealised ambition, in adolescence.

'When we get in the youth development phase, twelve to sixteen, one of the major challenges involves the coach's ego starting to kick in. Kids, who are already going through big changes in life, go from a world of creativity and experimentation to one in which there is pressure to win. All of a sudden you see people on the side of the pitch shouting, screaming and bawling, because they think it helps. I'm not convinced it does. There is no evidence to suggest it is an effective way to help people learn, but as you go higher up, the pressure felt by adults is transferred on to the pitch.'

Levett cites Eddie Jones, the England rugby coach, as a prime exponent of measured leadership. The Australian demanded the highest personal and professional standards in rapidly implementing a culture shift after a disappointing World Cup in 2016. Players were encouraged to take ownership of the gameplan and empowered to make instant decisions for themselves in highly pressurised situations.

The most promising young players need to be hauled out of their comfort blanket, kicking and screaming if necessary. Just as Ajax youth coaches tested Dennis Bergkamp's resilience by dropping him an age level, and ordering him to play at right back, a League One club took the advice of their sports psychologist and dropped the team's outstanding player to the bench for a Youth Cup tie to gauge his response to the disappointment. The importance of his development outweighed the importance of the result.

Similarly, Levett structured a series of challenging situations for Nottingham Forest's under-11 squad. In one drill they had to imagine they were a goal to the good with ten minutes to play against their greatest rivals, Derby County: how would they deal with the stress? In another they were losing 2–0 late in the game in an FA Cup tie against Manchester United: would they retain their spirit and ambition until the end?

The most revealing session involved Levett briefing the referee to be deliberately biased against one team: 'The biggest kid completely lost the plot. He walked off the pitch and wouldn't talk to his coach. He couldn't handle the unfairness but was left alone to think things through. After ten minutes he came back and apologised.'

Levett believes in giving even the youngest players the opportunity to organise their own warm-up sessions, instead of being overseen by academy support staff. The antithesis of such freedom is the goalkeeping coach who walked along the touchline at an under-14 tournament for Category One academies, so that he could line up a wall for his goalkeeper as he defended a free kick, twenty yards out on the right-hand side of the pitch.

'Now, when they release that goalkeeper for poor decision-making, who gets the blame for that? The goalkeeper coach is responding to his own ego, thinking, well, if I don't get this right then there's going to be an issue. Let the kid fail. Let them make mistakes. Then support them and talk to them about it afterwards.'

I had seen something similar in an under-16 game at Tottenham, when an away team coach came on to the pitch following the concession of a goal. He manhandled his central defenders into the positions that would have enabled them to better defend the decisive cross. It had the air of adult arrogance, and created the immediate, undoubtedly unworthy suspicion that the coach was showboating.

Talent doesn't necessarily announce itself with heavenly choirs or psychedelic colours. Progression can involve random chance or a decision made on nothing more substantial than a gnawing feeling that all has yet to be revealed. Gareth Bale was, for instance, a skinny boy from an external development centre in Bath who earned his Southampton scholarship by a single vote.

Levett's presentation highlighted one of Lionel Messi's earliest youth team photographs. He stood at the end of the back row; since at the age of 9 he was four inches below average height, he was dwarfed by those around him. Designed to reinforce the folly of releasing small boys too soon, the image took me back to a chilly evening in Doha in February 2016, and a meeting with Josep Colomer, Messi's mentor.

As Barcelona's youth director, he played a pivotal role in the development of a painfully shy and patently driven boy who had been discovered in Rosario, Argentina. Their relationship contextualises the familiar story of the creation of the planet's best footballer, involving a self-administered human growth hormone programme and a politically charged, financially driven eighteen-month delay before he was confirmed as a Barcelona player at 14.

Others, like Barcelona's former technical director Carles Rexach and the late Joan Lacueva, administrative director at La Masia academy, were significant advocates, but Colomer's bond with Messi has a familial feel. Bald and squat, he is the wise uncle who weighs his words carefully, uses his experience astutely and allocates his praise sparingly.

When we spoke, at the twelve-team Al Kass International Cup, the two of them had just returned from Senegal, where Messi supported Colomer's campaign to distribute a million anti-malaria nets as part of Football Dreams, a talent identification project spanning fifteen nations in Africa, Asia, Central and South America.

Colomer, assistant to Luiz Felipe Scolari with Brazil's World Cup-winning team in 2002, has the restless eyes and carefully cloaked emotions of his trade. Our conversation, conducted during a fraught under-17 match between Inter Milan and Estudiantes on the $1 billion Aspire campus in the Al Waab district of the Qatari capital, incorporated the wider cultural lessons of Messi's eminence.

His instinctive mistrust of modern European football, which he describes as 'a bubble of money and hysteria', puts him at odds with the orthodoxy of the English academy system, which is indulgent in nature and extravagant in its setting.

Colomer spoke of immediately recognising Messi's visualisation of opportunity, and the adhesive control that testified to hours of selfless, solitary practice. Yet of greater long-term significance, when he oversaw his initiation in Barcelona's under-16 team, was evidence of the unusual mixture of hardness and humility he seeks in those whose natural talent might otherwise mask weakness of character.

Like many of his generation, Colomer insists young players need the discipline of old-school chores, such as cleaning the boots of senior players or sweeping the dressing rooms. He uses Messi's example, of a naturally adaptable player developed on clay or threadbare artificial surfaces, to support his argument that pristine facilities can be counter-productive.

'Give too much to the boys, and they don't understand the steps they need to take. I have to tell people, "Look, Leo Messi was training and playing every day on very old, ugly pitches at Barcelona." Messi is Messi because we obliged him to earn all the steps, in football and in life. He even passed through Barça C, and nobody went there before I changed the philosophy.

'I have seen plenty of young players with his talent, plenty. Some had a little bit less, some a little bit more. They were at the top, top level, but they did not have his mentality. Leo, he was always a winner, he believed in himself a lot, but he also has a lot of patience for football.

'I remember when I put him in Barça B. They played on the Saturday. On the Sunday morning he took the bus with the under-16s, his team, to go and support them any place in Catalunya. He was living only for football. So I'm very happy for him because I love him as a person and a player. He is a model for many children who think this is easy. It is not easy.'

The fate of Messi's contemporary Leandro Depetris, another Argentine phenomenon who became a cause célèbre when he signed for AC Milan at the age of 11, is instructive. His career effectively ended at the age of 28 in the summer of 2016, when he was released by Sportivo Patria, a club in Torneo Federal A, the regionalised third division of the Argentine league.

His is a tale of homesickness, fecklessness, financial turmoil, over-expectation and underachievement. A striker, he is mocked not only by poignant footage of him as a joyful 8-year-old, weaving through massed ranks of defenders, but also by his professional record, of scoring a single goal at twelve clubs in Italy and his homeland.

'A cook sees a soup and only by smelling it he knows whether he is missing salt or not,' Colomer reflected, with faintly inappropriate lyricism. 'Our job is to discover players and of course we can make mistakes because we are not discovering a player for today, we are discovering a player for tomorrow.

'That is not only depending on the quality of the player. It's depending on his progression but also the style of the club, if it fits to his potential. Will a coach of the future like him or not? Will you be at the right place at the right moment?

'I will put an example to you: if there is a number ten

at Barcelona who is a very good young player, is he going to play in the place of Lionel Messi? OK, he has no chance. So the development of a player is not only about his quality. A player grows in a system, but more than a system, a philosophy. Messi has in his body the philosophy of Barcelona.'

One of the enduring issues with the English game is its indistinct philosophy, largely untouched by the FA's so-called DNA strategy. Levett, who admits, 'It is narrow-minded to think we have all the answers,' is at least seeking external examples from sport, business and the arts, to add weight to the case for change.

Strategic links with sports like rugby union, cricket and hockey, aligned to study of elite recruitment programmes at city investment banks, cover common ground in talent discovery and development. Pixar's corporate philosophy, which speaks of valuing experimental mistakes because 'without them we'd have no originality', has also been heeded.

It is doubtful whether football has the philosophical maturity to learn from the Knowledge Is Power Program, a network of free open-enrolment schools in underprivileged communities across the United States, but the attributes they demand in their pupils – social intelligence, grit, zest, gratitude, optimism and curiosity – are directly transferable to professional sport.

Why can't our gaudy game draw on the marketing-driven values of Red Bull, or the character traits that inform the recruitment programme of the BRIT School, which counts singers Adele, Jessie J and Leona Lewis, together with such actors as Blake Harrison, Tom Holland and Emily Head, among its alumni? Allow Levett to explain:

'The common lessons involve character. Red Bull, as a brand, invest in people with a story to tell. They might spend two years to really understand someone, to know what drives them, before they think of investing in that person. At the BRIT School I asked their director of dance who gets that last audition place.

'Is it the ballet dancer, trained since the age of two, or an urban street-dancer from Thornton Heath? She said, "Dancing doesn't get you in the building, your character does." Candidates are observed in different situations. They show something of who they are by interacting with other people, and asking pertinent questions. What comes through is the character, the person. Ironically that's the part that is under-resourced in professional football more than anything else.'

Academy managers, as a breed, are conditioned to trust hard numbers over soft skills. As support staffs have grown, data has been deified. The theory that the defining factor in success is one of mindset, supported by senior internationals in an impromptu survey conducted by Levett, was overlooked during his study visit to a leading Premier League club.

'They had all the data, graphs of the average speed in

the game of every player, comparing the goalkeeper with the centre forward, and that didn't make any sense. Where does this link to learning? Where does it show progression over the last ten weeks, linked to learning criteria, in order to become a first-team player? "Oh, we don't track that."

'They've got ten sports scientists who can churn out GPS data on how far players have run during a game. Kids are comfortable with technology, and could download that themselves. It would give them ownership of the figures. Support staff are experts in what they do, but professional clubs put people in silos. We need to be at the stage where programmes are built around the kids.

'Academy systems all have an element of psych support for the players coming through. It's important that it is embedded in the foundation phase so that the sports psychologist is just another coach. We've got to get away from the mindset of, you've got to go and see the psychologist if you're broken. Go and lay on the couch and they'll fix you. That's bollocks. We need a generational change, so that one-to-one sessions are seen as an aid to improve performance.'

Coaching is one of the fundamental weaknesses of English football, and Levett is the type of missionary worker who confesses to enduring occasional dark nights of the soul. He accepts the value of formal coach education is 'tiny' and estimates that 70 per cent of effective personal development involves making mistakes on the grass, learning about the nuances of language and communication with children. A good mentor and the collaborative mentality of the old Liverpool boot room also helps.

'I've got to get away from thinking that I'm going to change people's minds on certain things, and it bothering me that I don't. All I can do is give you the current thinking on helping players become the best they can possibly be. What you choose to do with that information is entirely up to you. The forward-thinking coaches will change stuff. The traditional ones, with more of a closed mindset, possibly won't.'

The mood is sombre. The England T-shirt he is wearing appears to take on the characteristics of a hair shirt. There is a constant urge to scratch the scab of yet another example of institutionalised ignorance. Levett recounts the rejection of a boy who, at the age of 9, amazed first-team coaches with the intelligence displayed in a ten-page document he had written, detailing his tactical dissection of three senior matches.

'That boy was released at twelve because he couldn't get around a massive pitch. They told him they didn't think he had the confidence to play in front of forty thousand people. This boy is the chairman of the school debating society. He played the lead role in the school play. Confidence? This boy will achieve in life . . .'

I didn't have the heart to share an all-too-familiar

story, outlined in the *Manchester Evening News.* Jaxon Lal had been headhunted by Manchester City scouts after his mother Joanne posted a video on Facebook of him playing football in the garden with his brother Riley. She shared her hope that her sons would have a career in the professional game. The accompanying photograph showed Jaxon posing, foot on a ball, in a Barcelona kit. Messi's name was on the back of his ludicrously over-sized shirt.

Jaxon Lal was 3 years old.

3
X Factor Every Day

The challenge to the conscience was framed by a deep, wide mirror in the men's toilet. Inscribed on white ceramic tiles above two washbasins, it was aimed at the only users of the facility – fathers waiting for their children in the parents lounge at Manchester City's impossibly opulent academy.

> Does your child getting selected or dropped, scoring the winning goal or missing an open net, getting man of the match or getting subbed at half time, represent your parenting? Or does a child who is a decent, polite, respectful, humble, hard-working teammate actually reflect the kind of parent you are?

Such a stark message, in a strangely logical setting since it addressed a captive audience, had greater impact than even the vast image which filled the facing wall in the gymnasium along the corridor. It was of Sergio Agüero scoring the goal that won City the Premier League title in added time against Queens Park Rangers in May 2012. The time, '93:20', was emblazoned alongside the invocation 'Every Second Counts'.

Other slogans in the performance centre are aspirational ('We are building a structure for the future, not just a team of all-stars'), motivational ('Practise again and again . . . make it count') and educational ('Train like a professional. Eat like a professional. Drink like a professional. Tweet like a professional').

In such concentration, in such an environment, they beg questions: is this a corporate PowerPoint version of football, or a sky blueprint for a dynasty? Is it an artfully packaged marketing initiative or a substantive socio-political statement? Does it represent enlightened thinking, or is it a billionaire's workhouse? In truth, it supports elements of many contrasting assumptions.

To the cynics, the City Football Academy, the CFA, to give it an appropriately modern acronym, is the Death Star, the manifestation of a malign and voracious philosophy that warehouses talented teenagers from around the globe. To the supplicants, true believers in the vision funded by Sheikh Mansour bin Zayed al-Nahyan of Abu Dhabi, it is Utopia.

In terms of social transformation, its impact on east Manchester is undeniable, and infinitely preferable to a short-lived alternative, a government-approved super casino. A total of 883 building contracts were placed with companies within the M60 corridor. Sixty-two per cent of the workforce, including ninety-three previously unemployed men and women, came from the local community.

When I first visited the area, twenty years previously, terraced houses beside the newly built Velodrome nearby were available for less than £10,000 on a 'buy one, get one free' basis. The 80-acre academy site was a polluted post-industrial wasteland. More than £200 million and 6,000 trees later, the complex is a world leader.

The detail is thought-provoking, product of unprecedented research into more than thirty sports development initiatives on five continents. Plans underwent nineteen drafts, and were informed by the culture of sports as diverse as American football, Australian rules football, basketball and softball. A 7,000-seater stadium dominates the entrance; sixteen more pitches are augmented by a half pitch on which to train goalkeepers.

All replicate the pitch at the Etihad Stadium, which is reached by a symbolic bridge. Three lengths of grass imitate conditions on opposition grounds. Six hydrotherapy areas, featuring a three-lane main pool and plunge pools with a temperature range between 4 and 36 degrees centigrade, aid rest and rehabilitation.

Two thirds of the building is devoted to youth development. Even the dressing rooms are aspirational; the first team's circular changing area, the only one used regularly on the right-hand side of the facility, is reminiscent of those in Major League Baseball clubhouses. The success of the project will be gauged by how many boys progress to the privilege of being able to toss their soiled kit down a centrally situated wooden chute into the unseen laundry rooms below.

City's under-10s, -11s and -13s were national champions in the 2015–16 season, the under-11s defeating QPR 29–1 in their final fixture. The under-15s won the national Floodlit Cup and the under-16s were undefeated. Though the under-18s were national champions, they lost in the final that mattered, the FA Youth Cup, to Chelsea. If you believe such dominance does not breed envy and resentment, give my love to the fairies at the bottom of your garden.

The Premier League took time to ratify City's transfer of Liverpool's under-15 goalkeeper Louie Moulden as part of a new Five Step Process, which involves formal interviews with players, parents and clubs involved in moves between Category One academies. Though they are reluctant to confirm their unhappiness officially, it is widely believed that Liverpool, Manchester United and Everton discussed refusing to play City at more junior levels.

City's recruitment is global and aggressive, especially around the pivotal age of 16, when scholarships are at stake and professional contracts beckon. Relocation packages, offered to families of boys as young as 11, are unprecedented in their scope and generosity. The golden eagle, which dominated City's club crest until a redesign in 2015, might have been consigned to history but its predatory tendencies endure.

Some boys are steeped in City's traditions. Tommy Doyle, arguably England's best under-15 midfield player, has two club legends, Glyn Pardoe and the late Mike Doyle, as grandfathers. Phil Foden, the winger who made the bench in a Champions League tie against Celtic at the age of 16 years and 192 days, has been with the club for a decade. Yet his classmate and international colleague Jadon Sancho, an extravagantly gifted winger signed from Watford at the age of 14 in a deal worth potentially £500,000, represented transplanted talent.

Unnoticed amidst the flurry of controversy inspired by Moulden, City signed a future rival, 16-year-old Polish goalkeeper Pawel Sokol, from Korona Kielce at the end of the summer transfer window in 2016. The delicacy of international transfers was underlined in September, when FIFA cleared City of illegally approaching Benjamin Garre, an Argentine midfield player signed from Velez Sarsfield despite the interest of Manchester United and Barcelona, when he was only 15.

This did little to quieten murmured accusations about the application of unreasonable advantage, extreme wealth in an inadequately regulated environment that invites greed and expedience. Mark Allen, the former

MTV executive who has been City's academy director since July 2009, chooses to confront such criticism head on:

'I'm going to be very open and honest on this, because I have a very strong view. I have two daughters, who are runners, and my overriding goal was to get them into the very best institutions that I could, based on their abilities. If I had a son who was, say, an outstanding cellist, I would want him to go to the best school I could find.

'That is going to be an ambition of most parents, I would say. They are looking to do the best for their children. Here we have an outstanding facility, a comprehensive football and non-football programme that probably very few match, even though they could if they wanted to. We're very, very strong about a holistic approach to development and investment in youth.

'We come up against criticism in terms of recruitment all the time. I know we have to face this, but I think it's less about poaching than opportunity. We are inundated on a regular basis by parents saying, "Look, how do we get our son to this academy?" And that's a fact.'

Equally undeniably, his operation will be obliged to justify itself financially in the medium term. At current, grotesquely inflated, market rates, it would take the emergence of four regular first-team players from the academy to write off the initial £200 million investment. Until then, the balance sheet will be supported by the sale or loan of fringe players who are good enough to realise what Grant Downie, the academy's Head of Performance, terms their 'asset value'.

The severity of the phrase hints at fundamental contradictions, yet Downie is a gently spoken, emotionally intelligent Cumbrian, who received the OBE in 2013 for services to physiotherapy in sport and young people. He has spent nearly thirty years in the professional game, progressing from Lilleshall's national rehabilitation centre to Glasgow Rangers and Middlesbrough before assuming a development role at City, initially as Head of Medical Services in September 2011.

Can hunger be sustained in such a paradise?

Downie has a singular reference point: 'At Rangers, we had boys from Castlemilk, a really rough housing estate. It's one of the most parochial places, but the fact of the matter is in these harder housing schemes in Scotland folk generally try to look after themselves, because they have values and appreciate things. You could argue, when you look around this beautiful facility, that maybe we're doing the opposite.

'We're not, but I can see why people would see this place as maybe being too good. If all we did was concentrate on the bells and whistles, we would be wrong. We've got to ensure that the scholars coming into it appreciate it for what it is, and maximise it for their benefit, because many will not be here in the longer term. Hopefully this can be the catalyst not just for their football career, but for their life.

'Football development is pretty straightforward. The boys who come through the doors here are pretty talented. What derails them is not necessarily football, but other things in their lives. It could be family, agents. It could be where they are from. We must develop the person. What would make me proud, and I'm sure Mark would say the same thing, is that when these boys are playing for Walsall, or Colchester, their coach can say to us, "Your boy is great. He knows how to look after himself, and conducts himself properly." '

City's academy squads are taught to cook, and put through bronze and silver levels of the Duke of Edinburgh award scheme. A life skills programme, aimed at those aged between 16 and 19, involves community work. Perspective is gained through serving at a soup kitchen, or playing on crutches and losing heavily to the club's amputee team.

The coaching syllabus for players under 11 years old is highly technical. It tests a boy's ability to operate in tight areas: can he take the ball on the half-turn? Is he two-footed? Has he an appreciation of space and others around him? To guard against the dangers of excessively early specialisation, boys undertake alternative activities like boxing, canoeing, judo, Pilates, yoga and freerunning.

Younger groups are let loose on an adventure playground alongside the main building three times a week. The aim is to recreate the organic pleasures of climbing, the accumulated resilience of falling. Play encourages a natural sense of balance but, above all, offers a cooling-down period in a hothouse environment.

On one of the days I visited a vanguard of half a dozen boys from the under-13 squad prepared to train on the largest indoor pitch in the UK. The timeless innocence of their childhood ritual, a game of headers and volleys which preceded the arrival of their coaches and cadre of support staff, masked the relentlessness of the scrutiny.

'I've often described this environment as *X Factor* every day,' Downie reflected. 'Big Brother is watching everything you do, and monitoring it. We are trying to provide a pathway that is challenging at every opportunity, but supportive. We have two full-time psychologists in the academy, plus additional support where we need it, so therefore there's a sense-check.

'Some lads, at times, are going to hit lows, but what we don't want to do is put so much bubble wrap on them they can't cope. You can go to the other extreme, where a footballer can turn up at a game and he doesn't have to do anything. He doesn't bring his boots and shin pads. He doesn't provide soap or a towel.

'Here things get done for you as you go further up the chain, but we use self-education, empowerment. Take soft-tissue massage as an example. We give them foam rollers, so they can learn how to do it themselves. Ultimately, when you're in front of sixty thousand people, and you've got to make what appears to you and I in the crowd to be a simple ten-yard pass, you rely on yourself. The difference between doing that in a match and in training is pressure. What we've got to learn is when to exert pressure.'

Such a delicate process, balancing sensitivity and cold-bloodedness, blurs boundaries and strangles language. Sir Dave Brailsford, embattled architect of Britain's Olympic cycling programme, employs 'compassionate ruthlessness' in the pursuit of perfection. City's strategy is one of exposing children to 'supported trauma'.

Downie used as an example their under-12s, who were at a tournament in Japan, playing in exceptionally hot, humid conditions, dealing with homesickness and the debilitating effect of jet lag. He consciously created additional pressure by imposing the target of winning the event (they eventually finished fifth) but took the precaution of briefing support staff to be compassionate in the event of failure.

Learning is contextualised. An experiment involving the under-15s tested their standing jumps before and after a video presentation featuring the heading ability of Cristiano Ronaldo at set pieces. On average the boys leaped 20 per cent higher when the images of the icon's impact were fresh. They couldn't explain why, but evidently understood the point, since it was not a training routine conducted in isolation. Similarly, nutritional messages are couched in everyday terms.

'It is about instant context, so we talk about refuelling

the body through food as topping up the battery on your cell phone. You recharge, revitalise, re-energise. If we delivered the same message using carbohydrate, proteins and minerals it would put a child to sleep.'

Downie's exchange over lunch with a 12-year-old, in the early phase of rehabilitation following the dislocation of his kneecap, was telling:

'CJ, do you ever eat fruit or vegetables?'

'No, I don't really like them.'

'What if I told you that if you ate that little pot of fruit every day you might get back five days earlier?'

The boy rose, made his way on crutches to the food bar, and took two.

'I don't sell it as, "This is going to make you healthy." This is going to make you play football better. This might actually help you play fifty league games. You will be stronger because of this. I spent twenty-five years working with senior players, and thought I was pretty knowledgeable, but my learning curve, working with this generation over the last five years, has been . . . boom.

'We've had boys from really difficult backgrounds. To try and influence them, you've got to understand them first. If they don't trust anyone it's probably because every time they've run out of the elevator in their block of flats they know a guy might be there, waiting with a knife. So how are they going to suddenly trust me? They aren't going to trust anyone. They can't – they can only trust themselves.

'Trust is not a word, it's an action. You know a boy is comfortable with you when he can cry in front of you. You don't judge him for that – because how many times have we cried in our lives? – but we have a private place, close to the main medical area, where we can take them aside. What a boy tells me there is completely different to what he tells me in front of his peers.'

Downie recounted the story of a boy who launched into a tirade at him because he was reminded, continually, that his laces were not fastened. Downie allowed him five minutes to calm down before ushering him to the quiet room. The boy apologised as soon as the door was shut. It transpired his best friend had just committed suicide, and his aunt had also passed away. He had bottled up his grief until it could no longer be contained.

'That's a person we expect to play under pressure. That's why I tell my staff that their principal role involves the welfare of people. Every one of them is a safeguarding officer. Football is a tough environment, and you must be there for everyone. It is not quite survival of the fittest, but dressing rooms can be brutal, and there are natural pecking orders.

'I've seen a lot of potential bullying situations in thirty years, working in football. They are creeping in earlier, and I'm sure the money streaming into the game is a reason for it. That will not influence the younger boys, but maybe it influences families. Has bullying ever occurred here? There's always going to be a certain form, but I think we're pretty good at seeing it, and arresting it. All we can do is try and be available.'

The intelligence operation relies on the simplicity of human interaction. Downie shakes the hand of each boy he meets, and makes a point of making eye contact. An experiment involving a wellness questionnaire, filled in on a mobile phone app, was abandoned when it became clear answers were structured to please the coaches, rather than inform them.

Two full-time academy taxi drivers, CRB checked, are gatekeepers. One is an army veteran, the other has experience of dealing with gun crime. The insight of teachers at the independent Roman Catholic school to which City send more than seventy pupils in a pioneering educational programme, provides another reality check.

If the CFA is a symbol of Mammon and modernity, St Bede's College is a fusion of the academic and the spiritual. Aspiring footballers enter a parallel universe though a red-brick hall, above which a Latin passage from Psalm 33, *Venite Filii Audite Me* ('Come, children, hearken to me'), is inscribed. They push back burnished wooden doors and walk to classes across a tessellated Victorian floor that reads '*Salve*', the Latin for 'Welcome'.

The school was founded in 1876, though tiny blue plaster fishes, engraved on the supporting columns, hint at the building's initial use as an aquarium. Sepia photographs from 1891, featuring stern priests and stiff-backed pupils, line the Our Lady Corridor, which leads to the chapel in which Roberto Mancini prayed privately before City's title-winning victory over QPR in 2012.

City meet annual fees of £10,785 per child, and, irrespective of whether a boy remains on their full-time training programme, guarantee to underwrite their education until they take their GCSEs at the age of 16. There are relatively few drop-outs since there is an element of self-selection; only the most promising players are offered a place. They must pass an entrance examination – tellingly some bring their agents with their parents to the introductory interview.

Richard Robson became headmaster in January 2015, following a traumatic period in which the school was the centre of a historic sexual abuse case involving clergy who taught there from the fifties. He has strengthened focus on the fundamental values that attracted City's Arab owners:

'We want grounded children that are courageous; not just in their faith, but in finding out what they are good at, what they need to work harder at. We want them to be courageous in being the best friend they can be, courageous in their kindness, self-discipline, self-motivation and self-moderation.

'It almost involves the ecology of the human being. It's not just about making decisions about right and wrong, working or living in a civil society. It's about gospel values, about a way of life. It's about producing children that are selfless, good communicators. They can work as a team, and don't take themselves too seriously. There is a fine line with young people, but they're confident, not arrogant.

'City's football terminology involves their growth mindset. We have a similar philosophy. We want our children to grow step by step, target by target. We're giving them an opportunity to realise the importance of how you behave, how you talk, how you present yourself, how sometimes your voice is not more important than another voice.'

That's a stretch target, given the travails of adolescence and the inevitability of City's boys being a distinctive, easily identifiable group. To counteract that, they must attend in full school uniform and are forbidden to wear club-branded coats. They are subject to standard discipline: if any are placed in detention they miss training.

The relationship entered its sixth academic year in September 2016 when an unprecedented thirteen boys from City's under-12s were enrolled. Their training programme was realigned for a week in the autumn when they undertook the compulsory retreat, at Castlerigg Manor in the Lake District. On average only 20 per cent of the City boys are Roman Catholics, yet this spiritual bonding was seen as critical to their integration.

The colour-coded timetable for the under-15s highlights the complexity and delicacy of the balance struck between the pastoral, educational and sporting demands on the boys. Their school week is divided into twenty-two hours of lessons, nine hours of football and three hours of physical activity. They spend one day exclusively at St Bede's, another exclusively at the CFA. Teachers shuttle between venues.

Andrew Dando, who, as Director of Studies, organises the academic programme, has the responsibility of rationalising conflicting challenges. A Manchester United fan, because he liked their kit when his family got their first colour TV in time for the 1976 FA Cup final, his sensitivity and grasp of character became apparent as we stood at the back of a class. He quietly pointed out two City players sitting in an informal semi circle around the teacher:

'Felix is a joker, a good student. He is unfazed by anything, and will be happy in life whatever happens. Nathaniel is a great student, intelligent and articulate, but he worries. He is really driven: am I good enough? Am I pushing myself hard enough? Will someone overtake me? I suppose you are only ever one bad game away from a problem.'

Ironically, Max Dunne, a pupil affiliated to Manchester United, provides the most compelling example of competing pressures. Initially informed he was going to be released, he completed revision for his GCSE examinations a week after his sixteenth birthday, while living on his own in a hotel during an extended trial for Southampton.

Despite the additional distraction of being courted by

nine more Premier League clubs, and thanks largely to online tuition by Jenny Hatton, his form teacher, he achieved two As, three Bs and two Cs. Football's capricious nature was confirmed when Nicky Butt, United's new Academy Director, reversed the decision not to offer him a scholarship.

City's coaches have noted an improvement in general levels of behaviour, and academic results have been above average, but the ambiguity of the situation is apparent. However exalted its ambitions and status, football does not exist in a vacuum; boys must deal with social issues and special pressures. Dr Robson acknowledges the difficulties:

'I sometimes see the petulant teenager, told he is brilliant at football his whole life. What I'm trying to do is make him realise that hard work, diligence, politeness, kindness, humility and mercy are the qualities he needs to exhibit, not an arrogant footballer's persona. Some of them, especially if they are very, very good and remuneration is going on, are not helped by their agents giving their ego a boost.

'There's a real sense of, I know I'm signed until I'm eighteen. I've got a really bright future ahead of me. We're trying to deflate that, bring them back down to earth by saying, look, it's about who you are as a person. It's what is on the inside that counts, not on the outside. I'm trying to build strength of character because generally, behind the bravado, there is insecurity.

'I see boys trying to make their way in life. They are very, very gifted and talented in one aspect but they are fragile, so scared that it is not going to work out. That's when they have to face their fear, and ask, "Please will you help me?" It can take a little time to get that point, because it is humbling and makes them vulnerable, the antithesis of what they want to be in the football world.

'At the end of the day I can't get away from the fact these boys are here because they want to be professional footballers. Do I see them as footballers? No. Am I actually even that bothered that they are good at football? Not really, because they don't play for my school teams. School is school and club is club, but we have similar expectations. Aspiration, drive and achievement.'

Mark Allen, as City's Academy Director Dr Robson's opposite number, stresses, 'We try and bring as much reality and normality to these boys' lives as possible,' but accepts that, 'Ultimately we know that not everybody is going to go on and have a glorious professional career.' Intentions are good, but the landscape is hazardous.

Allen has never forgotten the sense of alarm and worthlessness he felt when casually rejected by Swindon as an 18-year-old apprentice: 'It was an end-of-season presentation. We were invited on the pitch to collect the trophy. After that game, the coach in question said, "Listen, we'll be in touch." And that was it.

'I was distraught, so it stuck with me for a long time. I've been there. I've sat across that table. I know what it's like to hear the word "sorry". It's lived with me and been a major factor in terms of how I approach this and why I think it has to be as rounded as it is at City.'

Grant Downie is equally unafraid to acknowledge reality: 'We're entering into a new phase. Rewards are coming at an earlier stage in people's careers than ever before. That's partly dictated by economics, because competition for talent is intense. Big clubs chase talent around and reward it more. Does it concern me? If you're not concerned about it then take your head out of your bottom.

'If I think of three players here I would class in that [much-coveted] bracket, one of them, I know for certain, it won't affect. It's just the way he acts, the way he behaves. The other two I'm a little more concerned about, partly because we don't control the environment when they go home. All we can do is try and guide them on what will be a bumpy journey.

'On a more general Premier League level, and not specific to our club, if players are well rewarded at sixteen, and unemployed by twenty-two, as the case could be, what's the incidence of alcoholism, drug-related problems and even suicide going to be like? Pretty high. And that does bother me. I would have no pleasure in producing players for the first team if the rejects ended up being drunks who wanted to batter women and drive cars too fast. That's too big a price, in my view.'

Downie's is not a lone voice. The vast majority of those I have met in youth development dread the moment of rejection. They uniformly describe being troubled by the experience, even if, professionally, they accept it as part of life. City have a structured, humane exit strategy but the fact remains that the niceties of their nuanced corporate social responsibility programme cannot soften the blow they inflict on callow youths.

Benevolence is not an affectation, but the CFA, like all other academies, is judged objectively, on how many first-team players it produces. At least in City's case, there is a rare sense of strategic and philosophical harmony with the head coach. Pep Guardiola is a familiar figure at academy training sessions, and takes the Elite Development Squad at least once a week.

Ten academy graduates, including Sancho, the star of an exciting England under-17 team, and Colin Rösler, son of former City striker Uwe, were given four-year professional contracts on the eve of the 2016–17 season. 'Your future starts now,' Allen told them. 'These will be the most important years of your life.'

Five development players, including central defender Tosin Adarabioyo and England under-21 goalkeeper Angus Gunn, former St Bede's students, were promoted to the first-team squad in September. The gesture of faith prompted a reappraisal of an anecdote, shared by a fellow Premier League manager as the Spaniard was settling in.

When Guardiola met Roman Abramovich as part of an unrequited courtship ritual which lasted from 2012 to early 2016, he made two demands: 'Give me a hundred footballers and two perfect pitches.' The Chelsea owner agreed eagerly, and was further encouraged by the coach's lack of apparent interest in confirming his salary, dismissed as the responsibility of Pere Guardiola, his brother and agent.

A third demand, thrown suddenly into the mix, got the oligarch's full attention. Pep insisted that Abramovich and Chelsea's coaching staff list the best fifteen academy prospects; in return he promised to take personal oversight of the development of the best four players in each age group. The message was unequivocal: this would be a club run not by Abramovich's ego, but by the all-encompassing philosophy of Guardiola's mentor, Johan Cruyff. Reading between the lines of the corporate positivity that laces the language of one of the world's richest clubs, this is what is taking shape behind the tall black metal gates and security-screened turnstiles that guard the CFA complex. On a clear day, City can see for ever. The view for other, smaller if not lesser, clubs is ominously obscured.

4
Death of a Dream

Twelve 7-year-old boys, in red-and-black club track-suits, were paraded around Griffin Park at half-time with footballs at their feet. A public address announcer, alongside them on the pitch, babbled about the brightness of their future. Parents captured the moment for posterity on their mobile phones, and strangers in a 12,301 crowd, assembled for Brentford's 3–0 win over Fulham on April 30, 2016, applauded like indulgent uncles.

Cruelly, devastatingly, it was a charade, an illusion. The contracts the under-8 squad had signed for the 2016–17 season were worthless, since the decision to close an apparently thriving, well-respected academy was about to be ratified. Candour was considered impossible because HR protocols dictated that the club's priority, as part of a thirty-day consultation process, was to inform coaches and support staff they were to be made redundant.

It takes sixty-three minutes to annihilate innocence, for a dream to endure its death throes. That was the precise length of the meeting on May 11 that confirmed a 'restructure' that exposed football's family values as a façade. It had a false start because of microphone problems, and ended with tearful parents clinging to one another, like shipwreck survivors to driftwood.

They wished each other 'good luck' and with a final entreaty to 'take care', walked out into the night to counsel sons who were struggling to come to terms with the magnitude of their betrayal. Only a fortnight previously boys across the age groups had signed new contracts, celebrated their retention and basked in the measured praise of coaches who preached loyalty to the cause.

Three days beforehand, Brentford's under-13 team had followed Borussia Dortmund and Manchester City in winning the Elite Neon Cup, staged by AEK Athens. Suddenly, the boys' souvenir photographs with Pelé had become tokens of what might have been. On that same Sunday afternoon, the under-17s had lost only on penalties to Liverpool in the final of the Ipswich Town tournament. Bigger clubs were being upstaged.

The parents were addressed by departing academy manager Ose Aibangee: 'I am disappointed, frustrated, angry for you. It has been an absolute pleasure to work with such talented players. It is not a job. It is what we love, what we do. These are fantastic young men, who work hard. They are disciplined and respectful. That's a credit to you. Have a safe future.'

The parents' ire, directed at Phil Giles and Rasmus Ankersen, co-directors of football, had been raw, visceral and relentless: 'This is disgusting behaviour . . . shame on you . . . we were not considered . . . this is complete crap . . . my son broke his heart last night . . . you don't give a toss . . . this is not fair, it is not on . . . have you taken into account the psychological effects on our boys? . . . how can you say you have cared for our children?'

A supplementary statement, issued by the club, spoke of 'developing value'. It argued that 'the development of young players must make sense from a business perspective'. Yet the most telling moment of the evening came when Giles admitted: 'I have two sons. In your situation I would be exactly the same.' He 'regretted' the pointless parade of the under-8s.

The underlying strain was evident more than three months later, when Giles sat in a hotel coffee shop and dwelled upon 'a horrible experience'. His body language was not that of a corporate automaton; as he explained the background to the decision his neck became progressively flushed, and his unconscious habit of scratching the back of his hand and lower arm became more pronounced.

He sought context rather than sympathy: 'In a normal business there are not lots of kids, who need a clear message on their futures, involved in what is a complex process. HR law isn't set up to accommodate such a case, so it all becomes complicated to manage and very difficult to handle without making any mistakes at all.

'I had to explain the rationale to people who didn't care about the rationale. They were just looking after their kids. If I put myself in their position I would be caring for my son, not the business logic, not the owner's money. That's not important. It is such a grey area.

'Football clubs are effectively trading in children, trying to make money out of children. You can dress it up how you like, in terms of it being for their benefit, but as an individual I am not comfortable with being involved in that.

'I am sure there would be a moral outcry if HSBC or Barclays were involved in hoovering up eight-year-olds in the area, giving them specialist training as FX traders or money managers, and swapping kids between them. It is no different to what is going on in football.'

Piecing together the fragments of sorrow and concern felt like an intrusion into private grief. A father confided he had prepared a small speech for his son: 'I don't know for certain, but you may be without a club. Just steel yourself for that. It's not the be all and end all; there's a bigger world out there for you. It's not the end of the world, be proud of what you've achieved.'

It was impossible not to be moved by the anguished tone of a mother whose son had abandoned his A levels, after obtaining eleven A grades at GCSE, to take up a scholarship. An immediate promise by Giles that his contract would be honoured was met with scepticism, since the mood was dark, angry, bitter. The boy, Sean Bird, would eventually leave and join AFC Wimbledon.

When a loved one is compromised, explanations about the consequences of the Premier League's Elite Player Performance Plan, which expensively institutionalises inequality, are background noise. Giles' revelation that Manchester City had invested £2 million in youth recruitment in London alone failed to register, since tearful sons have infinitely greater impact than economic realities.

One boy had been through something similar at Wycombe Wanderers, Aldershot and Crawley Town, who had closed their youth systems around him due to economic necessity. According to his father, the timing of the latest setback was 'awful, a nightmare', and conformed to a forbidding pattern.

'It is their money and if they are seeing no short- or long-term strategic return on their investment they will make such decisions,' he reasoned. 'Clubs feel they don't owe you anything. They bring in trialists and if they find someone better than your son they have no hesitation in getting rid. Their job is to farm kids and find players who can potentially make the first team.

'At the end of the day it is a business, kids or no kids,

but that's not what we signed up to as parents. We were very happy at Brentford since they had developed him, not just as a footballer, but as a very considered, disciplined young man. They worked on his life skills for eighteen months. Now he might only have until Christmas to make an impression on another club.'

Other fathers, like Danny Johnson, whose 12-year-old son Alfie had left his local secondary school to enrol in the academy's associated school programme at Uxbridge High, were concerned by the educational implications. At the very least, the demands of ferrying his son to training at a new club, which, as a lorry driver, would require pre-dawn starts, had been immeasurably complicated.

The indoor facility at the school, featuring a fully enclosed 60-metre by 50-metre 3G pitch, learning zones, changing rooms, a gym and a physio room, was a monument to unfulfilled ambition, largely funded by the club. At the official opening on January 16, 2014 Brentford's CEO Mark Devlin had spoken of Brentford's 'strategic decision to invest in youth'.

The facility, essential if the academy was to achieve EPPP Category Two status, illustrated the dangers of being wedded to an ideal. Brentford's boys combined study with coaching sessions during the day; teammates from other schools attended on day release once a week. The annual taxi bill for ferrying them around London, met by the club, was £100,000.

Greg Dyke, then the FA chairman, was guest of honour on that Thursday evening, when the school's motto, 'making success happen', seemed apposite. He hailed the commitment to a new, homegrown generation. Devlin spoke of 'three or four' boys from the programme graduating quickly into the first-team squad. Aibangee's prediction that Brentford would produce a senior England international within five years mirrored the mood.

Now, despite the diligence of Allan Steele, who combined coaching duties with widely admired work as Brentford's education and welfare manager, the situation was fraught with uncertainty. Uxbridge High, rated 'outstanding' by OFSTED inspectors in 2011, had regressed in the following three years. An inspection undertaken on February 12 and 13, 2014 concluded the school 'requires improvement'.

The principal and his deputy resigned in October 2014, for failing to protect a 13-year-old pupil from abuse at the hands of a learning support assistant, former Commonwealth Games decathlete Kevin Sempers, but were allowed to resume their careers in April 2016. Sempers was sentenced to eighteen months' imprisonment after admitting two counts of sexual activity with a child.

The issues raised by the academy closure went straight to the heart of what a modern football club is, and who it represents. Is it a community asset, a commercial enterprise or a test bed for an alternative sporting philosophy? Is it a rich man's indulgence, a politician's plaything or a supporter's heirloom? Brentford's academy was deemed to be a stain on the balance sheet, yet it added colour, vibrancy and hope to the local area.

I had seen it flourish under Aibangee's leadership over several years, but the culture shift at the club, confirmed by the arrival of Giles and Ankersen in May 2015, left it vulnerable. Formative figures in the academy's development moved on; Shaun O'Connor returned to Arsenal to take up a youth recruitment role, head of coaching Stuart English left for Birmingham City and Miguel Rios joined Fulham's senior recruitment team.

They were badly missed, because rather than buying into the club, or its brand, the most balanced parents buy into the individual who sells the ethos of the club to them. Rios, in particular, was praised for his courtesy, integrity, intelligence and affinity with the ambitions and backgrounds of the boys he helped to recruit.

Aibangee was also held in huge regard. One father spoke for many when he said: 'I've always found him a very decent guy, very approachable, very regular. You could see that this had broken him. He looked tired, stressed. He feels it for the staff. He was leading the group. I hope he doesn't feel responsible for what's happened. He could only do what he could.'

Another parent spoke of how he had been convinced

by Aibangee's credo – of recognising the innate potential of the individual. He had been unsure about allowing his son to remain in the system, since he had been so concerned by his treatment at another club's development centre he had considered calling in the NSPCC. 'I felt I had a very good case against them,' he said. 'They mistreated boys, had them shivering in the freezing cold. One of the parents intervened, took his son away, and didn't come back. Looking back, I should have had the courage to do the same.'

A bag at the back of Andrew Mills' garage held clues to the contradictions that led to the closure. It contained Brentford kits and tracksuits of various vintages. They were once used by Barry Quin as tokens of esteem, given to boys he sought to recruit to the Centre of Excellence that preceded the academy. His was a hand-to-mouth existence, which included a three-game spell as caretaker first-team manager in 2007.

Quin is now Head of Coaching at Watford's academy. One of Mills' first actions, as Brentford's chief executive in 2010, had been to release him, following a review of the club's youth development strategy. Mills was obliged to lay the foundations for Aibangee's regime, but the decision weighed heavily.

'I wasn't particularly comfortable with that,' he admitted. 'Barry was a good guy. He had brought through so many boys from the estates. Like most in football, he had battled against limited budgets over the years. There was a wave of optimism about academies and EPPP, but I wondered whether it made business sense.

'I was brought into the club two years before I became CEO, on the basis of, we're losing £680,000 a year, can we break even before we go on to the next development phase? We almost got there. Brentford's catchment area gives the club a great ability to garner kids, but does throwing three million at an academy mean we are suddenly going to produce elite professional players?

'It just won't. It's going to mean that players will be better educated. It's going to mean that they have a better-structured pathway, but I don't think the end result is going to be any more positive. I was arguing against myself to a degree, because I believe in what a successful youth policy stands for, but from a purely business perspective I felt we couldn't afford to commit such revenue.'

EPPP is, in essence, a political and financial project under the guise of a philosophical statement of faith in English football, based upon enhanced coaching, youth development, education and performance. It was drafted by representatives of six Premier League clubs, including Arsenal, Chelsea and Manchester United, and is characterised by the certainty of the colonial bureaucrat.

Predatory clubs can sign products of smaller academies with minimal compensation, which ranges from £3,000 for each year a boy has been developed by a club between the ages of 9 and 11 to £12,500 or £25,000 for each year a boy aged between 12 and 16 has been developed by a Category Three or Category Two club respectively. Support of the scheme by Football League clubs was only guaranteed, at a meeting in Walsall in 2011, by threats to withhold the Premier League's £5.4 million annual solidarity payment, a contribution to the collective cost of youth development. Mills' memory of the process is instructive:

'EP3 was a fundamental change to a system that certainly needed improvement, but it was not the type of change that was required. The way the benefits for the bigger boys in the business were swept under the carpet destroyed the Football League's integrity in youth football. I, and others, thought it was time to draw a line.

'What happens in the Football League meetings is that you have a group meeting, you split off into your own divisions, and then effectively have a debate before returning to the main room. Ultimately, seventy-five per cent of the Championship vote is effectively the casting vote, so the lower leagues are always subservient.

'Football tends to throws around numbers. It's almost like negotiating with my girlfriend's four-year-old about how many carrots she'll eat. If I ask her to eat four carrots, she's going to eat one. If I ask her to eat ten carrots, and then work it down, there's a chance I might get her to eat five. So it's all about manoeuvring around reasonable chunks that you can digest.

'Here we were being threatened: "If you don't do this

there will be zero solidarity money." People were saying, "The money's not worth it for what we're giving away, and actually, they won't do this. The negative connotations of the Premier League pulling the money will be far too significant." I can't remember word for word but we were being urged by Greg Clarke that it was this or nothing. Shit or bust.'

Clarke continues to cling to a particularly greasy pole, having progressed from being Football League chairman to a similar position at the Football Association. The machinations of football politics, the power plays, financial forecasts and shifting allegiances, will have long-term ramifications.

Giles has been obliged to learn quickly, as an outsider in a sport suffused by the spirit of the insider. He was forewarned about football's introspection and conservatism, having spent the previous decade working as Head of Quantitative Research for Brentford owner Matthew Benham at Smartodds, providing consultancy services, statistical research and sports-modelling advice to professional gamblers.

Yet managing twenty mathematicians and operating with academic rigour in relative isolation is an entirely different commercial and cultural challenge to overseeing the contracts of players aged 8 to 35. He was obliged to transfer from a collaborative environment to a proscriptive, insecure world in which the focus changed from making money to trying not to waste too much of it.

Analytically, he supports the principle of affiliated boys being nurtured in local development centres, junior clubs given coaching support, until they enter the professional game at 15. Realistically, he appreciates such a concept would simply invite less scrupulous rivals to poach the most promising youngsters, without legal or financial restraint.

Brentford's experimental development model, involving a B team operating outside the system, is being studied closely by other clubs, since the average cost of running a Category Two academy, £1.5 million, can more than quadruple at the highest level. The iniquity of the current system led to them being poorly rewarded for losing their most prized young players, Ian Carlo Poveda and Josh Bohui, to Manchester City and Manchester United respectively.

Brentford received support for their stance in closing the academy from an unlikely source, a leading agent who, unusually, had no vested interest. 'Why should they spend time and money developing a young player they are probably going to lose for nine tenths of bugger all?' he asked. 'The old system worked because it offered due reward and kept the money circulating among the smaller clubs.'

Footballers have a sixth sense for the Chosen One and at 15, Poveda, a diminutive attacking midfield player with Colombian heritage who had earned England recognition, turned senior pros into spectators at training. Courted by Arsenal at 12, he played for Barcelona until he was 14, when legal issues led to his recruitment for Brentford by Rios.

His parents were measured and protective, steering him clear of agents attracted by the mesmerising skill that led to Steadman Scott christening him 'Messi' when Bohui took him to the Afewee Academy for an impromptu training session. Before the imposition of EPPP he would have commanded the sort of transfer fee capable of underwriting academy activity for a season; Giles passed him on for the guarantee of two fixtures against a City development team.

'At sixteen I have no control over whether he comes to us or goes to Manchester City. So in an academy you are committing millions of pounds in the hope, rather than the expectation or the certainty, that you will get a return on your investment. If you bring a good player through, the better he is the worse it is likely to be for you, since he will be playing for England. Everyone else can see him.'

Similarly, Giles failed to persuade Bohui's agent that proximity to first-team football at the Championship club outweighed the inherent uncertainties of a new era. Brentford received no immediate compensation when Bohui signed a three-year contract at United, who were rapidly restocking an underperforming academy with players aged between 16 and 19.

The vacuum at Brentford was partially filled by those surplus to requirements at bigger academies. Defender

Manny Onariase, released by West Ham, settled well and was given a more competitive outlet by spending the second half of the 2016–17 season on loan at Cheltenham in League Two. Nathan Fox, released by Norwich, revived his career in non-league football before joining from Cray Wanderers. Marc Río, a striker from the Juvenil A team at Barcelona's academy, signed a two-year development contract.

Ilias Chatzitheodoridis, a left back discarded by Arsenal, quickly progressed to the fringe of the first team; Danish youth international striker Justin Shaibu, signed from HB Køge for £40,000, made his senior debut in a League Cup tie at Exeter. The call-up of goalkeeper Ellery Balcombe for the England under-18 squad confirmed his status as the most promising survivor of the academy cull.

Brentford are pursuing a three-year plan, which will ultimately be decided by the quality of the relationship the club builds with agents, and the credibility of their unofficial games programme, leavened by regular exposure to high-quality international opposition in Southern Europe and Scandinavia. Giles depicts it as a relatively low-stakes gamble, a work in progress that will acquire greater relevance as it matures:

'I meet a lot of chief executives who don't like spending up to £2 million on an academy from a business perspective, but feel they can't do anything about it because everyone they speak to says it is essential to bring homegrown players into the first team. There is a moral and emotional aspect to the debate.

'Football academies, and the staff that run them, are fully aware that the vast majority of the kids are not good enough and are only there to support the very best coming through. Most of the kids, and to an extent their parents, are being used. My personal view is that the whole venture is morally bankrupt and I'm glad that Brentford is now out of it.

'In an ideal world, we would have made the decision sooner, but I made sure we met our educational responsibilities, and supported our Community Trust [where coaching is supervised by former Wycombe and Millwall defender Danny Senda]. I can take a fresh perspective. Certainly, there were a lot of upset parents who will never forgive the club, but in terms of the wider impact of the decision on our fan base, it didn't have a negative connotation.'

Such a conclusion may be bleak, but it fits football's myopia. Chairmen and club owners crave reflected glory. Coaches and managers are slavishly short term in their outlook. Fans care little for the game's harshness, as long as they have a result to toast in the pub. No one gave a moment's thought to the anxiety of those parents who struggled to restore their sons' morale.

Brentford provided them with contacts, but the parents' unconditional love led them into a netherworld of ignorance and rejection, where they blindly chased up unanswered telephone calls or emails in the hope of arranging a trial. Their vulnerability was blithely used against them by those who are accustomed to applying power without the encumbrance of personal responsibility.

Most parents were wary of publicly analysing the process, because they didn't want to jeopardise their sons' prospects. But one, who spoke on condition of anonymity because of the sensitivity of his job, was so affronted by its amorality he was prepared to provide a devastating insight into the hidden struggle for a second chance:

'There is very little common decency. They're all spivs. They have delusions of grandeur. What do they do between the hours of nine and five? Nothing. It's only between five and seven in the evening that they actually have a little bit of power and they abuse it. There are too many coaches playing God.

'One said to me, "You give me something and I'll get your son into a club." He was looking for a position for his son in my world. I can't do that. Sorry, it doesn't work that way. My son has been in an academy setup for a number of years, but that surprised me. It is a very, very murky and very incestuous world. It is not about how good the boy is.

'It is unregulated. There is a serious lack of duty of care and an element of, I've got my kit on, I've got my jacket on, you do what I say. For me, it was always going to be a love affair. It was never going to be a marriage to football, simply because I don't see football as being the industry that I want my son to go into.

'If I want him to go into a proper profession, where he can make his own way in life, a football certificate, or being player of the quarter, or a signed player, is not going to carry him anywhere in the world that I'm working in. Qualifications count, so he will make his way like that. Football is an add-on. If he prospers in that we will support him but school has to come first.

'I've seen parents with pound signs in their eyes. That's all they have, they don't see beyond that. Everything is geared up to little Jonny being the big professional footballer. They don't realise what's going to happen if he fails in his education. He's either a footballer, or he's nothing else. Now, I look at things quite differently.

'It has got to the point recently, because of the closure of Brentford, that I find they are trying to get me to beg. And I'm not going to beg you for a position. Take my son on for what he is, and for what he's achieved. I don't see him as a cash cow or a commodity.'

Happily, the majority of the Brentford boys were taken on by other clubs as summer ebbed into autumn. Their reputations preceded them and they dispersed to Norwich, QPR, Tottenham, Crystal Palace, Coventry, Fulham and Wolverhampton Wanderers. The intelligence system in youth football is so sophisticated that one under-15 player was given a chance to earn a scholarship at Southampton, who, like Tottenham, had compiled a player profile on him over the previous eighteen months.

But, just as a stormy sea can swallow a ship without trace, before subsiding into placidity, the restoration of calm was deceptive. A vision, indistinct but increasingly disturbing, was starting to acquire shape and texture. I asked a father what he expected of a football club, and could not get his expression of faith, and the fragility of his trust, out of my mind:

'The minute he crosses that white line, we entrust him to you. Do what you think is right. Educate him. Help him. Make sure his feet are firmly on the ground. Don't start throwing money at him, because at his age they take leave of their senses. Don't allow them to float around in cloud cuckoo land, because they will lack hunger and desire.

'Most of all, my son has got to be a boy. He's got to do things that little boys want to do. He's not manufactured for a football club. He's our flesh and blood and he belongs to us. We give him to you and we trust you to look after him. Forget about the house, and what we've got in the bank account, he's the most precious thing we've got in the world . . .'

5
Family

Can a logical limit be placed on parental love? When does the most powerful human emotion become too much to bear? What happens when the constituent cells of pride and devotion divide and mutate? How can intimate relationships survive external pressure? Are family bonds, tight and sacred, suddenly shredded by the strain?

There are no easy answers, but the questions intrude as the setting sun embroiders the southern bank of the River Don, and the valley in which Sheffield sits. Zak Brunt is being tutored by Miguel Ángel Llera in the far corner of the outdoor Power League complex, which overlooks the Hallam University athletics track.

Watched by his father, Glen, and his mother, Rachel, he warms up by caressing a football on a string hanging from his black body harness. Even at the required rate of sixty touches a minute it is possible to be languid.

The ball inscribes an arc as it is manipulated, first by the outside of Zak's orange boot and then by the instep. Left, right, left, right, left, right. Parade-ground perfect.

Llera, the former MK Dons, Charlton and Sheffield Wednesday defender, throws a second, unfettered ball into the mix. The boy, relatively slight but completely engaged, must pass it back while maintaining the rhythm. 'Keep watching the sky,' the coach urges, as he seeks to encourage flexibility, agility and sureness of touch. 'C'mon. Bap, bap, bap. Give me a half volley.'

They move to a plyometric ladder. Zak must dance through it at a high tempo, continuing to control the balls being tossed at him at different angles and speeds. 'High level of concentration . . . can you feel it? Of course you can . . . good touches . . . high knee . . . landing on your toes.'

Llera develops the drill, moving into the centre of the heavily rubberised five-a-side pitch to fire passes at hip height. The boy is expected to follow a deft first touch with an accurate side-footed finish into a portable miniature goal: 'Pivot. Get your body position right.'

They progress to resistance work. Zak is tethered to the main goalpost, ordered to run forward and leap over parallel lines of cones before the tension in the cord pulls him back to the starting point. He grimaces and sprints again, weaving through five more cones, set at 45 degrees to each other.

The coach's commentary has a complementary urgency: 'Quicker, quicker, quicker ... bend your knee ... bap, bap, bap, bap ... don't let the tension be stronger than you ... keep your focus now you are getting more and more tired ... this is when the challenge comes ... come on, don't stop the gas ... this is the ninety-fourth minute.'

Llera relents, and speaks softly to his pupil in Spanish as he frees him from the yoke, like a horse whisperer let loose in an unsaddling enclosure. Even in the sodium-shaded shadows cast by four-bulb floodlights, the sheen of sweat sparkles on the boy's forehead. He is breathing shallowly, exhaling before he swigs energy drink from a sports-capped bottle.

'I love watching him,' confides Rachel, a small woman who laughs at the memory of the chaos caused by his childhood habit of using the living room of their home in Chesterfield as a playground. 'We lost count of the number of ornaments he smashed, kicking a ball around. The dog couldn't get out of the way quick enough.'

Glen, who stands alongside the fence cupping his hands around a container of black coffee, has a natural intensity. As such, he is the perfect narrator for his son's story. Zak may only be 14, but he has crammed enough incident, opportunity and disappointment into his football experience to accommodate a lifetime.

His training kit, first worn during an open trial for

Chelsea in May 2015, offers a hint about the nature of the journey without revealing its harshness and complexity. The numbers, 215 on the light blue top and 214 on dark blue shorts, testify to the scale of the audition.

Zak had just turned 5 when he was asked to join a pre-academy group at Sheffield United. He was invited to breakfast with the first-team squad and posed for photographs with Gary Speed. At 6 he emulated a 12-year-old David Beckham, and won the world schools' skills title at Manchester United Soccer School.

Sky Sports News did a live link from his first training session back at Sheffield United. He continued to spend Saturday mornings there, but devoted two midweek nights to Aston Villa, at their Bodymoor Heath training complex, and a third night to Manchester United, at the storied old training ground, The Cliff.

'All I go on, as a football dad, is, oh, Aston Villa is bigger than Sheffield United. So, of course, we're going to give that a go. Then Rachel took a call from United, and rang me at my mum's. They wanted Zak to go up there. We were all United fans at the time, so we couldn't knock that back. When I consider it now, I think, what was I doing? I'm ashamed, to be honest.

'We didn't want to burn bridges, so it was a case of school, sandwiches and homework in the car. Zak was looking at me and his mum as if to say, "What do you think?" We're new to it, naïve, so he picks up our excitement. He's a good kid. I've spoken to him about it since, and he felt that he needed to go on with it because it was what we wanted him to do. Mum and Dad want to take me here, there and everywhere. I don't want to let them down.'

The tone is confessional, unstinting, lacerating. Glen Brunt is prepared to admit to what is usually regarded as inadmissible evidence of parental weakness. That takes a distinctive form of moral courage, and unstinting self-awareness, because his demeanour suggests it triggers potentially self-destructive emotions:

'During Zak's younger years I had a lot of fury at him. He generally played up an age group and did well. But on this day, at The Cliff, he was not on it. We were coming down the motorway and I completely lost it. I'm screaming and shouting at him. He has a vacancy across his face, which just makes me more angry.

'I'm going, "Don't you realise? Best and Charlton played on that pitch. Do you know what I mean?" Of course he had no concept of what I was going on about. He was just six. Rachel had a word with me when we got home. She said, "It's not him that needs to change. It's you."'

He realised his relationship with his son had become dangerously constricted, since it depended on whether Zak had reached perceived standards of excellence. His immediate response, to enrol on a sports psychology course at the Open University in an attempt to gain a deeper insight into the power of the mind, did not alter the priority: choosing the club at which Zak would take an academy place.

'We had the bright lights, big city syndrome, and were torn between Villa and Manchester United. We had met no bad individuals at that stage. Everybody was hunky-dory. There are good people in the system, but there are also a lot of second-hand-car salesmen. They crawl all over you to buy the vehicle, and get the signature, but when they've got it they're suddenly busy. They're not interested.'

The Brunts opted to accept a contract from Villa, and moved into rented accommodation in Staffordshire, closer to Bodymoor. It was a fundamental family decision, since Glen and Rachel are officially registered carers for two profoundly disabled sons. Each has cerebral palsy; Niall is wheelchair-bound and reliant on twenty-four-hour care while Rees, his twin, is partially sighted, registered blind. A fourth son, Liam, almost died when he was run over at the age of 4; Glen still suffers flashbacks from pulling him out from under the car.

Zak, an academically bright child, enrolled at a local junior school and excelled in his first six months at the Villa academy. A pivotal problem arose when he set up a goal with a look-away pass during a training match. The coach stopped the session, criticised the extravagance of the gesture, and alienated the child.

'Zak, being a nine-year-old, took that as a personal

jibe. It wasn't, because we saw other kids get the same treatment, but they were looking for conventional play. Pick up, pass, look to receive. I didn't think there were too many better than him at running with the ball, and being tricky, so I worried they would take away what was good about him.

'Was he going to be another statistic, and fall away? I realise, even as I say that, I was lost in the process of how he was going to get through. Zak started to feel his coaches were on at him. I was instructing him another way, saying, "Don't let your skills go. It's about bums on seats in this game."

'I've changed, thank God, but I'm just trying to be candid. I don't like a lot of what I see in myself back then. It's very difficult for a nine-year-old to do what his dad is asking, when people at the club are saying, "Don't do this, don't do that." In the end he said, "Dad, I am not sure I want to do this any more."

'We did have more time together as an immediate family because of the relocation, but we missed the respite care we received from our extended family. We didn't realise how much they did for us, minding the boys at the weekend. I started suffering from anxiety. Me and Rachel started, you know, falling apart a little bit. I felt I should know what to do, but I didn't. I just didn't.

'When we went to see the club, to talk about the way Zak was being treated, we were just sort of palmed off, when we were welcomed with open arms before. It became a real tug of war. I was told, "You need to show more commitment." So I'm like, well, you've not suggested we move down, but I've relocated my family . . .'

The decision to leave, exacerbated by a dispute over mileage expenses, was complicated by a far-reaching disagreement over the nature of Zak's contract. The club rejected his father's contention he had been promised his son would be released without compensation; the boy was unable to play for ten months while Villa sought a fee.

Manchester City eventually recruited him, on the recommendation of Sheffield-based Kristian Wilson, one of their elite development coaches. His registration was initially rejected by the Premier League, because the family lived outside prevailing one-hour travel time limits due to a difficult journey across the Peak District, but accepted the Brunts' counter-argument on appeal that relocation was impractical because of the twins' need to be within reach of hospital treatment.

City were welcoming. Zak was invited to meet Roberto Mancini in the dugout before a league game, ironically against Villa. He met Joe Hart and was presented with David Silva's signed shirt. Yet his form in his first season, in the under-11s, was lukewarm. His problems during the second season were compacted by the disintegration of his father's relationship with a co-ordinating coach for the under-12s and -13s.

A confrontation, triggered by disputed accusations of favouritism and a perceived lack of game time, marked a point of no return. Glen admits he sent City an anonymous letter of complaint, which was not acted upon. He was left to pick up the pieces when the club acceded to his request that Zak should be released.

'Don't get me wrong. There are some good people at City, but Zak's self-esteem suffered. He doesn't stay low for very long, because he has an intrinsic ability to bounce back, but that doesn't make it right. He was known in Chesterfield as the kid that plays for Man City. All of a sudden he's the kid playing grassroots football. There were snide remarks towards him. He found it difficult.'

A YouTube clip of him as an 8-year-old in a red England kit, demonstrating his ball skills, was used against him. An ill-advised caption read: 'Remember his name. This boy is going to be a star.' Innocence acts as incitement on what should really be termed anti-social media; commentaries were crass, callous and barely literate:

> It's one thing kicking a ball around in your back garden. I'm pretty sure he won't have the time to be doing pointless tricks in the middle of a game . . .

> A lot of kids his age are better. For all we know, them videos could have took hundreds of takes before any of them worked . . .

> I see all these videos of kids having mad skill and that there the next Messi or Ronaldo but in reality there probably gonna suck . . .

Even someone like me, inured to the rough and tumble of opinion over decades observing sport at the highest level, treads warily in the comments section, beneath the line. Such forums offer a platform for cowards and charlatans, the deluded and the plain nasty. Experience would have cautioned Zak against plunging into the cesspit, but his strength of character, in directly answering his detractors, was admirable.

> This boy is crap he isn't going to make it to pro won't even come close . . .
>
> *Thank you very much for your support I will use it to drive me.*

> It's so annoying when he finishes doing his skill and he just stays there staring at the camera happily.
>
> *You got a problem with me being happy? I'm sure last time I checked football was a hobby in which your supposed to enjoy yourself.*

> Kid kill Your Self for once u know im better boi whitey im asian boiiiii you look like a burnt white sweet potatoe with your crocodile HAIR
>
> *Thank you very much for your comment I appreciate it . . .*

This, remember, is a boy approaching his twelfth birthday, a blood sacrifice on the altar of so-called public opinion. Zak stayed at home, watching videos of Paul Gascoigne and falling in love with South American football. The sense of a family being sucked into a vortex of unfeasible ambition heightened when he announced he would like to study at a Brazilian academy. Even now, more than two years later, Glen shakes his head at the surreal nature of the subsequent conversation:

'I said, "You know where Brazil is. That's obviously not going to happen." So he said, "Where's the second best place in the world to learn, then?" It has to be Spain, doesn't it? My wife is as barking mad as I am, and she is privy to this, so she just said, "Take him." I said, "What do you mean, take him?" She said, "Just take him. You don't want to go into another English academy, do you?"'

Glen reasoned that an approach to Spanish clubs by a father seeking advancement for his son would be doomed to failure. Instead he used his recently earned diploma in sports psychology to give applications for a trial the veneer of professional distance. It worked: Real Valladolid, Villarreal and Atlético Madrid were prepared to take a look on those terms.

His first session was staged in 35-degree heat, but by the time Zak reached Madrid, following polite rejections by the other two clubs, he had acclimatised. He played outstandingly well over two weeks, impressing with his diligence and technical quality. Atlético's offer of a youth contract, contained in an email received forty-eight hours after their return to Chesterfield, gave the adventure sudden gravity.

'We had viewed it as a bit of a vacation really, but that's when the enormity of it hit home. We couldn't relocate as a family. We were reliant on the NHS, which is wonderful despite its woes, and had a decision to make. Rachel told us to go. She would make it work at home, for however long it lasted.'

The family agreed to regard the first fortnight of Zak's return to Spain with his father as an extended experiment. It went well. He was allocated to Atlético's B squad, and, once the formalities of his education were established, signed for them. Money was tight, but they paid 600 euros a month to share an apartment with an elderly Argentine couple.

Football was the easy part. Zak excelled in a series of tournaments and enjoyed the emphasis on mastery of the ball. Yet everyday life was hardly the stuff of soft-focus cinematic fantasy. He cried each morning on his way into a local school, in which little leeway was allowed for his lack of language skills. He had only had a couple of Spanish lessons before they moved to Madrid, and struggled initially to make friends. Homework was an ordeal.

His father failed to find work, and filled the time

between academy sessions by studying for a long-distance psychology degree. It took more than six months before the artlessness of the exercise became apparent. The club called Glen into a meeting at the Vicente Calderon Stadium. They had bad news to impart.

FIFA had noted the absence of an answer in the section of the registration form devoted to the father's employment. Glen had left it blank, since he had none, without grasping the reality that this would make Zak ineligible to play. Despite an attempt to argue he intended to use his qualifications to set up a sports psychology practice, FIFA ruled he had moved to Spain for football-related, rather than work-related, reasons.

This was a breach of Article 19 of FIFA's regulations, set up to tackle child trafficking. In essence, no player under 18 can be transferred internationally unless the family are relocating for employment purposes. A statute drawn up for the most honourable of reasons, to protect minors being enslaved by unscrupulous agents or unprincipled clubs, was being used against him.

'In my total and utter naïvety I thought nothing about the regulation concerning the protection of minors. We'd simply done things off our own back. We tried to fight it, but I absolutely understood the principle. I've read the stories of African kids left on the streets when things do not work out, but it is a case of one net catching all. It doesn't seem to be looked at on an individual basis.

'I had gone through the immigration procedures. We were welcomed into Spain, as long as we were not going to feed off their social care system, which I totally understand. Zak soon loved it there. The football was made for him. I could see so much progress in him. His language skills were improving, and he was socialising with Spanish friends. Rachel had flown over a couple of times with the twins, and we had gone back to England every three months. It was starting to work.'

In limbo while the appeals process was underway, Zak played informally at a semi-professional club in Majadahonda, a town on the north-western fringe of Madrid. He played alongside the son of Guti, the former Real Madrid player, who, ignorant of the broader picture, offered to arrange a trial at his old club. Like Zak's previous Spanish coaches, Guti recognised the boy's long-term potential as a number ten; in the more literally minded English system, Zak's skill had seen him pigeonholed as a winger.

The irony of another unsustainable opportunity arising in such random circumstances was characteristically cruel. The family was offered the chance of taking their case to the Court of Arbitration for Sport in Lausanne, but could not afford the legal fees. They were forced, in Glen's words, to 'come home with our tails between our legs'.

The final submissive gesture came just before Christmas 2015, when Glen drove alone to Madrid in a completely empty car. He loaded as many of their belongings as he could, settled his outstanding rent with his landlady, and pulled the shutters down on an impulsive, impossible dream. By then, Zak was back in the domestic system. Arsenal had offered an official six-week trial, and Chelsea were sufficiently interested to want to monitor his progress, but endless hours on the motorway network had finally lost their allure. He trained with Sheffield United for a short spell before joining Derby County, a progressive academy flourishing under Darren Wassall, their former defender.

His father's comfort in relative normality is reflected by a self-deprecating summary: 'I've plenty to compare it to, but it's very difficult to find a negative with Derby. The staff are very approachable, reliable. Zak had a good first full season with them, and is really enjoying it. He's quite vocal and quite forward without being rude, but, unlike some, the coaches there say they appreciate that.'

The past is, literally, another country. Though he cannot officially be represented until he is 16, Zak has an association with Ten10 Talent, an agency that counts Pelé, Gareth Southgate and Glenn Hoddle among its clients. They facilitated a minor kit deal with Adidas, in which merchandise was also made available to his brothers.

The family's collective challenge is to retain perspective and stability. Though football, as an industry, is uncomfortable with candour, their openness is refreshing. On this particular night in Sheffield it didn't seem impertinent to ask Glen to outline the enduring lessons of his role in his son's irregular development.

'I had a sort of inner arrogance, because Zak was showing a certain level of promise, but I am not an arrogant person. I thought, we need to look for Premier League. He's better than Chesterfield, Sheffield United, Rotherham, whoever. Maybe if I had not taken that path Zak's path might have been different. He may just have gone to Derby at an early age and loved it. The grass isn't always greener. Don't let pride get in the way. Bigger clubs don't treat players any better. The coaching is not necessarily any better.

'I am much more relaxed about things now, a totally different person. I still get anxious before a game, and let a little grunt go if he skies a free kick. I still feel like I'm out there with him, so I've still got some progress to make, but I enjoy it more now. The one golden thing I try to remember is, I've still got a relationship with my son if football doesn't work out. We have our little tiffs and fall-outs but I'm very close to him, irrespective of how it goes on the pitch.

'If I had my time again I wouldn't get as emotionally involved. I'd actually ask Zak what he wanted to do, which is what I do now. He has the final say. I wouldn't discuss things in front of him with Rachel, or anyone for that matter, because a child naturally wants to impress his parents. He tends to think, oh well, they're thinking that way, so I'm going to go with that. Some things have been bad for him, but he's learned a lot, very early, about who you can and can't trust.'

His study of sports psychology continues. He offers advice to other parents, free of charge, and knows he is a powerful case study: 'I see the parents as I was. It's like dealing with an alcoholic. You need them to get to a point where they say, "I've got a problem." The amount of parents that won't acknowledge they've got an issue with their son would surprise you.

'Some are in football for the right reasons, but others are doing it because essentially they live through their son. They see a pension plan and all sorts. They get caught up in it. It goes through me, some of the things I hear parents do and say . . .'

He trails off, the inference of his having learned from past mistakes a beacon in the gloom. A group of Asian lads are waiting to take their turn on the five-a-side pitch. Having packed the kit into four bags, Zak and Finn Hunter, a school friend preparing for a trial with Rotherham, are absent-mindedly scuffling for possession, kicking footballs against the fence.

There is always time for another lesson: 'This is the English culture,' Llera exclaims. 'You should be resting, cooling down after a good session. Now, boom, you are running around again, smashing balls. You are treating your body like a car that has been driven at two hundred kilometres an hour. It ticks over at thirty for a short while, and then you accelerate it up to two hundred again. No wonder things break.'

Lecture over, he lowers his voice and considers the merits of his principal pupil: 'Zak wants to be better every day. He gives good feedback and works really hard. His desire is very strong, but he is also a boy. He tries to fuck with me a little. In Spain there is more discipline, more respect for the coach and manager. But if he listens to me, maintains his focus and concentration, he can adapt to the football life. He must be true to himself.'

That is a difficult concept for any adolescent to come to terms with. Glen asks me to pose for a photograph with Zak, and is eager that his son and I should chat. In truth, I'm uncomfortable with conducting a formal interview, but I play down its significance by suggesting to him that it will be good practice for the future.

He speaks softly, but smiles readily, almost as a self-defence mechanism: 'It has been rough at times. It has been a long journey, a great experience, and I have enjoyed the ride. Looking back, it has made me stronger as a person. It has developed me as a player. Different aspects of my game have improved.

'There were times when I thought, this is too hard. When I was training at Manchester United I looked around and thought, wow, this is unreal. I thought it was too difficult at times in Spain, when I was missing my mum, brothers and friends, but I got through it. Scoring a hat-trick for Atlético in front of my grandparents and brothers was my best moment. I'm buzzing, thinking of it now.

'My dad used to be aggressive at times. The worst time for me was in the car on the way home from United. I'd had a bad session. He had a go, and I cried my eyes out all the way back home. I didn't want to go out of my comfort zone, but if that involved me doing something for him to be happy, I did it.

'Now I have grown up nothing bothers me any more. No other lad has been through what I have been through over the last eight years. It is unique. I am stronger than a lot of people out there. I have also got my brothers behind me, which is a big drive for me. I do think I am going to be a footballer. It is going to be really hard to make it, but it has got to be done.'

Go well, young man. You have earned the right to dream. Stay safe out there, for there are still many swirling rivers to cross.

6

Ghosts in the Machine

The air in the Cozy Stadium, home of St Neots Town, is scented by chips, simmering in puddles of malt vinegar. High-speed trains on the East Coast Main Line, inadequately hidden by immature trees behind the dug-outs, are an intermittent blur. The Rowley Rabble, a terrace tribe closer in spirit to *The Archers* than the Ultras, idly taunt a teenaged winger.

'We'll give you a rusk at half-time, number eleven,' shouts one, when the youth disputes a throw-in decision. Darren Foxley can't resist a glance in the general direction of those teasing him, which makes their night. He is compensated by the belief that, one day, they will have cause to remember his name rather than his number.

His father Derek sits in isolation, close to the halfway line. He is blissfully unaware of the gentle joshing endured by his son because, in a ritual that combines superstition and pragmatism, he is listening to eighties guitar rock on a miniature MP3 player. Headphones are only removed at the interval, when, right on cue, Thin Lizzy announce over a tinny tannoy that 'The Boys Are Back in Town'.

Foxley is one of three players from the Newbart project turning out for Soham Town Rangers, a club from the eighth tier of English football, the Isthmian League Division One North, which is happy to offer a refuge for the waifs and strays of the academy system. The 2–1 win in a friendly against St Neots, a team from tier seven, completes a successful trial for his companions, Billy Harris and Kieran Bailey.

Their pedigree was obvious in a match that featured several of the clichés of non-league football: the well-upholstered goalkeeper, the shaven-headed midfield enforcer and the striker whose paunch suggested he was not a stranger to a 2 a.m. kebab. The trio were technically sound and thought fractionally faster than their opponents, without having the confidence and personality to consistently impose themselves on the game.

That hint of uncertainty was understandable, given their need to mentally re-attune in the early stages of the rehabilitation process they were each undergoing, but they still figured in the decisive moments of the match. Soham fell behind, but equalised midway through the second half when Foxley made a break down the right before setting up Harris to score with a well-struck, marginally deflected shot from the edge of the area.

Five minutes remained when Bailey, running intelligently between the lines, was crudely hacked down. Much to his apparent surprise, substitute Will Gardner channelled his inner Gareth Bale to direct a curving, dipping free kick inside the angle of post and crossbar. When it was over, and the club bar reclaimed its patrons, players meandered to the dressing room to the accompaniment of Biffy Clyro's anthem 'Many of Horror'. A fragment of the second verse seemed mockingly relevant:

> My bruises shine
> Our broken fairytale
> So hard to hide.

The three academy rejects are 'ghosts', a term coined by Professor Ross Tucker, the eminent South African sports scientist, to describe youngsters who become lost in the maze of muddled thinking and short-termism that defines the professional system. They hope to emulate Jamie Vardy, who recovered his ambition and equilibrium playing for Stocksbridge Park Steels, by recalibrating in non-league football.

Foxley joined Charlton Athletic at the age of 7, but left for West Ham, who released him at 16, citing a lack of pace. Soham took him on the rebound from Dagenham & Redbridge, who put their praise and promises over two seasons as a scholar into perspective by opting not to offer him a professional contract, following a retrial at the age of 18.

Harris, primarily an attacking full back but a viable option in central midfield, was captain of the under-16s at Southend United, the club he joined as a 6-year-old. He was passed over for a scholarship following an ill-timed change in senior recruitment staff at the academy, which signalled a strategy shift.

Bailey, arguably the most naturally talented of the three, was picked up by Colchester when West Ham let him go at 18. He was undermined by a season-ending injury, in which a calf muscle repeatedly peeled away from the bone. The problem was traced to faulty posture, and John McGreal, Colchester's first-team manager, thought sufficiently of his promise, in a number eight or ten role, to allow him to continue to train with them while they waited for his future to become clearer.

Foxley's father spoke with revealing bitterness: 'These boys are commodities, full stop. That's how clubs look at them: can we make money? Important decisions have very little to do with football. They are personality-driven – does this manager or that coach like you? Being released is a lovely pleasant use of language. It means you were kicked out.

'Forget the pretence that people care. Rejection feels like being kicked in the balls. The system sucks because it has so much wealth. Why persevere with one of your own when you can pick up the phone, bring in a fifteen-year-old from Mexico, and give him a hundred grand?'

Fred Harris, Billy's father, conceded he was in danger of losing his religion. As a youth scout for West Ham, he was becoming burdened by ever-accumulating evidence of the imperfections of a game that engaged and enraged him in equal measure. Natural loyalties were being stress-tested; the undertone of sadness was unavoidable when he admitted quietly: 'When Billy goes, I might go with him.'

The Newbart project is funded by Birmingham-based brothers John and Peter Finnegan. Newly established agents, or intermediaries to use FIFA's preferred nomenclature, their philosophy is based on a holistic approach to sports management, in which their complementary business and sporting backgrounds are used to revive the faltering careers of easily forgotten young players.

For the avoidance of doubt, John, who has built and sustained a successful IT company over thirty-five years, insists, 'We are in this to make money, no two ways about it.' He handles all contract negotiations and organises support services, but recognises profit is a long-term goal. In the short term representing a stable of up to thirty young players, the majority of whom are redirected into the top end of the non-league pyramid, is a loss-making exercise.

Football nous is provided by Peter, a former non-league manager and club owner who ended a ten-year association with Aston Villa, as a senior scout in the UK and Europe, to help set up a venture 'which knows it can't change the system, but tries to put a dent in it'. Bold words, in keeping with a distinctive set of values.

Newbart operates on word-of-mouth recommendation, and adheres to the strict policy of not representing a player until any existing relationship with another agent expires. Even the story behind the initiative's name is highly individual; the New element of the company title pays discreet homage to a spiritual inspiration, Cardinal Newman, the nineteenth-century theologian beatified by Pope Benedict XVI in 2010, and the Bart reference is a reminder of their Irish grandfather, Bartholomew.

The filial intimacy of their conduct is striking. They often defer to each other in conversation with the simple term 'brother', and argue that their status as outsiders sharpens their instinct for the amorality and duplicitousness with which they are regularly confronted.

'You really get to know very quickly the clubs you want to do business with,' said John, the more quietly spoken of the pair. 'Forget the setting, football, for a moment. You have in your hands the life of a vulnerable, often lost, young man. This is about how you deal, how you communicate, how you respond, the information you are willing to share. I'm not afraid to have a hard conversation to cut through the bullshit.

'There are some, like Stoke City, West Bromwich Albion and Bournemouth, who are brilliant. They engage honestly and openly. At the other end of the spectrum there are clubs where I don't trust a single thing they do or say. They go behind your back because they are so desperate to get a player or parent's information. They don't understand how stupid that is, because we get to find out about it.'

Football's back-of-the-hand cynicism and knee-jerk cronyism is so deeply ingrained that many in the game will dismiss the projection of such a combination of realism and idealism as hopelessly naïve or deliberately deceptive. Parents straddle a natural fault line; they become so immersed in the career path of their sons that a significant percentage is seduced into a sense of personal entitlement.

Peter, stockier than his brother, also has interests in the building trade. He is neither artless nor unworldly. He draws on his experience as co-owner at Redditch United where, in addition to managing the first team and expanding the youth programme from three to twenty-one teams, he accepted an informal invitation from a scouting contact to mentor a richly talented 11-year-old. The relationship was in its fifth year when it fractured under pressure from competing clubs and agents.

'I don't blame the kid, because parents get sucked in so easily. I'd advised the family what they should be looking for from a scholarship at sixteen and spoken about the pros and cons of going with an agent. Then, over a meal, the dad suddenly said, "What's in it for me? Does a signing-on fee help me?" I told him it wasn't about him, but I'd lost him.

'I don't like the dishonesty in the system, the lies, the backhanders. That's not me. I am an honest person. I couldn't get involved in something where I could destroy a boy's life, maybe not immediately, but somewhere down the line. That is what happens in football.'

The brothers employ so-called associates – coaches and scouts who will contribute to the ultimate aim of establishing a national network of development centres. The pivotal figure in their planning is Mike Linley, my companion at St Neots. This is a vocational exercise for him; he spent five years funding a low-key but ethically similar scheme in the south of England before accepting a job with the Finnegans, whom he met while watching his son Joe, a full back in Villa's under-23 team. A natural networker, who lives on his mobile phone from 7 a.m. to 11 p.m., charging it three times across the course of an extended working day, Linley has turned down a series of prominent jobs in youth recruitment because he believes in the power of personal commitment.

Life, for him, is about fashioning the next opportunity rather than securing the next result.

Some boys can't afford public transport, so he picks them up and takes them to training, or to trial matches. The majority are registered on what is colloquially known as 'a seven-dayer'. They are essentially non-contract players, and trade the lack of security for the ability to respond rapidly to the chance of advancement.

Typically, during the ninety-minute drive to Cambridgeshire from his Essex home, Linley was called by Sonny Shilling, an 18-year-old winger released by Scunthorpe. He placed him at Cambridge City, where his mentality and potential could be properly assessed. It can take time to detect the extent of the hidden damage to those unwillingly set free.

'They don't know what to do. They look lost, half the player they once were. Scholars become used to going into training every day and suddenly they have nowhere to go. It is no different to you and I working for twenty-five years, and coming into the office to find an envelope on the desk telling you you're out of the door. The kids can't take it. There is no aftercare. It destroys them.

'They should not be bringing in kids at five years of age. Every parent thinks their boy is going to go all the way, even at that age, and the boys easily become disillusioned. They get all the hype and none of the realism. A boy should not come into a club until he is fourteen.

'I see boys of thirteen who think they've made it when they've not reached the first rung on the ladder. Make them sub and their dummies come out of the pram. All these people with all these badges don't seem to know it is really all about how you mentor the child. There are no man-management skills. Coaches are in it for the wrong reasons, for themselves.

'There are too many kids in the system. Clubs are taking too many, too early. They are building their hopes up too high, too young. They're telling ten- or eleven-year-olds that they're fantastic and dropping them when they're thirteen. It is just all wrong. People treat their greyhounds better than clubs treat these boys.

'They are training far too much when they are maturing. It is absolutely ridiculous. I hear of scholars being in every day for two weeks. They are pounding, pounding and pounding them to get the hours in. They run them too much. Judgements are made too quickly and too many parents can't handle the rejection.'

The talent trawl can occasionally be taken a little too literally. Linley recounts, with an enduring sense of wonder, the tale of a boy whose father was twenty miles out in the North Sea, working on a fishing boat, when he took a phone call from an agent who had been passed the number by an anonymous official at his son's parent club. In so many words, the agent wanted to poach the boy, and was disinclined to take into account the surreal setting for what was a short, understandably fractious, conversation.

Linley's empathy with his charges stems from the experiences of his son, who, after overcoming a fractured tibia and stress fracture of the back, was facing a critical season at Villa, a club in meltdown following relegation from the Premier League. He is attuned to signs of stress, and calls each player with whom he is associated at least three times a week to gauge their mood and progress.

'Agents have already taken their money out of most of the boys we take on. I get more pleasure out of seeing them run out in places like tonight than sitting at home moping, or going down the pub. They've all got decent parents, and they have to have mental strength to get as far as they have. They've been able to take the abuse, the hard work.'

But for how long?

Fortunes fluctuate on a week-to-week basis. Clarke Bogard, a goalkeeper parachuted briefly into Soham, joined another of Linley's special projects, the former Millwall and AFC Wimbledon central defender Jake Goodman, at Braintree Town in the National League. Clarke made a stellar debut, and quickly attracted scouts from several league clubs, led by Brighton.

Josh Smith, a goalkeeper released by Leicester following his scholarship, was undermined by intermittent hot-headedness during a subsequent spell at Brighton.

Linley had high hopes of his earning a professional contract at Cheltenham Town, but by the autumn of 2016 he had slipped off the radar.

Similarly, the original Soham trio splintered in October 2016, when Billy Harris, who had won admirers for his energy and application, decided his apprenticeship as a plumber offered greater scope than playing football in front of crowds of 150. The grind of 160-mile round trips to training and home matches, and a burgeoning relationship with a new girlfriend, swayed the decision. Ultimately, he simply craved what passes as normality for an 18-year-old.

His father, on the horns of a dilemma, kept his counsel while Linley got to work on his son following a two-week absence from the game. 'You are going to regret this later,' he told Billy. 'I let it go at twenty-three and should have done more with my talent. Don't make that mistake.' The short speech worked, since Harris quickly agreed to join Great Wakering Rovers, a Ryman League North club close to his Southend home, under newly installed manager Keith Wilson.

The teenage generation is married to social media, for richer, for poorer, in sickness and in health. Ben Marlow, a technically gifted, strong-willed midfield player regarded by Linley and Peter Finnegan as having the greatest promise of their summer intake, unwittingly emphasised the inherent perils of inadvertently allowing strangers into his life.

He was catching the eye at East Thurrock United in the National League South, and played for a strong Leicester City team in a behind-closed-doors friendly. Mark Venus, Coventry City's caretaker manager, made several scouting trips to watch him, yet Marlow's social media activity hinted at underlying insecurity. Most starkly, he shared this Twitter post by Blair Turgott, a friend attempting to revive his career with Bromley: 'They all think football is this smooth sailing ship with beautiful scenes . . . you better bring your umbrella and life jacket.'

Retweeting such fortune-cookie philosophising is, of course, harmless. In the same spirit, Marlow, who was impressing with his diligence as much as his natural ability, gave an insight into his value system by sharing the sentiments of boxer Chris Eubank Jr: 'Two things will define you as a person. Your patience when you have nothing & your attitude when you have everything.'

Yet by choosing to comment publicly on the acquittal of Welsh international footballer Ched Evans on rape charges in mid-October, he was entering more dangerous territory: 'Ched Evans found not guilty. The woman should get put away for ruining his whole life, just for a bit of fame for a couple of years, bitch.'

The post, completed by an emoticon depicting a raised middle digit, doubtlessly reflected the views of many in his infantilised profession. Marlow may have, at the time of writing, only 1,666 followers, but, in an age where employers comb Twitter, Facebook and Instagram searching for clues of character, he had no control over the size and nature of his audience.

I am conscious that by highlighting an indiscreet intervention I am leaving myself open to accusations of mean-spiritedness at best, and malevolence at worst. There is no intention to demean or cast doubt; the point at issue here is that had a Premier League player posted something similar the howl of moral outrage would have registered on the Richter scale. It is never too early to learn the lesson that football and footballers are placed under an unforgiving microscope.

The game can positively highlight social issues, as I know through my contacts with Martin Ling, the former Leyton Orient, Torquay United and Swindon Town manager who has emerged as a compelling and courageous voice in the mental health debate. His son Sam, a defender who caught the eye along with Marlow in a series of pre-season friendlies for a Newbart select side, had broken into a Dagenham & Redbridge team seeking an immediate return to the Football League after their relegation the previous spring.

Martin Ling had, by way of return, managed some of the early Newbart composite teams, in conjunction with coaches Garry Clancy and Steve Southgate. He was held in the highest esteem by Peter Finnegan, who was actively considering the purchase of a non-league club of appropriate stature, with the intention of installing him as manager.

Linley, meanwhile, was bullish about the prospects of Ross Elsom, an attacking midfield player whose promise was confirmed by former Arsenal full back Lee Dixon, a family friend. Undeterred by failure to win a contract in extended trials at Glasgow Rangers and QPR, he was parked at Bishop's Stortford, where he was being monitored by such clubs as Stevenage, Gillingham and Cambridge United.

His backstory was the English development model in microcosm. His was the first year group obliged to deal with the practicalities of the Elite Player Performance Plan; in the words of his father Mike they were 'guinea pigs'. Ross dutifully changed schools to one aligned to his boyhood club, West Ham, but, according to his father, canteen lunches occasionally ran out before academy players arrived from late-morning training sessions.

Young footballers obliged to visit the local fish and chip shop to stave off hunger pangs was hardly cutting-edge custom and practice. Ross suffered from asthma during puberty, and seemed to have been written off well before the end of his two-year scholarship. His availability was signalled on the PFA website, but nothing came of three fleeting requests for further information from the union by interested clubs.

Linley, who had helped facilitate a work experience loan at Histon while Elsom's scholarship was winding down, took pride in his proactivity. He helped Ross move on again in early November, to join Billy Harris in what amounted to an entirely new first-team squad at Great Wakering. Further up the food chain, one of Linley's most productive areas of partnership was AFC Bournemouth, who were attempting to build an academy in the modernistic, intelligent image of first-team manager Eddie Howe.

The Premier League club took Will Dennis, an under-16 goalkeeper released from Watford, and showed significant interest in the Soham experiment. Foxley continued to excel for the Cambridgeshire team, which improved incrementally after a slow start to the season; Bournemouth gave him a two-week trial and agreed to examine his progress.

Bailey moved to National League South club Poole Town on the recommendation of Stephen Purches, manager of Bournemouth's under-21 team, for whom he also played in what amounted to a fruitless three-month audition. When he tired of the commute to Hampshire, which involved overnight stays in a budget hotel, Linley arranged for another transfer, to Cambridge City, so that he could 'enjoy his football for a while'. That lasted until mid-December, when he left 'by mutual consent'. The incestuous nature of non-league football was reinforced the following month when Darren Foxley, who had scored four goals in thirty-three appearances for Soham Town Rangers, moved to

Cambridge City, who were being managed by former Soham manager Robbie Nightingale.

Other such 'last chance' schemes were starting to emerge like mushrooms after summer rain. Komarni, an agency operating out of the south London suburbs, were experiencing notable success in placing young players in the non-league game, at clubs like Grays Athletic, Greenwich Borough and Godalming Town.

FAB Academy, established at Bisham Abbey National Sports Centre by Nas Bashir, a former Reading player and coach who briefly assisted Stuart Pearce with the England under-21 squad, recycled youngsters into such clubs as Sheffield United, Nottingham Forest, Birmingham City and Kidderminster Harriers.

The Kinetic Foundation, a charity that seeks to help disadvantaged youths in Croydon, where one in five young people under 16 are classified as living in poverty, placed boys at Barnet, Charlton, Ipswich, Reading and Sunderland. Their most eye-catching, headline-seizing success story involved Yeboah Amankwah, an under-16 defender spotted playing Sunday league football.

He joined Manchester United on trial, and helped them win the Premier League's Football for Freedom trophy in October 2016 before accepting Manchester City's offer of a scholarship in early December. This did little to smooth relations between the neighbours, exacerbated a fortnight earlier, when City beat United 5–0, 6–0 and 9–0 at under-13, -14 and -15 level respectively.

The Strachan Football Foundation, run from a junior club in Rugby by Gavin, son of Scotland manager Gordon, operated a typically diverse model, which offered BTEC educational courses in conjunction with opportunities for academic advancement, through football scholarships to the US. Junior Boyaback, a left-sided full back or winger, was capped at under-20 level by Cameroon; five clubs competed for striker Jordan Ponticelli, who signed a two-year professional deal at Coventry City.

Bobby Bowry, a midfield player who had a sixteen-year professional career at Crystal Palace, Millwall and Colchester, manages to combine commerce with coaching. He is a director of Volanti, an agency that represents, among others, Bournemouth defender Charlie Daniels, but he also oversees the development arm of the organisation.

The flagship for the Volanti Academy, which aims to nurture previously undiscovered or undervalued talent, is Shelton Athletic, a grassroots club in Croydon which runs up to twenty-four youth teams. Like Newbart, Volanti field composite teams against professional academies, giving what Bowry terms as 'second chances to those who have lost direction in life'.

It is easy to be sceptical, especially when some, like Anthony Hamilton, father of multiple world F1 champion Lewis, make crass attempts to make commercial capital out of the yearning for football eminence. He spent the autumn promoting KickTrix, in essence a football tethered to a console that enables children to practise ball skills indoors. At a minimum list price of £199 the sales pitch had to be robust.

His invention, designed to build muscle memory and encourage deftness of touch, was hailed as being 'revolutionary' with notable over-eagerness. The principal promotional theory, that the keepie uppie is 'one of the most crucial skills in football', may not bear too much scrutiny, but the modernity of offering a data app and performance log, to track progress, suited the five-colour marketing strategy.

Hamilton made sensible points about the priceless gift of parental time, and understood intimately the delicate balance which must be struck between inspiring and intimidating talented offspring, but was on distinctly unsure ground when he extrapolated the benefits of his machine to the prevailing problems of domestic football.

'I looked at the plethora of players that come into football and into the Premier League and all the British kids that aren't playing in the Premier League and I'm wondering, what's the difference?' he told CNN. 'Maybe it's the weather? When you're abroad you can play longer but you can't play when it's raining outside in the UK. There are a lot of good young players but a lot of them don't make it because they don't have the skills necessary to control the ball.'

Football in the rain? He was right. It will never catch on.

Back in what passes as the real world I asked Peter Finnegan to articulate the more profound feelings stirred by his work. He described the transformation of a young man he first met as a troubled 13-year-old, misbehaving during a club night at Redditch United:

'The boy, Lauren, was ruining my training session. His parents had split up. He was on drugs, robbing cars, the lot. I told him I could help him become a man, but he had to play ball with me. The kid had never heard this before. When I said I wanted to help him get somewhere in life I could tell he was looking at me, thinking, what's in it for him?

'Most people would have ditched him, chucked him out. But we persevered. The way that kid turned himself around, through the discipline he learned and the direction he gained through football, was unbelievable. I saw him recently. He is in the army and he told me, "You changed my life." This isn't about me, and football isn't necessarily about making a living. It can be about making a life.'

On the page, stripped of the emotion with which they are delivered, those words can appear bland, bloodless, even calculating. But try telling that to those, like Linley, who have seen what happens when latent powers are released or, more damningly, suppressed:

'The best thing about doing what I do is seeing a boy

go out there and become the person he was six months previously. He understands he has someone behind him, and that he is not doing it on his own. Out there on the academy field coaches are just looking at the one boy they think is going to make it. The others are just numbers. To me, every boy is the same. It doesn't matter whether he is playing for Manchester United or Soham Town Rangers.

'The worst thing about this job is a boy having all the ability in the world, and we can't turn him around because he is too far gone. He is ruined and walks away from it. He will wake up in ten years' time and regret what he has done. There's a lot out there like that. Often it is one little setback that changes their life.'

He pauses when I ask him to delve deeper, and expand on those moments when he despairs of the sport in which he operates. He takes the path less travelled, and provides me with a name: Kieran Bywater.

7
A Parent's Warning

Everyone has their breaking point. Kieran Bywater reached his on a nondescript park pitch in Buckhurst Hill, fifteen minutes into a match designed to showcase his talent and renew his ambition. He stopped suddenly, and walked slowly around the touchline. At the moment of submission, behind one goal, he sank to his knees, clutched his head in his hands, and wept.

'What am I doing here?' he asked those, like Mike Linley, who instinctively came to his aid. 'A couple of weeks ago I was playing against PSV Eindhoven. Now look at me. I can't do this.' He was inconsolable, and led to the sanctuary of the car park by his father, Simon. In professional football, no one likes to be around to hear you scream.

Rejection by West Ham, in unexpected circumstances, had the deadly efficiency of a depth charge. It took time for its percussive force to be fully felt, since

Kieran was sufficiently well regarded, as a high-scoring midfield player with leadership qualities and first-team potential, for Manchester United, Norwich City and Aston Villa to register an initial interest.

He underwent a series of trials, at Villa, Coventry and Sheffield United. He spent a week at Crewe Alexandra, who had a change of heart and signed two older players at his expense. Mark Robins, Scunthorpe's manager at the time, delayed his decision until after the summer break. Kieran's best experience was a five-week spell at Manchester United under Warren Joyce, head coach of United's second team before he left to manage Wigan Athletic.

Joyce recommended him to Barnsley, but as an under-21 player, requiring a salary and the security of a contract, he was not as attractive a proposition as a loanee of similar age, whose parent club were willing to underwrite his wages. Villa's under-21 coaches, Gordon Cowans and Stuart Taylor, were impressed, but the political dynamics of the academy ensured priority was given to promoting from the under-18 group.

The new reality became unavoidable during an invitational trial for Cambridge United, undertaken because of its proximity to the family home in Sawtry, a village eight miles north of Huntingdon. The dressing room was full of familiar figures, second-year scholars and first-contract pros released from Premier League clubs. Mutual expressions of surprise that they should share such a fate were placed into brutal perspective when none were offered a contract by the League Two club, or even an extended examination.

The first four stages of grief, in a football sense, are denial, anger, fearfulness and depression. The fifth involves defiance, in those determined to pursue an increasingly distant dream, or acceptance, in those who let it go, and realign their life. That final step involves a deeply personal, uniquely painful, decision. Though taken in isolation, its impact is felt by those who share the journey.

Simon Bywater's response to his son's plight was to post an article on his LinkedIn account entitled 'A parent's warning – football academies'. It was a 3,156-word *cri de coeur*, designed 'to highlight a side of football only a few see and even less talk about'. It began with a simple statement: 'I can't sit back and bite my tongue any longer.' It touched a nerve, and quickly went viral on social media.

A poignant study of devotion in adversity, his story was driven by a series of deeper truths. These were put into context by Simon's description of bringing his son up to aspire to the ten defining values of the Royal Marine commandos, with whom he served in Iraq in the first Gulf War: courage, unity, determination, adaptability, unselfishness, humility, cheerfulness, professionalism, fortitude and humour.

Football's contrasting culture took little time in manifesting itself once Kieran signed for West Ham at 9.

According to Simon, the club circumvented prevailing travel rules by offering to register Kieran at a local address instead of his home, which was outside the one-hour time limit for players under the age of 13. It cost £400 a month in fuel to ferry him to training and matches. Invariably, he did not return from training until 11 p.m. on school nights; homework in the car was virtually impossible in the winter darkness.

'How could I turn around and say, "No, you can't go any more?"' Simon wrote.

> 'It would have broken his heart as an eleven-year-old and, given our location in the country, where else could he have gone for his football, as West Ham would have sought compensation? So in effect we were caught in a catch-22 situation over his registration if he wanted to leave.
>
> 'Family life begins to revolve around the club. As a parent, school holidays are full of football tournaments and games. You have to be prepared to arrange things at minimal notice. Dropping family events is the norm. The sacrifices as a family will be unseen by most and certainly ignored by the club. With hindsight we were naïve but like many we couldn't see it.'

Despite the difficulties, Kieran progressed rapidly, regularly playing up an age group. At 13 he moved into a club house in Romford from Wednesday to Saturday. The family funded a maths tutor to support his preparation for his GCSEs. By 16, when he was offered a two-year scholarship and the guarantee of a subsequent one-year professional contract, at £500 per week, he was in the ascendancy.

He chose not to have an agent, despite his parents being pestered at each home game. 'We avoided these individuals who circled training grounds like vultures,' Simon recorded. 'There was a lot of pressure from agents to sign and explore avenues with other clubs. We truly didn't have a clue who to turn to for advice and nobody spoke about it. It was as if it was some kind of a dirty conversation to have. At the time, our son wanted to remain loyal to West Ham.'

He captained the under-18s and, latterly, the under-21s. He was nominated as academy player of the year and played a behind-closed-doors first-team game at Upton Park against Queens Park Rangers. Even his most traumatic moment, laying a wreath in the centre circle at a home game in memory of his friend and housemate Dylan Tombides, who had passed away from testicular cancer, was a symbol of his status.

The replacement of the universally admired Tony Carr as academy director at the start of the 2014–15 season proved to be of pivotal personal significance. Terry Westley, Carr's successor, had worked with West Ham's powerbrokers, David Sullivan, David Gold and Karren

Brady, at Birmingham, where he restructured the academy and instigated such innovations as joint training sessions with Aston Villa and West Bromwich Albion.

While at St Andrew's, he was one of six club representatives responsible for drawing up the Elite Player Performance Plan. He subsequently became the Premier League's head of professional development, a position from which he was able to dispense the informal patronage that is rarely forgotten in football's cloistered world. Regime change at a football club is invariably brutal. It is an accepted part of life at senior level, but a relatively new phenomenon at junior level. Westley had a clear brief to impose change at West Ham, which was to lead to the departure of two of Kieran's previously influential supporters, senior development coaches Trevor Bumstead and Nick Haycock.

According to Simon Bywater, Westley was initially supportive of his son. He praised his goal-scoring record, and seemed concerned that Kieran had only a year left on his contract. In December 2014 Kieran represented the club at a function celebrating the Bobby Moore Foundation at the Grosvenor House hotel. His father reflected that 'there was no indication that he would be leaving the club or hadn't been performing'.

He confirmed his son's contract status, at Westley's request, when they met at a game against Cambridge United. Soon afterwards, in a meeting in the academy director's office, Kieran verified that he had no agent.

According to his father, Westley advised Kieran that he would find a representative for him, and extend his contract for a further two years. In January 2015, Westley called Kieran into his office and informed him he was free to leave the club. He claimed he wanted to keep him, but had been overruled by Sam Allardyce, the club's first-team manager at the time. 'Who could we believe and where did our son stand in all of this?' Simon wrote. 'He was devastated and once outside the office door cried his eyes out. Our phone didn't stop ringing from people stating they had heard the news and couldn't believe it. All the clichés came out, "One door closes another one opens." "He will have no problem finding a club and be snapped up." "They have made a huge mistake." Privately, this didn't ease any of the pain for him.

'So why this article? I want to warn other parents going down the academy football route. You will hear so much storytelling and false promises. Trust nothing you are told and always have a plan B outside football. Clubs will say one thing but do something completely different. One minute you're top dog, the next you're bottom of the pile and your son could become very isolated overnight for no apparent reason.

'Some will think I'm a bitter dad because our son didn't get an opportunity at West Ham. That's not the case. What I'm bothered about here is the way clubs conduct themselves during the academy process. I say this because I was recently on the touchline in the

Midlands, at an under-21 trial game. I spoke to parents of lads from Villa, Chelsea, Fulham and Arsenal to name a few. They all had similar stories to tell, young lads facing the depression of isolation having given everything to a club from the ages of seven, eight or nine.'

Simon Bywater's clarion call for an improvement in the game's duty of care to young players had potentially far-reaching consequences. His background as a former detective, dealing with gangland murder cases involving teenagers with MAC-10 machine guns, and his current practice, as a private investigator, enabled him to retain perspective when the club threatened legal action. The miscellany of the dispute, carefully annotated files and indexed statements, is spread out before him, on a well-polished walnut dining table in a neat house that occupies the corner plot in a modern cul-de-sac. A small white dog has been indulged before being ushered into the adjoining kitchen.

He speaks of the 'horrendous' experience of being branded a liar, the unsolved mystery of how and why his LinkedIn account was hacked and various items deleted. To be clear, West Ham and Westley deny all knowledge of, or involvement in, this. Simon maintained his comments were in the public interest, and argued the article could not, as was suggested, have harmed Westley's reputation, since he was given a new five-year contract, as Academy Manager and Head of Coaching and Player Development, two weeks after it was published.

'I'm used to dealing with lawyers because of my job, but if I was your run-of-the-mill parent I would have potentially panicked, submitted, rolled over and had my tummy tickled by them. Don't get me wrong. I felt alone, the only one prepared to put his head above the parapet. I had sleepless nights over it because they were just trying to bully me. I'm an ordinary bloke who earns an average living and they are a multi-million-pound business, but I could see the bigger picture here.'

That picture is given sharp focus by one of the ring-bound folders, which contains email printouts and handwritten notes. A vicar promises pastoral support. A father asks for advice because his 7-year-old son is being pursued by a posse of clubs led by Arsenal and Newcastle. Correspondence features senior players who identify with Kieran's setback, and parents who are close to despair.

One parent writes: 'Our son is quite frankly being treated awfully. He has suffered so much at the hands of his academy, both educationally and psychologically, due to the underhand tactics going on. Your article resonates with my wife and I, as parents. You are so correct when you say that people outside just don't realise the stress it causes the whole family.'

The dossier includes the testimony of a League Two player, driven to share his fate at the hands of a new academy director at his first club: 'He came in and started slating everything. There wasn't a player in the building, and the academy wasn't good enough, which was a load of rubbish. Not many people realise this but what that does is buy him some time in his job. It lets him get his feet under the table and takes the pressure off him.

'He then brings in his own players, from his previous clubs, and starts scouting around elsewhere for players who he signs, and puts a clause in [their contracts which states], that if those players play in the first team, he gets a bonus. The way he sees it, if I played in the first team, he wouldn't get any credit or money, because he wasn't the man who signed me, so there isn't anything in it for him.

'I was top scorer in the under-18s team, I captained the reserves, and in the last year I was training with the first-team squad every day, and playing in pre-season friendlies. Everything was going fine, exactly the same as Kieran. There was no one left at the club that had been involved in my development, and I was seen as a threat. When the first-team manager changed, the academy director went to him, and I never played again.'

Objectivity is virtually impossible to sustain, since parents are understandably obsessive about the welfare of their sons, and clubs like West Ham have every right to protect and project a philosophy summed up by the 'Be Inspired' strapline on the playbook given to every player at the club aged from 12 to 16. Yet one admission, contained in correspondence to the Bywaters from a stranger, acts as a haunting challenge to the game itself:

'I can't watch football now because every time I see a young player, I think, how many casualties have there been?'

Jamie Herbert, the Premier League's Head of Legal – Football and Regulatory Services, interviewed Simon and his son at the family home about their experiences, paying specific attention to the alleged breach of travel rules, which included suspicions of false documentation. The Bywaters refused Herbert's request to attend a disciplinary tribunal due to a damning sense of pointlessness.

'I said, well, what's in it for Kieran? He's been released by West Ham. You've got EPPP rules and regulations that you should be enforcing. You should be checking that information is correct when it's submitted to the Premier League. I'm not putting Kieran in, to be cross-examined for a day. He's not going to get anything out of it. Even if they find West Ham guilty, what are they going to do, fine them thirty grand? It's nothing to them, is it?'

West Ham categorically deny circumventing the existing travel rules at the time by offering to register Kieran at a local address instead of his home. A statement also stressed: 'Terry Westley categorically denies that he instructed Kieran to take one specific agent. It is the club's policy to distance themselves from appointment of agents.' The Club insists: 'Kieran was released by West Ham because it was agreed by the senior management team that he was not the exceptional standard required to make the step up to become a professional footballer at the club.'

Simon Bywater attempted to use his experience positively, by liaising with Simon Andrews and Peter Lowe of the Players' Trust. They lobbied the Premier League to introduce a standardised exit strategy at academy level, and suggested scholarships should be awarded at 15, rather than 16, to avoid distractions in the GCSE academic year. The Premier League responded to concerns about educational welfare by monitoring GCSE results, and comparing them to national and regional averages.

'I joined the Marines at sixteen, so I understand that you've got to stand on your own two feet, but when you're being talked to by people who you've looked up to, it's very difficult to negotiate. Kieran's exit strategy was, come in, sit down, yeah, we've had a chat about it, Kieran, you're not getting a new contract.

'If we are talking about a nationwide procedure, look at what Southampton do. They bring the player, the parent and the agent in. They have a couple of staff there, and minute the meeting. Everyone signs it, to show everyone's happy with it. Everyone has the opportunity to contribute to the discussion. It's not back-of-a-blinking-fag-packet stuff, see you later, mate.

'The football industry reminds me of the BBC during the Savile era. Let's be clear it's nothing to do with sexual offences. It's to do with a similar culture of everyone knowing something bad is going on, but it's easier to keep quiet, and ignore the problem. A question might come up from a lone parent or player but they are easily muffled and quickly swept under the carpet.'

Managers and players have their own peer support organisations, the LMA and PFA respectively. Simon Bywater's proposal that the Players' Trust should be given a viable long-term role in independently representing young players and their families is a challenge to a range of special-interest groups, accustomed to influence without true accountability.

The Trust is the brainchild of Simon Andrews, who forged a secondary career in the financial services industry following his release by Manchester United at the age of 19, and Peter Lowe, former Head of Education at Manchester City. It was shaped, in its inception, by the concerns and curiosity of Sir Alex Ferguson, who saw the need for transitional support for young players going out of the game, and a structured antidote to the chaotic, entourage-driven lifestyle adopted by many prematurely rewarded Premier League starlets.

Andrews formulated ideas about education and mentorship programmes with Gary Neville, Ryan Giggs and former United chief executive David Gill, an important advocate at the highest level of the game's administration in the UK and Europe. The most easily overlooked requirement, for an instantly available confidential counselling service, is the most pressing.

'What everybody sees is about ten per cent of what is there. As soon as something happens to a player there is a headline test, but no one concentrates on the hidden aspects of a particular problem. There is, for example, a lot of parental bullying going on. I know this will sound very harsh, but the socio-demographics are such that you've got parents living their failed existence through a son who is now a lifeline.

'The meal ticket syndrome puts more pressure on the boy than sometimes the club does. There's peer pressure at school, bullying within clubs or between players. These are real issues for a young player who is simply trying his best to make it. They don't feel able to come out and say, "Well, actually, my dad, or my mum, is making my life a misery because I had a bad game. They haven't talked to me for a week."

'It's not exactly the Samaritans, but a boy needs someone to pick the phone up, so they can tell them, "Look, I'm feeling really shit. I'm having a bad time, things aren't good." We can use former players who have experienced similar issues as mentors. Lifestyle is another obvious area, because footballers are naturally addictive personalities; I still am.

'It doesn't necessarily mean to say that you're having ten pints of lager every night or on drugs or gambling recklessly. There is good addiction, to training, winning, and competing, and bad addiction, where you find yourself in areas that you shouldn't really be. There has got to be a better model than the one that exists, because at the moment it is every man for himself.'

The system is swamped by what Andrews terms 'a tsunami of money'. Agents are wielding greater influence, opening fissures within clubs struggling to cope with the pace of financial change and the residue of a feudal philosophy. Chief executives are preoccupied by protecting their multi-million-pound investments in first-team players while lesser-paid employees are prey to temptation.

Andrews captures the contradiction: 'There are clubs that feed agents. There are individuals within clubs who are introducers to agents, and what they get back differs from the odd thing here or there, to potentially a commercial arrangement. You've got to remember that in football clubs, not everybody earns huge amounts of money, but, equally, they are part of an aspirational environment.

'Environments trigger behaviour, don't they? So what you've got is a relatively low-paid individual compared to some of the players, who is in close contact with the players, who can feed the player into someone he knows, and there's a deal done, for whatever reason. The feedback we're getting from people who care about the game tells us this has to change.

'Agents are controlling players, being responsible for moves. There's no education process for parents. What does a good or bad agent look like? If they're saying to us, "I've been approached by three agents and I don't know how to choose," we can provide somebody to talk to. At the minute they can't pick the phone up to the club, because of what I described earlier.'

United funded a pilot programme, which involved seminars by financial, legal, media and security specialists. These ranged from basic advice on investment strategies and crisis management to pre-nuptial arrangements, tax issues and addressing fears about the vulnerability of highly paid footballers and their families to burglary or even kidnap.

It was augmented by the development of an app, which Andrews refers to as a 'player passport'. This, in essence, is an emotionally intelligent CV, in which a player records the minutiae of his progress through the system. If necessary he undergoes psychometric testing, so he can understand the complexities of character and culture.

'Speaking to young players, they trust technology more than they trust people. The passport is really a catch-all for whatever a footballer has experienced in his life, so that if he's moving to another club, or if he's moving to another career, he can say, "This is me. I've built this, this is mine. I own it." He understands himself. He can sit down with a prospective employer and say, "This is what I've experienced. These are the highs, these are the lows." Currently there isn't a way of capturing that.

'Clubs do really well on statistical information around playing, but this, in my opinion, is more important, because this is about him as a person. Whether he makes it as a footballer isn't irrelevant, it's really important to him, but, in the long run, given the stats around the game, what's more important is that he has a platform, literally a technology platform, for his future life.'

Kieran Bywater had reached that crossroads. He had been worn down psychologically by the accumulated stress of post-rejection trialling. In the words of his father, 'He was just living in hotels and traipsing around really, and it wasn't doing his mental health any good.' Lowe provided advice about further education, in a football setting, and a family conference provided the perspective.

Anger lingered over the lack of meaningful feedback. Scars were scoured by such hidden indignities as the sudden loss of a sponsored boot deal with Adidas. The Bywaters' solution was to summon the simplicity of childhood, the innocence of 'going to the park and playing, and scoring goals, and enjoying it, having fun'.

Enforced detachment from the professional game encouraged broader thoughts, a focus on wider horizons. Kieran accepted a full soccer scholarship from the University of Charleston in West Virginia to do a four-year degree course. He realigned his ambition to one of academic excellence and, in the medium term, a potential career in Major League Soccer.

He was one of seven British players recruited in January 2016 by Chris Grassie, head coach of the

University of Charleston's Golden Eagles, a nationally ranked NCAA Division II team competing in the Mountain East Conference. The twenty-eight-man roster features ten different nationalities and trains in a new £6 million Innovation Center and Sports Arena.

As a freshman, to aid integration and come to terms with the polyglot nature of the squad, Kieran was obliged to have a roommate from a different culture, in his case a midfield player and native of São Paulo, Bruno dos Santos from SC Corinthians Paulista, the legendary Rivellino's club. Kieran had to sit out the 2016 College season, because fifteen appearances for Bishop's Stortford following his release by West Ham made him initially ineligible under NCAA rules.

Grassie, whose Geordie accent has softened during his time on the other side of the Atlantic, has built his own life in North America in two phases. He attended the school of excellence that preceded Newcastle United's academy before his family moved to Canada when he was 15. He graduated from Alderson Broaddus, a liberal arts university in Philippi, West Virginia, in 2002 and spent three years as an assistant coach before returning to the UK.

He played semi-professionally for Northwich Victoria in what was then the Conference, but when Martin Allen had to suspend his offer of a contract at Brentford in 2006 because of financial problems he faced a choice: indulge himself as a penurious lower-league journeyman, or supplement his studies for a master's degree by developing a coaching career in the US.

In truth, it wasn't much of a choice. He still visits England annually, on recruitment tours of Category One academies, organised for college coaches by the Premier League. He looks for players who are problem solvers, unafraid to look at things in a different way. They are not immediately obvious, since the young men in the audience tend to be in denial:

'You look around the room and they are all sure they are going to make it. You talk to them about this great opportunity, the cheerleaders, our analytics and our A licence coaches, but they don't hear you. They know your name and have your number, but they don't realise it is probably not going to happen for them.

'It takes time to hit home when they are released. The grieving process usually lasts for a year. Then you are meeting them at their lowest point. They're thinking, what am I going to do with my life? Hopefully you can build them back up, reignite the spark. This is their lifeline. It gives them something to believe in.

'We know about most of these kids, and I have to admit I never thought someone like Kieran would be available to us. The way they were speaking about him, the way I saw him performing, he didn't seem to be someone who would fall out of the professional game. He has had a great football education. He is a special player, a special lad, a happy, positive guy who works very hard at his craft and seeks to challenge himself. He will probably be my best player; if not, top three. He is captaincy material, without a doubt.'

On the day we speak, unseasonably warm for late October, Grassie is formalising his recruitment for the following season. He conducts back-to-back interviews with first-year pros who know they are likely to be released from clubs like Manchester City, Sheffield Wednesday, Huddersfield Town and Queens Park Rangers. He suspects the exodus from England will gather momentum in the years to come.

Kieran is on campus, enrolling for two new classes, since he wishes to stretch himself intellectually. He is cryptically quoting Socrates on social media ('Be slow to fall into friendship but when thou art in, continue firm and constant') and promoting World Mental Health Day. Few will grasp the haunting eloquence of his Twitter bio, which reads: 'You see my mask, not the story behind it.'

If the scars are covered by the foundation powder of easy friendship and impending achievement, Kieran has dealt well with the immediate frustrations of the hiatus in his football life. He relished a summer season away from NCAA restrictions in Tennessee, playing for Chattanooga FC in the National Premier Soccer League, the amateur fourth tier of the US game.

He was accompanied by two of his Charleston team-mates, Jake Young, younger brother of former England defender Luke, and right winger Will Roberts, a former Wales under-19 international who had a single substitute's appearance in the Championship for Coventry City in 2012. The experience was certainly different.

Supporters, self-styled 'Chattahooligans', marched into matches in unison, and ritually observed an a cappella version of the US national anthem before kick-off. Bywater was hailed as a 'two-way midfielder', scoring twice in seven games as they qualified for the national play-offs, where they lost to a ninety-first-minute goal in the semi-finals before a home crowd of 12,251.

Disappointment has become a relative experience. Bywater was being judged on his own merits as a potentially pivotal player in the Golden Eagles' attempt to claim national honours in the 2017 season, which stretches from April to November. Though, inevitably, he is occasionally ambushed by memory, he is bullish because he has learned to compartmentalise failure:

'I'd had the stuffing knocked out of me, and trying to motivate myself was incredibly hard. There had been no warning signs that I was about to be flushed down the toilet. I wasn't ready mentally to start trudging round new clubs when I had naïvely thought I was going to be OK, but I've not looked back since moving out here.

'It is a fantastic university and the setup is akin to any pro team back home. I'm training like a pro with players who have a similar story to mine. England is not the be all and end all. My advice to anyone released from a British academy is to think long term, rather than flogging it out in the lower leagues on poor pitches for short, bitty contracts.

'I'm working for a degree that will give me a plan B when I can't kick a ball. I'm not chasing money and I'm not motivated by it. What's motivating me is the happiness of playing in a completely different environment. This has made me fall in love with my football again.'

8

Shiny Gobshites

There is, sadly, no star on Hollywood Boulevard, no place in the Rock and Roll Hall of Fame, for La Rocca, an indie piano-rock band named after a damp downstairs bar in Bristol. Their anthems of twenty-something angst drew comparisons with U2, Keane and Supergrass, but they had only a solitary hit single in Australia, a 129-second thrash entitled 'Sing Song Sung', to show for a five-year, two-album exile in Los Angeles.

The lead singer and principal songwriter, journalism student Bjorn Baille, insisted on being known as BjÃ¸rn in what can only have been a loosely parodic attempt to channel the creative genius of Prince. Tony Hoffer, a producer borrowed from Beck, and Belle and Sebastian, impressed Alan Redmond, the drummer, with his sagacity when he decided he liked the aural warmth of guitars recorded in a toilet.

Redmond, whose beard, braces and coarse waistcoats

preceded the pheasant-shoot chic of Mumford & Sons, had a self-confessed 'band manager head'. He saw the business logic of constant gigging across the United States, even when the stricken tour bus was ambushed in 8 Mile, Detroit, and their equipment was stolen in Philadelphia. The less said about a five-day gambling binge 'in a big B&B' on the Nevada border the better.

A decade on from the release of La Rocca's first album, *The Truth*, the self-styled 'Alan Whicker of Shitsville, Arizona' is a singular football figure. Now 41, and owner of the R10 agency, he works primarily in England, Italy and Spain, with a small stable of twenty first-team players, nine academy players, and renowned development coaches such as Rodolfo Borrell at Manchester City, and Pep Segura, who has returned from Liverpool to Barcelona as technical secretary to oversee the latest evolution of their academy.

Redmond has a Dubliner's natural eloquence and brings an interesting mixture of vivacity and intelligence to professional football, where he is in little danger of being confused with senior members of his relatively new trade. They have affectations of dignity and authority, despite the cigar-sucking, proverb-quoting, deal-cutting clichés, and are unlikely to be impressed by his acute portrait of a particular breed of modern agent:

'There is one class of agent that is, for me, almost a joke. It is like they have come off a conveyor belt. We refer to them as shiny gobshites. They are immaculately turned out. Even beyond the age at which they should start dressing respectably they still squeeze themselves into skinny jeans and very expensive shoes, trousers rolled up and no socks.

'They have the manicured beard and the Southampton players' haircut, shaved on the side with the little sweepy fringe. There are a lot of these guys and there is no substance there at all. I don't know where their personalised BMWs come from; they must be on lease or bought with some family money.

'I tend to see a lot of the same faces on the sidelines. There are a few of them where I think, he's a good guy, he's not on the take. If his player has a career further down the line, then of course he's going to take his five per cent, but he'll contribute to that player's progress. But quite a high proportion I look at and think, God help the players that are with them.

'I might have an alien background, but on a serious note there are a lot of parallels between music and football. I spent a large part of my youth practising and trying to get a deal. Once we got the deal we realised that only got us to the foot of the mountain. Talent, luck or a combination of the two takes you the rest of the way.

'We sold so few records I think we shocked our label. When we first started playing we turned down a couple of adverts because we were ethically against them. By the time we released our first record it was needs must.

Every song on that album bar one has been used in an advert, video game, TV show or a film.

'It qualified me a little for football because at a relatively young age I was given a big chunk of money, simply because I was good at doing something unusual. I watched some people handle that quite well, and I watched other people handle it quite badly. The only difference for me is that some of the best musicians I ever met never made any money and some of the worst footballers make great money. There's guaranteed money in football, whereas in music there is never that guarantee.'

His eclectic approach was forged during degree studies in English and Italian at Cardiff University, where the band was formed by three Irish students and a garrulous Lancastrian, keyboard player Nick Haworth. The course entailed a gap year in Parma where, in the late nineties, Carlo Ancelotti was shaping a young team around such stellar prospects as Gianluigi Buffon and Fabio Cannavaro, in a 4–4–2 system pioneered by the great AC Milan and Italy coach Arrigo Sacchi. Redmond 'wanted to speak football' and collated a glossary of simple terms, which gained in relevance when he started a language school in the UK following the end of his musical career. Liverpool FC were among his first clients; he translated legal documents and recruitment DVDs in five languages for the club's global scouting network and acted as an English teacher for players and support staff.

The gap in the market was immediately obvious. One senior coach, struggling to transfer his knowledge and experience, confessed that his previous English tuition had essentially consisted of learning the children's song 'Head, Shoulders, Knees and Toes' by rote. The problems of international transition for highly priced foreign players were also tinged by farce:

'I went to see one Argentine player, who was really down in the dumps. He tried to explain to me that he felt that he was being bullied because of the size of his head. He said that the players were calling him "melon" because he had a big head, like melon head. I was looking at him and I thought, if anything, his head is quite small. I couldn't understand it.

'When I investigated it, his teammates were shouting "man on", but he just heard "melon". So, every time he had the ball, he felt that they were on at him. I thought, what the fuck? But then I realised there were so many stupid things to sort out. There are so many critical football phrases used every second of the game, which are so easily misunderstood.

'They are not going to hear those terms in a general English class. Coaches will never stop and take the time to explain. So, for example, if a midfielder plays the ball to a striker with his back to the goal, and there is a player running on who wants to shoot he might shout "set". But the guy doesn't know what he's saying, he's got no idea, so the moment is lost in his confusion.'

Redmond was used in an advisory capacity by the Premier League, and together with Sean Warren, compiled an Oxford University Press book, *English for Football*, with a foreword by Sir Alex Ferguson. Distilled into eight chapters, covering different positions on the field and roles within a modern club, it formed the basis of an intense thirty-hour introduction to a sanitised version of industrial language.

Goalkeepers were taught the vernacular of eternal verities, such as 'narrow the angle' or 'stay on your line'. They were informed that a clean sheet had nothing to do with their laundry. Midfield players were given a list of personally relevant terms, including instructions to track back, play a through ball, cut inside or play on. Basics, such as how to ask for advice or even how to apologise for an error, were paramount.

He gained an insight into the mentality of the top professional by teaching Luis Suárez and Fernando Torres. Martin Škrtel, the Slovak defender, was so committed to fitting in as smoothly as possible he had Redmond visit his hotel for English lessons each day during his first month at the club. They had families to help them assimilate; academy players, allotted to house parents, were more vulnerable.

They were usually aged 16, although some younger boys were at the club on extended trials. Redmond would take them on a tour of their host city, and later test them on place names and street signs. As his experience extended to include work with Everton, Stoke City, Bolton Wanderers and Wigan Athletic, an obvious opportunity beckoned.

Players began bringing their contracts to him for translation. This developed organically into broader advice, since he had won their trust as a tutor. Pep Segura, summoned to Liverpool by Rafa Benítez as technical director of the academy following a spell as Olympiakos manager, sought to put their relationship on a more formal footing.

A seed, carefully planted, germinated when Segura suggested he should take the agents' examination, which underpinned FIFA's global licensing system until it was scrapped with chaotic consequences, appropriately enough on April Fools' Day in 2015. Redmond's diverse career had reached another crossroads:

'Pep was a bit of a mentor to me. It's not like I was Mother Teresa, trying to set the world to rights. I could see the way things were moving, and was one hundred per cent aware that there was a lot of money to be made. I won't lie to you. That was definitely a motivating factor. I would see players arrive at a big club, requiring some form of mainstream education, and the agent, who had made a lot of money from the transfer, just disappearing.

'On a basic level, being unable to communicate because of the language barrier, the frustration is huge. Clubs do a lot for their players, but I never understood how a care package was never considered to be part of the agent's responsibility. At some of the really big agencies it wasn't part of the job. It was just like, there you go. Get on with it.'

The examination consisted of twenty multiple-choice questions, mainly on contract law and football regulations. He studied for it for a minimum of five hours a night, seven days a week, over a two-month revision period in which his only release was to put his children to bed. It was an instructive process, since he detected the slackness in the wording of the Football Association's rulebook, compared to that of the global governing body.

At that stage there were approximately 400 licensed agents in the UK. Now, in a deregulated age, there are 2,000, who pay £500 to pass 'go' in what they envisage, optimistically in most cases, as a lucrative form of Monopoly. Being charitable – admittedly difficult in the circumstances – the catch-all qualification that the newly branded intermediary is of 'immaculate character' is too imprecise to inspire complete confidence.

'I'm glad I did the exam because I don't know how anyone can do the job without having learned the stuff within it. You can always check things, but it's good to know them first. It gives you a reference point, where you can confirm that you're right, rather than wondering what the hell you should do in any given situation.

'It is a mess. FIFA haven't helped at all. The money in

the game means that people will do desperate things to get in on deals. I've had a Portuguese agent contact me saying, "Look, I represent this player at Benfica. Manchester United have offered fifty-five million euros for him. We know you've got UK contacts, could you speak to these clubs for me?" When I've done due diligence, he's got nothing to do with the player. I get an email a week from some fairly high-level bullshitter, trying to connect A with B and somehow jump in the middle.

'I was waved through the new intermediary process because I passed the exam. I haven't seen any positive effect of doing away with it. I can't understand any business coming to the conclusion that removing knowledge as a barrier of entry is logical. If you do so, what are you saying? We welcome people with no knowledge, is what you're saying, and it's not rational.'

The Spanish system, in which Redmond works for around 10 per cent of his time, is no less fraught, but his dealings with Barcelona have reinforced his respect for their talent identification process. He believes such familiar stories as Manchester City coveting three of their best academy prospects, Pablo Moreno, Ansumane Fati and Nico González, miss the point.

'Barça look at English teams in youth tournaments, and are envious of their athletic level and cultural diversity, because their teams are very Catalan, but they regard any young player lured away by money as having a flaw. I suppose in the nicest possible way they feel they are smarter than everybody else. I'd probably go along with that. They really believe in the old rule about it being a narrow stride from the academy to the first team.

'In terms of expertise, I've never met scouts like theirs. It's no accident they spot players because occasionally I've had a chat with a Barça scout about an English player, and they know him better than their English counterparts. They've no interest in signing the player, because they trust their traditions and philosophy, but their knowledge is unmatched.'

Such lucidity and reason are hardly calling cards of a game in which material wealth is matched by intellectual poverty. Redmond, who works alongside Bertie Foster, son of former England defender Steve, may be arguing against himself to an extent, but as someone who is not afraid to think counter-intuitively he detects danger in the shift of the balance of power from the player to the agent. One particular incident was telling:

'A lot of agents are now attracted to younger players. To be honest, when I first started working with the academies, maybe I drank a little at that pool as well. I thought, this kid is going to be huge, and then he wasn't. Then there's another kid. He goes on loan to Cheltenham and it doesn't work out for him either.

'I saw the good and the bad, and it was predominantly bad. I wouldn't say that I saw certain players being mistreated, but I certainly thought I could make a good living, and could contribute to their career, if they'd have me. On this particular night, I was in the apartment of a very promising academy player at a Champions League club when the teenage son of his agent arrived.

'As the player opened the door, the agent's son said, "I thought you were supposed to drop off fucking tickets at my house after training." That's incredible, awful behaviour, in any business. I'd been having conversations about this sort of thing with my wife and other friends within the game, and this confirmed to me that things have gone too far the other way.

'Players now feel like they are working for the agents. This is totally wrong. Some agents take ten per cent when for me it should always be five. I've seen Premier League players, discovering a couple of years down the line that the agent has taken more from them than they realised, being afraid to phone them to discuss the issue. They are in awe because he's this major broker, as they see it.

'One first-team player whose contract with his agent had expired told me he was afraid to leave him because he had all the connections. When I looked into it, the player had been trying, unsuccessfully, to move for three transfer windows. From doing a little snooping around, I found out that this agent had been looking for an agency fee of two million quid.

'When I spoke off the record to a couple of clubs they said to me, "Oh, we like the player, but the agent is a fucking lunatic. He's a megalomaniac. We're not giving that sort of money to anybody." So the agent, the person the player thought had all the connections, was actually working against him getting the move he wanted.

'If anything, the pastoral side is even more important when you are dealing with young players. I'm confident on the legal side, the contractual side, but I have learned most from seeing things done badly rather than by looking at someone and saying, "That's how to do it." Does that tell you anything?'

It is an indication of a strange combination of complacency and desperation, greed and financial recklessness. In such circumstances it is not a huge shock that Redmond, a member of the Association of Football Agents, which is trying to become more transparent under the chairmanship of Mike Miller, spends a lot of the time either on the phone, or pretending to be on it, during breaks in their meetings:

'There are a handful of agents I know and trust. I have the odd coffee with them, and talk generally about football. We don't really talk about each other's clients. I don't really like many agents. Sometimes I'm judging a book by its cover. I might be wrong, but it's in my interests to keep a professional distance because I don't want to be accused of trying to get their players, and I don't want them anywhere near my players.

'There's a lot of desperation. The oldest trick in the book is the bullshitter who goes around with a car boot full of football boots. He hands them out to players with a line about him knowing the top guys in the company, when he has actually paid for them out of his own pocket. It is fantasy when the reality is any agent worth their salt can get free boots for a reasonably well-regarded player.

'I don't initiate conversations about that with parents, but if they raise it I am happy to assist them. The mum of a young player I'm helping at Everton came to me, saying that he was costing them a fortune, going through six or seven pairs of boots a season. At two hundred pounds a pair that was a burden because they are not a rich family. That was something we could fix straight away by having boots sent to him.

'But I never use that as a basis for a relationship, because if you do you're just offering what everybody else has. You've got to be careful. It's very easy to say, "Oh, listen, happy birthday, here's an iPhone and this and that," but if you start doing that someone else will start getting him an iPad, and you look shit. You've always got to be judged on the quality of your work and the support you give.

'I got a call the other day from the company which supplies boots to a young player I have just signed. Their rep was laughing his head off. He told me that when the lad was called up by England, he had ten people call him to say they represented the player. Of course, he knew differently. Five of them were from the same major agency, and didn't realise the others had been on.

'It is ambulance chasing, really. I don't know the structure of some of the agencies, but I guess a lot of them are on commission only. They desperately want to work in football, and consequently will do whatever it takes. Most of them are pretty transparent, and parents have become a lot more savvy.

'They talk amongst each other. If you are a parent of a promising under-16 player, you will get to know about the agent who is unscrupulous, or a liar. Word gets around. I don't make people promises; the only thing I promise is that I'll work my backside off for them. I'd never say to a parent, "You know what, your son is going to play for Barcelona one day." I'd never do that.

'I'm pretty consistent. I tell the boy his first fight is to have a career as a player, at any level. Once he has got out of the academy system and is playing football with grown men, he will find his level. That may be going straight through to the first team, at an Arsenal or a Tottenham, or it might involve being released, and going to a Swindon Town.

'Every player needs a starting point at first-team level and that is what a lot of them don't get. My starting point is that nobody makes it. The trick is how to navigate the system to give yourself the best chance to do so. You never know what the future holds, so I stress to them that good work is never wasted.'

At times, this involves bordering on being a professional nuisance. Redmond calls opposition academy managers, or heads of recruitment, before matches, to brief them on his client's status. No selection secrets are disclosed; it is merely an insurance policy, designed to keep the player's name at the forefront of an influential individual's mind.

'If I've got a player who is sixteen or seventeen years old, and he's playing, I'm not shopping the guy out. I don't want him to agitate for a move. But what I am doing is speaking to clubs he is playing against, and saying, "Just keep an eye on him, because you never know." The player could hit eighteen and go through a period when he is not playing very often, so he can't be scouted. That means he has to go trialling, if he is released. At least this way when they are in the spotlight I make sure people know they exist. That's all you can do.'

Redmond speaks quickly, occasionally forcing his words into a traffic jam around his vocal chords. He works in a world of deceptive courtesies, flagrant phonies and poor character actors. Though some in football will doubtlessly be distracted by his ardour, and appalled by his candour, there is something refreshing about an individual prepared to puncture the game's pretty balloons:

'Maybe I'm unusual, but I choose not to work with even potential arseholes. Maybe when I first started I took a gamble on a couple of situations, and regretted it. Maybe it was a parent that was a nightmare to try and work alongside. To give you an example, I was phoned by the dad of the captain of a national under-18 team, who was a defender at a big club in the UK.

'I know the player. I've got no interest in taking the player. I could make some money out of the player but I don't want to. I don't like him. When I say I don't like him, I've seen enough of him to see that he thinks he's arrived. And in my opinion, although he's at a big club now, his level is League Two. I've no interest in being the guy that delivers that player down the slope.

'A player hasn't got have Champions League potential for me to work with him. If I think that Swindon Town is the top end of a guy's potential, I'll take him if he's going to work his arse off to get there. In the last year I'd say I've probably done maybe a dozen contracts that I haven't taken money for.

'Some of the players have been relatively young, others a little bit older, but if he is on a low salary, why would I take five per cent if I don't need to? It might sound a little naïve and that's probably why I'm better outside of the large agency structure. You hear stories of certain agencies talking about each player having six individual revenue streams.

'I just laugh when they talk about a brand, because that looks after itself if you've got a player who plays for a really big team. It's simple: people will pay that person to do shit if he's very good at football. If he is an ugly bastard, fewer people will pay him to do certain things. If he's a handsome guy – and there's no way to manipulate that – he does what he wants. You can't build a brand around nothing. You can't build a brand around a sixteen-year-old who has never kicked a ball with men.'

His experience of working with young players in an educational capacity crystallised his conviction that clubs could do more to assist academic development. He believes concentration on BTEC courses lowers the bar, and that players between the ages of 16 and 18 would benefit from the additional responsibility of studying for at least two A levels, or further GCSEs if that is more educationally appropriate for the individual.

Temptation is omnipresent in such a materialistic, status-conscious culture. Redmond was aghast to hear one of his 16-year-old players was selling his complimentary boots to less celebrated teammates, 'and absolutely ripped into him'. His lecture on the importance of mutual respect and the warped morality of 'treating people like dirt' was part of a thematic approach:

'To be honest, it is easy to come up with these little things that sound like bumper stickers. I challenge my players by saying, "I know you've got your career plan and your dreams, but did anyone train better than you today?" And if they go, "I don't know, I didn't really think about it," I tell them to start thinking about it. Don't let it happen again. If you trained really well on Monday, don't celebrate it on Tuesday. Do it again, because that's what top players do. You can't do the impossible but you can do your best every day if you focus on it.'

He works on personal recommendation and on average takes on one new player each month, 'because with not so many mouths to feed I don't have to go chasing'. He learned from early mistakes, dealing with the neuroses of mid-career cast-offs from other agents, and has followed the market trend, which dictates that the best players are recruited earlier.

'You've got to do a lot of work to reinforce the point they are not really on the road yet. They feel like a pro, because of the professionalism of an academy environment in which everything is just incredible, beautiful and touch screen. They think they've arrived and they haven't. They're miles away.

'I tend to know in the first meeting if a player or a parent is for me or not. I fully expect the parents to have their say, and beyond that make major decisions. I never presume they're going to hand their son over to me and walk away. That is not the way it should be. Sometimes, you just get the feeling that the parent isn't going to listen to anybody anyway.

'I walk away from the start, in a nice way. Instead of saying, "I don't want your brat," I usually ask who else they have spoken to, or worked with. No matter what they say, no matter which name they come up with, I tell them what a good job he would do for them. That's the best way of handling a delicate situation.'

Occasionally, the chemistry is benign. Redmond has strong links with Arsenal, and had been aware of Vontae Daley-Campbell's reputation as another outstanding graduate of the Afewee Training Centre in Brixton for about a year when he received a text message from the boy's uncle, Nathan, seeking advice. Their arrangement is informal, but integral.

'The text was pretty straightforward: "We have a lot of people circling us at the moment. We've been told that you're honest. Would it be OK to have a chat?" We took it from there. People ask – and it is a good question – what the hell do you do for a young player? In Vontae's case it was simple initial things, like stopping him having to pay for boots and getting him additional nutritional advice.

'Rather than say, "We will step in from here and do everything," as others had suggested, I am happy to help prevent him making any mistakes. If the family thinks it is worth us working together more formally closer to the professional phase, and we still feel the same way about them, then that would be great. I've been really straight with them.

'He has the potential to go directly through to the first team at Arsenal, I am certain of that. Will it happen? Let's see. I never make a promise of that to any player I represent. Look at any team: you can see three players with first-team potential, and many without even a one per cent chance of making it. Vontae is lucky he is in the group that has the potential but it just takes one bad injury, one poor decision, one night out that goes wrong, one coach that doesn't really fit in with him.

'Arsenal might sign a Portuguese under-19 international in his position when he is in his second year as a scholar, but I believe in Vontae a lot. I believe he has an excellent chance. An excellent chance for me is still maybe less than twenty per cent, but considering that I think most players have zero per cent, the odds are good.

'Players always think they have time. They don't. They have to have a real selfishness, and never really trust that the club have their best interests at heart. They have to have their career's best interests at heart, and not take any shit. If you are performing well, training well, and you are still not in the team you have to find a way to get out, because that kills a young player.

'Some of my youth players might be a little more high profile because they score more goals and play in an attacking position. As a defender you tend to be naturally more in the background, but I do think Vontae is the player who will keep quietly doing the right things. He just doesn't make mistakes. There's no physical resemblance, but he reminds me of Denis Irwin. Come to think of it, Nathaniel Clyne has those attributes as well . . .'

There was an unintentional symmetry in the comment. Even the most tenuous connection with the

Liverpool full back, Steadman Scott's greatest ambassador for urban youth, echoes in the tight, cluttered streets around the Brixton Recreation Centre. It begged an altogether more complicated question, of whether another of Scott's protégés could succeed against the odds.

9
Hope

The clock on the wall in a sparse office beneath the main stand at what will be known as the Checkatrade.com Stadium for the duration of a five-year sponsorship deal reads fourteen minutes to three. Dermot Drummy, manager of Crawley Town, has a final team talk to deliver in the dressing room along the corridor, but one last thought to impart before he does so.

'Tell him what he means to people,' he says, rising from behind a desk on which sits a dormant laptop, a team sheet and a concise scouting report on Notts County, a streetwise but ageing League Two team that would struggle badly in the winter months, when the club was convulsed by a change in ownership. 'It will be good for him to hear that. He needs know this is about more than him.'

A little under three hours later, following a 3–1 home defeat in which he conceded a late penalty, I am directing

Andre Blackman, Crawley's left back, to a seat in the visitors' dugout. He is freshly showered, a little nervous, and oblivious to the hypnotic quality of the small bead of sweat trickling down the outside of his nose.

He smiles slowly, revealing a slight gap between his upper set of front teeth, and chuckles softly when I do his manager's bidding, and emphasise the wider importance of his struggle to permit his talent to conquer his temperament. He has heard the lecture before, from figures of far greater authority than me, someone with whom he has been in intermittent contact since he was tracked down to a hotel in Fez, a Moroccan city in the shadow of the Atlas Mountains.

A fortnight previously, he had returned to the Brixton Recreation Centre, where his name and his progress were spoken of in hushed tones, as if to avoid the danger of tempting fate. He coached the boys who had come off familiar streets to train under Steadman Scott, the man who was there for him when he was a 7-year-old taking a bus, on his own, across the borough to play football for the joy of it.

'You can change all these boys,' Scott told him, when the Afewee Academy session was over. 'They can relate to you. Three quarters of them will have issues with self-worth. They don't feel part of this society. But they look at you. People won't talk about your colour. They will talk about your talent. Dedicate yourself to showing the goodness of this community.

'Go as far as your ability can take you. Your mother is a good woman. My responsibility is to help you be a man. There is an end product, and that's why I can be strict with these boys, as I was with you. They will be attracted to you. Making it as a footballer is their ultimate dream. You have that chance. It's important that you settle down, shut your mouth, and take instruction. Let it happen.'

Drummy, a dapper silver-haired man in an open-necked black shirt, first knew Blackman as a 13-year-old training at Arsenal's Hale End academy, where he began a career in development coaching that led to his overseeing FA Youth Cup and under-21 Premier League titles at Chelsea. He had spoken to him in similar terms in July 2016 when he decided to give him a one-year contract at Crawley, the latest club in a chaotic career.

'All I can do is give you hope. I'm not going to pull any punches with you. I am not going to give you false hope. Connect looking after your mum, and the welfare of your family, to your football. This is your opportunity to earn a living, to look after yourself. Money is not our god, but we need to earn it. Don't ever neglect that side of life.

'Sit down, anyone who ain't made a mistake in the world. You've been in the wrong. You've mucked around and your past ain't glorious, but let's step through it and move on. In ten years' time you could be a role model for someone in Brixton. If I can give you a cause, a connection, that's the biggest thing I can do for you or any of my players.'

Many managers have tried, and failed, to solve the riddle of a gifted, athletic player and the conflicted, restless young man. His pockmarked CV doesn't match his post-match persona, since Blackman engages earnestly in a conversation monitored by a young club official silently searching for scraps for the following week's programme, but it contains too many blips to ignore.

Blackman lasted five years in the Arsenal academy, flirted with Chelsea and spent a further year at Tottenham before he joined Portsmouth at 16. The arrival of detectives in first-team manager Paul Hart's office, with a request to interview him in connection with an investigation of a serious crime in Streatham, proved the last straw, despite Blackman's innocence. 'A lovely lad,' recalled Hart, 'but too much.'

His Bristol City contract, signed in the close season of his release by Portsmouth, was cancelled within three months for what manager Gary Johnson termed 'disciplinary issues'. An unsuccessful trial at Leicester City was followed by a thirteen-game spell at AFC Wimbledon in what was then the Conference, where his pledge 'to sort my life out' remained unfulfilled.

Another unproductive trial, at Oldham Athletic, presaged a difficult spell in which he paid to attend an academy in Tooting run by Jamie Lawrence, a former right winger who accumulated sixteen clubs in a journeyman's career. When the money ran out, he returned to his roots, and played five-a-side football with friends in Larkhall Park, close to Union Grove in Stockwell.

He was out of the game for nearly a year before repeating the cycle of contrition, determination and rejection at Celtic. Signed on the strength of assertive performances in several development games, he made his Scottish Premier League debut in a 1–1 draw at Aberdeen, when the club were already twenty points clear at the top of the table.

He is best remembered at Parkhead for winning the supporters' 'tackle of the year' award for a sliding challenge in a reserve-team match, where he was unable to prevent himself colliding with manager Neil Lennon, who was pitched, face first, into compacted ground close to the touchline. Lennon's humour remained intact, but Blackman was to play only three first-team games for him.

The carousel continued. Man of the match on his debut for Inverness Caledonian Thistle, Blackman managed only one more appearance there before his loan was cut short three months early. Terry Butcher, a ferociously competitive player and a notably disciplinarian manager, cited his 'poor attitude'.

Quietly released by Celtic in November 2012, he was without a club for a further eight months before he signed a short-term contract at Plymouth Argyle in

League Two. Discarded after six starts in five months, he spent the rest of the 2013–14 season in the Conference South at Dover Athletic and Maidenhead United.

Owner Massimo Cellino orchestrated an extended trial at Leeds United, which included a pre-season training camp in Italy, but Blackman was overlooked and picked up by Blackpool, who installed him in a hotel with a weekly living allowance of £125. The club and his personal life were in similar disarray. In April 2015 he was convicted of what he described as 'a moment of madness', stealing a £1,225 jacket from Harrods; he was sentenced to forty hours' unpaid community service after the court heard he was apprehended by police, attempting to flee the Knightsbridge store. His future appeared bleak. Raw material – physicality matched by the sort of pace which enabled him to recover quickly from occasional lapses in positional discipline – was being undermined by reputation. At his lowest ebb, when he was a transitory figure, intermittently sighted as what coaches refer to as a 'body' in training games, he needed the faith and friendship of men like Chris Ramsey.

Ramsey had wanted to keep the teenaged Blackman when he was Head of Player Development at Tottenham, but, in a scenario that was to become all too familiar, 'he probably didn't do himself any favours. The club thought it was going to be difficult to deal with him.' Having retained contact, he gave him breathing room in the autumn of 2015 by inviting him to train with QPR, where he was promoted from the academy to manage the first team before becoming Technical Director.

'Do you know how good Andre was? He was fantastic. One the best players I have seen as a kid. His social life and his lack of emotional control stopped him. He couldn't keep his mouth shut. I got on all right with him, but what he has to remember is that people don't care about your life. You have to play the game. He is only realising that now.

'When you are in the game, and there is a way of manipulating your image, there is a chance. When you are outside, looking in, it is more difficult. It will be hard for him to make it in the football world because his reputation goes before him, but I have a soft spot for him. He would be brilliant in the community. He is a good kid, but he has just not been a good kid, if you understand what I'm getting at. He has a lot to offer.

'The best players, the best sportsmen, use their environment to make themselves better. Those who have the silver spoon, the rich ones who have the best gym and the best nutrition, will use those advantages. Those who come from nothing will use whatever they can get hold of.

'What we have in the academy system is kids who have never experienced that horrible side of life, kids who think they have a God-given right to be in this clean, kind, supportive environment. Somewhere along the line the fight goes. The ones who are the quickest and the strongest see beyond the veneer.'

Blackman had such vision. He also had the street smarts to text Drummy when rumours of his impending appointment by Crawley reached Morocco. 'He knew a lot about me, on the pitch and off it,' Blackman reasoned. 'I asked if it was OK if I came in and showed what the new Andre is all about.'

The manager smiles at the memory: 'He started calling me Gaffer. I told him I was going to take my time because I needed to make it right for everybody. I wanted to see how hungry he was. I knew his background. Mine was being brought up on a Stoke Newington council estate. All we had was a ball and hope.

'I guess I've never forgotten that I didn't have anyone to mentor me when I didn't make it at Arsenal. I left at nineteen and six weeks later was climbing up telegraph poles as a British Telecom engineer. I went semi-pro and then became a London cab driver. Doing the Knowledge makes you very humble. As a coach, I develop people. I don't develop footballers.

'You have to be skilled at, and knowledgeable about, what you do, and point lads in the right direction. Things change. In our generation you stood still when a policeman came down the road. You went into the army. Boys learn in such a vastly different way now.

They are thrown into adulthood by the world in which they live.

'They have to have someone they believe when they are talking to them. I think you can pick people up if there is a trust – and there is a trust between Andre and myself. His mother was ecstatic when we signed him because she knew we would give him a reason to get out of bed. He knows now that talent is never enough.'

Crawley is a homely club, unpretentious and welcoming. Kelly Derham, the chief executive, cleans the toilets when the need arises. Drummy espouses the benefits of sports science on a limited budget, expects his players to fetch and carry on their solitary training pitch, and believes in the power of human contact.

'I see myself taking time out for my players, not just Andre, but when his gran passed away the other day we made sure Crawley sent flowers. I wanted Andre's mum to know her son was in a family. Andre is going to be looked after. Andre has guidelines. There is no easy stroke for him. He gets treated the same as everyone else, but he has a shirt to pull on, a cause to go for.

'There's many a person who wants to grab a young kid in the spotlight and make some money out of them. The best coach is a community worker, whose best interests are in the kids. Then you make sure they are linked into the right environment with the right guidance. If there are no role models in their life, and crime in the background, there will be opportunities to take the easy way out when things go wrong.'

Blackman's response may contain customary promises, but they are delivered in a manner that suggests lessons have been finally learned. Arsène Wenger argues the optimal age to gauge a player's long-term potential is 23, and though Blackman lags two years behind that schedule, his self-awareness gives reason for cautious optimism.

'I have learned how to control my emotions, and I've improved my decision-making in the heat of the moment. Whereas in the past I was more reactive, I have a strategy to count to ten and just focus. Everyone's journey is a bit different, you know? Obviously some will say I have gone the long way around it.

'I wouldn't say I'm one hundred per cent, but I am nearly there. Some people understand things a bit quicker than others. I have been around younger boys who are really mature. A group of people is about the right mix, different minds and different decisions. Some don't have the mental strength to push through and fulfil their potential.

'I come here where people are professional and understand what you have to do. Then I go back to Brixton, and I don't know what Brixton is going to offer. Sometimes, someone's been hurt. There's a lot of boys right now just in and around it, and that's all they know. I have seen some really, really good players. They are more comfortable just following the cycle.

'Obviously I have had my ups and downs but I have always known what I have wanted to do, which is to play football. I went to Morocco out of sheer love of the game, to show everyone I still have that drive and hunger. I have been out of the leagues and been abroad. Some players are released and that is it. I look at that and say, how can that be?'

Drummy knows the score: 'There is no doubt about Andre's talent, his physicality, but he blows up. It happened a couple of times in training when he first joined us. He was emotional. I had to tell him, "Oi, come on. What the fuck are you doing?" He has performed brilliantly since. If he keeps performing people will start looking at him again. This could be a stepping stone for him.'

Scott knows the scene: 'You've got to look at the positives. Bearing in mind the environment that he's exposed to, this boy has done a wonderful job not ending up with a criminal conviction. If it wasn't for football, Andre would either be in prison, charged with murder, or dead. For me, he deserves chances because of where he comes from.'

Ramsey knows what is at stake: 'If, through Andre, Steadman can convince these kids that your environment doesn't need to hold you back, he will do a fantastic thing. I came from Holloway. It wasn't the best. People I know are in Pentonville and places like that. Those Steadman has saved have had to want not to be in the gang.

'There is an age where you do have to come to terms with the fact you have no money. If you have illegal money it is not sustainable. Do you have that "aha" moment when you say to yourself, "Do you know what? I can't keep robbing because I don't want to do five years in prison. At some stage I am going to have to be a civvy-street person who works in Costco, stacking shelves, earning a decent amount, driving a modest car and living in a modest flat."

'The norm isn't the norm for the lad from the leafy suburbs. The norm is hanging around, doing the wrong thing. It is wanting trappings that you are not prepared to work for, getting the BMW by selling drugs. That's why I admire people like Steadman. There are a lot of good parents who don't want their kids to be stigmatised, but it is a scary place.'

Being tossed into an overheated, overstretched job market at the pivotal age of 20 is a fundamental test of character; when that struggle involves something as visible as professional football, the strain intensifies. As winter crept closer, Leo Chambers, an accomplished Afewee graduate, was at least being medically supported during his rehabilitation from a persistent leg injury by West Ham, the club which had released him in the summer.

Nathan Mavila, whose contract was also not renewed, as he expected, underwent trials at Perugia and Spezia in Italy and trained informally with Charlton Athletic before signing for National League club Maidstone United as a free agent in September. He struggled to hold down a first-team place, yet sought a deeper connection to the world around him by volunteering for St Mungo's, a charity dedicated to providing food and shelter for 2,500 homeless individuals each night.

His search for spiritual solace took him to the French Christian Assembly of London, a Pentecostal church in Stockwell. The congregation was strikingly young, overwhelmingly black and typical of those drawn to an exuberant form of New Evangelism. Faith, shaped by cultural challenges and economic hardship, had a telling relevance.

Mavila, accompanied by his brother Gaius, preached regularly, and often played drums in services that switched between English, French and Lingala, a Bantu language spoken along the River Congo in Central Africa. On this particular Thursday evening, clad in white collarless shirt, trousers and canvas shoes, he sought to link the spiritual with the sporting:

'In the industry I am in a lot of the boys like to party, so I went out with them all the time. That's what I used to do. Amen. So, one thing I realised was, as I accepted Christ, I had to change my surroundings. 1 Corinthians, 53. Do not be misled. Bad company corrupts good character. Amen. If you are a good person at heart do not be around people that do not have the same heart as you.

'My dad always told me this: you are a footballer. Do

not mix with people who do not play football. Surround yourself with people who have mindsets like you. We are moved by the things that are around us. Amen. We need to discern and distinguish who we need around us. What do you establish around yourself?

'If you are not around good people then how are you going to get to where you need to be? One thing I have realised is that Church is cool. When I was growing up, Church was my home. Satan is everywhere. Do you know that? Sometimes a fool goes a different way and you think, why? Try to be around people who focus and love God.

'A lot of the time we are not focused. That's why we miss the target. In my career I have been around a lot of established players. But some people don't get that far. They are the ones without the right focus and mind-set. If you focus on the money you will miss being a player. If you focus on the best bits you will miss God. Chase him and the rest will follow.

'Focus on what you love. I love Lionel Messi. He is one of the greatest footballers in the world. As soon as he steps on the pitch photographers follow him. Sponsors follow him. The world follows him. He doesn't care about anything else but the score. The greatest have standards. Be the best you can be. But how great can you be without Christ? You are limited, very limited. Amen. In Christ you have no limits.

'I was born in sin. The only way to get over and out of

that is to accept Christ, right? God has given each and every one of us free will. God knows what you are going to do but he has still given you free will. That's mad, isn't it? The mind is led by the things you see and the things you hear. Amen. If you are exposed to crazy things, the wrong people, they can change the way you will be. In this life you have one shot at it. Give Him service.'

As he led prayers, speaking into a handheld microphone while walking either side of a transparent dais, he exuded a revealing serenity. His eyes were wide, exultant. An equally broad smile stretched a trim moustache, and dared the congregation not to share his devotion. The mood was as far removed as it is possible to be from the despair that, at the age of 17, triggered Mavila's renewal of faith.

The death of Dwayne Simpson, a close friend and football partner since primary school, was a consequence of the random violence, warped relationships and festering resentment that characterises gang culture. Simpson, nicknamed Squirrel, went to the aid of a boy nicknamed Laughter, who was being chased along Brixton Road by Rio Julienne-Clarke.

Simpson, who armed himself with a steering-wheel lock before jumping out of a passing car, was attacked in an alleyway when his friend escaped. CCTV cameras captured Julienne-Clarke giving up the chase and pulling out a knife before turning to confront him. Simpson was stabbed three times, through the heart and lungs, and died two days later, following an ineffective emergency operation. He was 20.

The jury, which found Julienne-Clarke guilty of manslaughter, took into account police intelligence that he and his victim were former members of the Brixton Guns and Shanks gang. Sentenced to twelve years' imprisonment, the perpetrator argued he was a target of the gang because he had acted as a police informant. It was also suggested in court that he had set up his own drug-dealing operation in defiance of the gang code.

According to his mother, Lorraine Jones, Dwayne, who had slipped into criminality during her divorce, was in the process of rehabilitating himself. He was coaching football informally to local children, and involved in the establishment of a boxing club for disaffected youth. She had been shopping in the Iceland supermarket, close to Brixton Tube station and within walking distance of the stabbing, when word reached her of her son's plight.

She found paramedics attempting to resuscitate him where he lay, in a pool of blood, and was prevented from touching him. The haunting image of his hand hanging inertly from a stretcher stays with her, though she continues to take comfort from the faith that sustains her as an ordained minister at the Lord's Church International Ministries in Brixton.

She told Premier Christian Radio: 'I thank God because in those two days, even though he was on a life support machine, I was able to speak to him, kiss him and pray with him. He was with us, but couldn't communicate. I said to him, "Death is a transition from earth to heaven. It is nothing to be afraid of. When a person dies, it is just their flesh that goes into the earth, but their spirit goes to our maker."

'So when he was on the life support machine, I said, "You can't speak, but call on Jesus. Jesus will be with you through the transition." When you lose a child, the grief affects you emotionally, physically, psychologically, your whole being. I thank God that I am a Christian because truly the Holy Spirit has helped me and my other six children to get through this grief in a positive way. My son died a hero, a Good Samaritan.'

The grief was collective. More than 300 local residents gathered inside and outside the family home on the Angell Town estate for nine nights, following his death. Some, no more than teenagers, showed her the bulletproof vests they wore as a matter of course. A peace march was held at dusk to a local church, where birdsong provided evocative backing to public prayer.

Lorraine Jones spoke of 'turning pain into power'. She received a police commendation at New Scotland Yard for her anti-knife-crime advocacy, and received a Point of Light award from David Cameron. Nathan Mavila sought spiritual advice from his mother's pastor, and resolved to change. He asked himself, 'Is this the life I really want to lead?' and discovered that, 'God spoke to me.' He returned to the embrace of his church, shed dangerous friendships, and helped relaunch Dwaynamics, a boxing gym in a local railway arch designed to mentor vulnerable children, who receive life skills coaching and attend employability workshops. 'We're trying to open doors,' Mavila explains, outlining work experience opportunities, apprenticeship programmes and homework classes offered by the scheme.

Sport, as so often, silently fills a social vacuum. Yet Afewee's success, embodied by Rinsola Babajide, who started studies at the University of East London and starred for the England under-19 team which won the Women's International Cup with victories over France, USA and Northern Ireland in late October, can easily be marginalised, under-appreciated.

Steadman Scott's community campaigning intensified following the transmission of a Channel 5 two-part documentary entitled *Gangland*, which risked the glamorisation of gang members who filmed their activities with GoPro cameras supplied by the producers. He attempted to balance images from a lavish, live-fast-die-young lifestyle by issuing a statement in the name of the organisation he helped found:

> 'Showing young people killing each other off, without offering a solution, or an explanation why this is happening is sensational and exploitative. It is also a counsel of despair. Young people need

hope. They need to see and hear from people who have succeeded against the odds. They need role models who will uplift and inspire them. There are many people that could have been interviewed to show that there is a way out.

'Things are tough for young people growing up in the inner cities. The reality is that in this country young black people are still held back by racism. The kids in the film were clearly intelligent, educated and enterprising young people. If they are in gangs it is because they don't see an alternative.

'Children need to believe that there is another way. They need to be armed with knowledge about the realities of the society and understand how to counteract barriers put in their path. I have lived in my community for fifty years. I have a duty to speak out about the problems facing our young people. But as a "big" man I also have a duty to do something about the situation.

'Nobody will guide these young people or instil in them a belief that they can succeed, if we, the community, don't do it. Government-funded schemes are designed to let children have "fun", not push them to reach their potential. Having low expectations of children is one of the worst forms of oppression.

'Youngsters respond to challenge. They can accomplish excellence, if excellence is asked of them. Afewee has proved that time and time again. We see youngsters develop self-discipline, focus, application, confidence and competitiveness because they are in an environment where it is required.'

Football has the sort of sheen that can change narratives and shape attitudes, but footballers are not social workers. Nathaniel Clyne, who was being linked to Barcelona as a potential transfer target in the 2017 winter window, acknowledged his background in a series of interviews, without fully engaging in the social significance of his success.

'The boys know where he comes from,' Scott reflected. 'They hear his name, see him on television. But we have not seen him here for so long.' There was no hint of censure in his voice, merely exasperation at the practical difficulty of securing meaningful interaction. Andre Blackman, for all his flaws, is a more powerful symbol of advancement because of his availability, and recently acquired humility.

Though he was sent off for two bookable offences in a 1–1 draw against Bristol Rovers in the first round of the FA Cup in early November, his second dismissal of the season, Blackman was a regular in a Crawley team with play-off ambitions in League Two. His coaching sessions at the Brixton Rec were irregular, but invaluable.

'Oh my goodness, we used to fight, constantly,' Scott said, with gentle, ruminative laughter. 'Andre's problem was that, because his father wasn't there until he was about ten years old, he was spoiled. But if I didn't have those years with him, he would be worse. If he comes in and coaches the young boys it will help him in his football, since he will be looking for discipline. He will teach them it is not about your ability but your mentality.'

Drummy, an alternative father figure, was on the same wavelength: 'When I talk to Andre he is a very conscious young man. Sometimes the behaviour is misleading. I tell him, "If the guys you are rolling with love you, they will leave you alone and let you get on with your career." I think his mum is his rock. He has a younger brother, and he sees himself as a man. Cometh the hour, cometh the man.'

Identifying Blackman as a rallying point for an entire community seems an unfair burden to place on someone who admits, 'I am not an established player and I still have some things to learn.' Experience counsels against idealistic expectation, yet hope dies hard where it matters most.

10

Education, Education, Education

They were seduced by the trappings of fleeting success, the flattery of strangers, and promises of fame and fortune. Instead of gracing the great stages of the Premier League, as they anticipated, they are incarcerated in a bleak prison cluster on the Isle of Sheppey in Kent, or lingering in such privately run jails as Thameside, in south-east London.

Albert Barnes visits them regularly, shares their pain and hears their fears. It is a forbidding ritual, because of the unanimity of their desperate, doomed responses to rejection by football. They played for big clubs, had big ideas and an even bigger fall. They are landfill, human wastage in an industry that cannot claim a clean conscience.

'These are the boys who are given a taste of what is available to those who make it. Are we letting them down? They come through top academies, don't get it right, get released and then tend to cry. Football has been their area of safety. Now it is denied to them. They're trapped, and feel they cannot go back to where they came from.

'We live in a society where lies thrive. We don't tell these boys the truth. Football basically says to them, sorry, you didn't make it. Get on with your lives. Out of frustration, with no education and nothing to do, they come out, and the first thing they do is look for the quickest way of making money.'

Barnes tends the casualties on the front line of a war that can be found on no map. It straddles the fantasy of inevitable enrichment and the reality of probable failure. He combines academic rigour, developed during a seven-year study of criminology in which he rarely slept more than three hours a night, with paternal experience – his son Aaron, a second-season pro who began at Arsenal, has just been given a first-team squad number, 33, at Charlton Athletic.

Between 70 and 80 per cent of the inmates he counsels from a sporting background are imprisoned because of drug offences, or armed robbery. His current caseload involves boys who were in academies at Tottenham, Arsenal and Chelsea, but the problem cannot be defined by geography or club policy.

His mobile phone carries depressingly familiar news on the late-summer day we first meet. Nathan Ashton, who made more than twenty appearances for England youth sides and played on the wing for Fulham in the Premier League before joining Crystal Palace and Wycombe Wanderers, has been jailed for fifteen years for a series of armed raids on betting shops.

Together with an accomplice, former Scottish Premier League player Ohmar Pike, he terrorised cashiers, one of whom fell to his knees, had a panic attack and begged for his life when the demand that the safe be opened immediately was accompanied by a black handgun being jabbed into the back of his head.

Barnes is a pleasant, singsong-voiced man whose non-judgemental manner reflects the philosophy of UKresettlement, the charity he has established to assist ex-offenders and vulnerable young adults. He visits prisoners to gain an understanding of the issues – which run parallel to those facing military personnel unable to deal with discharge from service – and is there for them when they are released.

He has established a safe house in Folkestone, where residents are eased back into society through such basic community work as tending the gardens of local pensioners. They learn to cook, to trust, to look beyond themselves. Known to all and sundry as Uncle Albert, Barnes seeks to recreate a family environment that is too often fractured.

'So many problems can be traced to the family unit. Many of these guys are where they are because they didn't have love from the beginning. Mum and Dad may have not been there. We do everything together. I say to them, "You are all brothers, living in one house. Start thinking." The idea is to re tune their mentality, the way they think, the way they see things, because everything that they want, they want now. They have never had the patience of working through certain stages.'

He works to ingrain and enhance basic skills and attitudes such as communication, self-reliance, personal responsibility, teamwork and rational decision-making. It is a decompression chamber, a place of emotional cleansing since they come from a world that encourages self-defensiveness and suspicion.

'Football is about survival of the fittest. It's an industry where everyone is selfish. You look after yourself because of the competition. It is so fluid; your best mate in the playground becomes your enemy because you both want the same thing. Parents bitch and bite, do anything to push their sons ahead. I'm a realist, not an idealist. The real world is tough. Everyone is fighting his own corner. Nobody will ever fight for you.'

His survival instincts were honed when he fled Liberia, via Côfe d'Ivoire and its capital Abidjan, as a political refugee in the early nineties. He settled in Streatham, worked night shifts in a factory making gas meters, and studied at the Open University for a year before enrolling on a full-time degree course at Westminster University during the day.

He chose criminality as his subject because he was disturbed by the demographics of the drug trade on local streets, and had decided to do a master's degree at Leicester when he was bundled into a toilet by his factory supervisor. The subsequent lecture seemed to summarise the self-generating pessimism of a community stigmatised by the casual acceptance of crime and institutionalised racism.

'When I was in Streatham I would always get stopped near the bus garage in the high street and be offered drugs by black people. That seemed to justify the slurs and made me question why. My supervisor at Sweet Meters was from Saint Lucia. When I told him I was leaving to study he said, "You are a black man. You'll never get a job you want in your life." That was my trigger point, my motivation, my challenge.'

While at Leicester he was mentored by Professor Martin Gill, a security management expert, and inspired by the resilience of a fellow student, Chris Moon. A former British Army officer who survived capture by Khmer Rouge guerrillas, Moon lost the lower parts of his right arm and leg while clearing landmines for a charity in Mozambique. He has subsequently specialised in such endurance events as the Great Sahara Run and the 135-mile Death Valley Ultra.

Albert's lifestyle might not have been as dramatic, but his daily durability, as the only self-funded pupil in a class of twenty-four, was remarkable. Having set up his own cleaning company, he slept between 'nine-ish' in the evening and midnight, cleaned offices until 7.30 a.m., and then left south London to attend lectures in Leicester until mid-afternoon. He then completed a 280-mile round trip and returned to Streatham, where he studied in a local library for another four hours or so.

'I am very, very conservative. Conservative with a small "c" – that's me. I have this mentality that no one is better than anyone else. Rich people don't have thirty hours in their day. Poor people don't have ten. We all have twenty-four hours. How you use those hours, day and night, is what determines your future.'

The ethos transferred to his sons, Aaron, Ashley and Alex, who were put through King's Rochester, a cathedral school. All are high achievers; Ashley, the youngest, is an outstanding athlete and Alex, who gained seven A*s and three As in his GCSEs is aiming to study philosophy at Cambridge University. House rules are clear: in bed at 7.30 p.m. up until the age of 16, an hour later thereafter, with only occasional concessions.

Aaron's educational compromises began when, against his father's instincts but at the insistence of a German PE teacher with links to Bayern Munich, he moved into organised football at the age of 10. His speed, as the Kent 100-metre champion, and his burgeoning physicality were obvious gifts; his understated nature belied leadership qualities, which came to the fore when he captained a public schools' select team.

Chelsea and Millwall made approaches, but he signed for Arsenal, his boyhood club, and moved to a grammar school at 11 because King's were unwilling to release him from Saturday-morning lessons. Liam Brady, Arsenal's academy director until May 2014, recognised Aaron's lack of street wisdom, but understood his potential as an attacking full back.

Football's innate conservatism only became an issue when he achieved four A*s and six A grades in his GCSE examinations. After Arsenal released him – despite retaining faith when a knee injury cost him a season in the under-15s – his father came to an accommodation with Charlton, who agreed that he would be allowed to study independently in the evenings for a single A level, alongside the traditional BTEC day-release programme.

Aaron was hardly stretched academically, and gained distinctions, the equivalent of A grades at A level, in his two BTEC modules. Coincidentally, on the day I first saw him play, in an under-21 game at West Bromwich Albion, he had just learned he had earned a B grade at A level in Geography, his supplementary subject.

Albert was elated, since this triggered an offer to study sports management at Loughborough University from the autumn of 2017: he had his plan B, in case Charlton failed to take up the option of an additional year on Aaron's professional contract. Albert's sunny mood and pleasant personality enabled him to talk around some unusually accommodating security guards, who were initially insistent no spectators were allowed into Albion's training ground.

As it turned out the only other neutral observers were a South African agent, resplendent in the white trousers that seem de rigueur in his trade, a Dutch coach, and two random scouts. They would have gleaned little of enduring value from another example of the film-set football that passes as youth development in a rebranded Premier League Two.

Both sets of performance analysts pored over their cameras and laptops on a hill overlooking the plateaued pitch. There were too many support staff, substitutes and coaches to cram into the transparent dugouts spread beneath them. The match, played in a strong crosswind and intermittent rain, had a familiar sterility.

Albion have a locally driven youth policy, and genuine prospects in Sam Field, an England under-16 midfield player, and his international teammate Kane Wilson, a versatile full back. Tony Pulis, Albion's first-team manager, spent most of his thirty-minute vigil with his coaching staff on the touchline taking a series of calls on his mobile. There was little sense of opportunity or continuity. Charlton, who took the lead and were denied an obvious penalty before drawing 2–2, were contrastingly cosmopolitan. They fielded a Bulgarian goalkeeper, an Australian centre half, a Dutch defensive midfield player, an Irish playmaker and a French striker. Aaron, well built, deliberate in possession and purposeful in his movement, was played on the left to allow a triallist from Manchester City to operate from his normal position, right back.

There is always a transitional feel to development football; too often teams consist of passing strangers. The exception to the rule was provided by Charlton's midfield player Regan Charles-Cook, one of three footballing brothers. He signed on at Arsenal's Hale End academy on the same day as a 10-year-old Aaron Barnes in 2006.

'That's quite cool, isn't it?' Aaron remarked. 'He's like a little brother to me. We've spent half of our lives playing football together, and to keep going, at such a high level, is unusual. It is hard to have that type of relationship in football, because you see so many friends and teammates released. You don't tend to keep in contact with them.

'It is a delicate subject. You have your contract and although you are in a team environment everyone has their own objectives. Everyone is on a mission. You see people leave and they are a bit bitter about it. They are uncertain about their futures. It is a tough situation, and it is hard to talk to them about it.'

The pair's careers continued along parallel lines later in the year, when each made the first-team substitutes' bench in the Checkatrade Trophy, a risible attempt to promote homegrown players through the admission of development teams from a smattering of Premier League academies, alongside Football League clubs. Aaron was shadowing one of Charlton's few realisable assets, former England youth international Chris Solly.

Aaron hides the requisite inner steel well, though he lacks the flip, supposedly knowing, attitude projected by his peers. He admits to being uncomfortable with bad language and his father praises Paul Hart, Charlton's former academy director, for having the foresight to 'place a coat of armour' around him.

Albert's distinctive loyalty prompted him to leave a high-level job at the Home Office so he could devote more time to overseeing Aaron's progress. He appreciates that internal dynamics tend to count against strong-willed parents at many clubs, but sees no reason to be apologetic about his protectiveness.

'It took a long time for me to allow Aaron to be a footballer, because in the culture I come from, to be a footballer means you have no hope in life. I gave up my job to be as supportive as I can. So many parents don't want to take the risk, but they want their children to succeed. You spend your life worrying about how to pay the bills, but my wife is working, so we live on only one income.

'It's a sacrifice that we all have to go through. I don't want to do it half-half. I have the charity but my job is to take the pressure off Aaron, so he has the energy and mentality to concentrate on his football. I don't care how much money I have. I don't care what house I have. If my children are not respectable, then I'm sorry: I have failed. You make the decision to have children, therefore it must be your responsibility to provide them with a positive future.'

Roger Hosannah, son of a British soldier based in the Ruhr, bases his parenting skills around the military discipline to which he became accustomed during his upbringing. He was a sufficiently promising footballer to be scouted by Schalke 04, but forged a career in professional basketball after taking up a scholarship at the University of South Carolina.

Now back in the UK working as an intermediary in the sportswear industry following a spell, as head of clothing for T.K. Maxx, he is shepherding his son Bryce, a second-year scholar at Crystal Palace, down a similar pathway. He sees sport as 'a tool to develop a boy's personality', and has maintained a healthy scepticism about football's feudalism and self-importance.

He accepts other parents might have succumbed when, at the age of 14, Bryce was told by Palace that it was in his best interests to transfer from Trinity School, part of the academically acclaimed Whitgift Foundation group, to Oasis, a school linked to the football club's academy. His father, who had already defied club coaches by insisting his son develop multi-sport skills in rugby, cricket and athletics, was unequivocal:

'No way. You don't need to sacrifice your fundamental

right as a parent because of what a club wants. That would be wrong. Too many parents have a sheep mentality. They fall prey to the bullshit. Boys get caught up in the bubble when there is nothing wrong with being different. There are too many automatons in the system, with structured thought processes. Everyone was telling me I was in the wrong, but I told Bryce, "You have to trust me." Fortunately he has.'

Roger knew the family pact he had engineered, which guaranteed his son a two-year window to concentrate on winning a professional contract if he was successful in his GCSEs, had reached fruition when he sat in his car outside Trinity School, one anxious morning in August 2015. He looked in the rearview mirror and saw Bryce running towards the vehicle:

'I know my son so well, I could read his face. He had six A stars and three A grades. All those years working towards that point had paid off. We simultaneously burst into tears. It was the greatest moment of my life, because I had completed my first task as a parent. He is living on the edge as far as football is concerned, but he has a network around him.'

Parental influence and ill-concealed concern about the depth of the talent pool is a global constant. While England's newly reinforced inferiority complex was being worked through at St George's Park, before the tribal rite of passage against Scotland at Wembley in November, I was assailed by the woes of Norwegian football in the unlikely setting of Skudeneshavn, a small fishing village on the island of Karmøy on the south-western tip of the country.

Rain, presaged by a chill wind and dark frontal clouds, rolled in across the white-capped waves of Skudenesfjorden, and battered the warren of 225 white-planked wooden houses. Its familiarity did little to improve the mood of a standing-room-only crowd in the former public bathhouse. The locals had gathered to discuss the underlying reasons for the national trauma of conceding a World Cup qualifying goal to San Marino.

The domestic game was deemed to be at its lowest ebb. The presence of three Norwegian players, Ronny Johnsen, Ole-Gunnar Solskjær and Henning Berg, in Manchester United's Champions League-winning squad in 1999 seemed, like mermaids, trolls and meadow elves, to belong to ancient, unlikely, Norse mythology.

Complaints ranged from poor pitches to conservative coaching, youthful indolence and a lack of cash. It seemed easier to wallow in imported televised coverage of Premier League football. In search of greater insight, a more revealing example of potential, I was advised to seek out Frode Samuelsen, who lived across the Karmsundet Strait in the town of Haugesund.

His son Martin, on loan at Blackburn Rovers having signed a four-year contract with West Ham on his release by Manchester City, had at least helped rescue the national team from irredeemable embarrassment by scoring one of three late goals in that 4–1 win over San Marino. He was attempting to buck the system, with variable results.

For twelve years, since the age of 7, Martin had progressed along what his father described as an Exposure Ladder. This involved a systemic, individualised approach to skill development, in which he would assimilate video clips of key skills, taken from a clinic by Wiel Coerver, the acclaimed Dutch coach, and stored on his father's mobile phone.

Martin practised close control in cage football or on his own in the playground. He learned how best to turn and feint, and dribble the ball using either foot. Once the basics were ingrained, he would increase the pace of his runs, and incorporate different angles. Frode engaged him by devising a scale from one to ten, which ranged in difficulty from basic apprehension of the technique required, to the ability to master it consistently, so it could be employed competitively. A minimum 80 per cent success rate was required for the top mark, which was logged on a spreadsheet.

The intimacy of contact between father and son can never be recreated in a coaching session overseen by a virtual stranger. The Samuelsens visited leading academies in England and Europe to assess training methods; clubs of the stature of Chelsea, Liverpool, Manchester United and Real Madrid were beguiled by a boy who had scored

1,500 goals, often playing three years above his age group, between the ages of 7 and 14.

'Every story in youth development is different,' Frode explained. 'There is not one solution or formula that solves everything, but key elements have to be in place. We operated on the slogan, "If you want to be extreme you have to go extreme." The issue is how extreme you can be without being seen as too big a problem for your environment.

'You have to push limits, test rules, and everyone has an opinion about what you are doing. There are social elements to take into account. You need coaches who understand. You meet opponents who feel the pain of being beaten heavily. Parents talk to other parents and they get fed up with coaches concentrating on one player. In a small place like Norway that is a problem.

'Martin has a different mentality from other kids. He is extremely gifted, an outlier in every test of mental capacity they conducted at national level. He was very mature intellectually and confident socially, even at the age of seven. But it is not enough to be positive. At some point you have to make a decision to stick to your character and become the person you want to be, or just accept being like everyone else.

'To stay true to the footballer he has become, Martin presents an intellectual threat to the coach. He operates outside the box, so that he approaches his training differently. His errors must be accepted because he is doing complex things. He is motivated by improvement, is very honest with himself, and has always had a mental picture of how he masters his skills.'

Scott Anderson, Director of Athletic Training at Stanford University, uses data from military and sporting sources to support his theory that the quality of an athlete's eye movement determines performance at the highest level. His explanation, contained in the following excerpts from a paper delivered to a Leaders In Sport conference in London, is accessible and plausible:

'The brain operates by planning 2.5 seconds into the future. It is constantly assessing its environment, in anticipation of what is about to happen. This predictive brain function is critical in synchronising incoming information from the outside world with one's actions. It is required for simple tasks such as driving a car and riding a bike but also for complex sensorimotor tasks often seen in sport.

'For example, if I throw a ball to you, you don't see it in real time. Your brain is predicting the speed and trajectory and anticipating the point at which it will arrive, and co-ordinates receiving the ball with the motor system. This sequence is a highly co-ordinated effort that results in a fluid output of cognitive operations, based on the ability to predict.

'This state of orientation is the by-product of the brain operating in the future. People who excel at this are highly co-ordinated, move efficiently, and acquire skill through repetition with ease. Those that are not adept at this exhibit poor co-ordination and are injury prone. The eyes are the most directly accessible motor component of the brain. The brain uses the eyes to orient itself in time and space, and since visual tracking and attention share similar neural networks we can perform assessments on the eyes to determine the quality of brain performance.'

To put that into context, it is thought the average professional footballer has between five and ten mental images to process in the split second before he receives the ball, and decides what to do with it. The essence of Lionel Messi's genius is that he is believed to have in excess of 100 options running through his brain in the same timeframe.

Football is resistant to a frontier mentality, though the 'brain-centred learning' advocated by Belgian coach Michel Bruyninckx for more than a decade is chipping away at the rock face of conventional wisdom. His approach, based on the premise the brain is at least 1,000 times faster than any computer, has been recently refined through his work with seventy or so players, aged between 12 and 19.

Selected from clubs in the top two divisions in Belgium, and based at a secondary school on the outskirts of Brussels, Bruyninckx's pupils are expected to touch the ball 500,000 times a year, five times more than the boys at Barcelona's La Masia academy. The programme's most successful product, at senior level, is Steven Defour, the midfield player who joined Burnley from Anderlecht in the summer of 2016 for a club record fee of £8 million.

Drills increase gradually in difficulty and are designed to 'multitask' the brain. Boys often play bare-footed to develop sensitivity of touch, and are asked to complete simple mathematical tasks while exercising. Should they neglect their academic studies they are banned from training for up to a month. Counter-intuitively, they are told not to dwell on the mechanical reasons for their mistakes.

Thomas Tuchel, the Borussia Dortmund coach whose stock is high in several Premier League boardrooms, is a disciple. He deliberately compresses space in twenty-a-side training sessions, limits wide players to a small area of the pitch to test their flexibility and ingenuity, and matches two full teams in one half, to enhance touch, quickness and suppleness.

England, it seems, remains a province of closed minds and short attention spans. Samuelsen was regarded as too much of a maverick by Manchester City and though he has broken into senior international football at the age of 19, he has not been trusted in the Football League, apart from a mutually beneficial loan spell at Peterborough, to whom he returned in January 2017. Promises that he would play regularly at Blackburn, a chaotic club with an unpopular manager, Owen Coyle, were not kept.

Frode believes academy football militates against

ambition, flair and self-reliance. He uses his son's experiences to argue that the system abhors honestly made mistakes which, addressed intelligently, would lead to long-term improvement. Coaches prefer the short, safe pass to the surging, jinking run that shows the defender the ball and carries the risk of loss of possession. Their command-and-control culture militates against any young player who prefers to develop his skills by working on his own.

'Many clubs forget this is meant to be about development, so the story repeats itself. Martin needs to be with a manager who looks at football in a modern way. If you look at his clips and study his match analysis he runs more than most and makes fewer errors, yet he has a reputation for being risky because he doesn't do the conventional thing as a wide player, and throw the ball into the box. Bias builds up against you.'

This cultural predisposition to narrow horizons extends to the classroom. Teachers at St Bede's College in Manchester found Martin had an aptitude for learning not shared by British players at the school as part of City's development programme. In the words of Director of Studies Dr Andrew Dando, he was 'respectful, polite, but absolutely driven educationally'.

He was 'gutted' to attain B grades in Maths, Physics and Chemistry A levels, despite having to do homework and revision on the bus, going to matches for club and country, and relying on distance learning during a loan spell at Barnsley. Less than four months before the end of the academic year in the upper sixth he announced that he wished to study for a GCSE in Biology as part of a contingency plan to enter the medical profession if football didn't work out.

He was effectively self-taught, since he could not be accommodated in the timetable at such short notice. Dr Dando gave him a textbook and arranged an email account to allow him to ask questions of a specialist teacher, Christine Hennity. He sat the first paper in Manchester, but was in Norway, assisting Wayne Rooney in a coaching clinic, when the second half of the examination was conducted.

There was no room for administrative manoeuvre, and Dando was amazed when Samuelsen still earned a C grade. This meant he had scored above 90 per cent in the half of the examination he was able to take: 'That must have something to do with what was instilled in him when he was younger, through the culture in which he grew up.'

Too many academy footballers are over-indulged to the point of social impotence. They complete wellness questionnaires each morning and are shielded from realistic criticism by the superficial positivity of support staff. When the going gets tough, they lack the toughness to get going.

Samuelsen wasted no time when City informed him he would not be retained at the end of his under-18 season. He personally organised a ten-day trial at West Ham, a fortnight's stay at Schalke 04 and a week of scrutiny by the coaching staff at Inter Milan. All were completed despite the duress of his being in the final stages of revision for his A level examinations.

Professional football may ultimately be unable to process his individualism, but he will remain true to himself. The importance of such comfort in his own skin cannot be underestimated, since everyone has his own path to follow, in sport and in life. Some may end up in a cell, but the survivors reach for the stars.

11

Ground Zero

The years fall away on a cold, clear afternoon, when a northerly wind carries the portent of winter. Tony McCool has returned to reminisce, and begins at the house in which he grew up, on the Lewsey Farm estate in Luton. He retraces countless childhood steps, along Hereford Road and past the Hindu Community Centre where the elders used to allow him to chalk a goal on the wall, and play football in the car park.

He ventures across Pastures Way to reach the grassland that was once an imaginary Wembley. It is now overgrown, because the council claim they lack the resources to tend it in an age of austerity. Another former playing field, not too far away, is rutted and unusable, the consequence of a bureaucrat's bright idea – rotivating it in an attempt to create an urban meadow.

The justification for such social vandalism is the architecturally impressive, academically optimistic local college, and the new 3G pitches, funded by the Football Foundation and the National Lottery. The facility is well used during weekday evenings, by portly pub players and club teams of varying standards, yet on this particular Saturday, as on many such Saturdays, the gates are padlocked.

It costs £56 an hour to rent, which, on an estate blighted by social exclusion, vandalism and gang-fuelled violence, is the sort of legitimate disposable income no one possesses. A publicly funded facility is paralysed by market forces. The high, green metal meshed fencing is a forbidding symbol of missed opportunity.

This is England, our England. Our children are among the least physically fit in the world. When the government finances a £200 million anti-obesity drive through sport the money is squandered on an inane marketing campaign and the administrative chaos that accompanies it, rather than invested in coaches on the ground.

When the Football Association partner with Tesco, for a programme of free coaching sessions aimed at children aged between 5 and 11, the project is hamstrung by the necessity to stage lessons between 4 p.m. and 6 p.m., when working parents are unable to provide transport. The reason for the time restraint is simple and damning: private leisure facility owners make the majority of their money on the post-work, conscience-cleansing rush between 6 p.m. and 10 p.m. Their profits are sacrosanct.

McCool has worked in all aspects of football over two decades. He was one of the pioneers in performance analysis software, coached at Luton Town's consistently productive academy before moving to Queens Park Rangers, and scouted first-team opposition for MK Dons. Now, in addition to youth development work for Norwich City, he supervises in-school activity programmes.

He is understandably wistful: 'Like most people, I tried and failed to make it as a pro. When you have a tough childhood, it is your dream. Every day, I'm out with a football. I want to get spotted, so I'm in the park playing football. If I tried to play there now, I'd lose a size-three ball in the undergrowth.

'Now it is pay to play. My mum and dad struggled to feed us, let alone pay for football. Elite athletes can come from any background, from the stockbroker belt to a high-rise council flat, but kids around here are dealing with all sorts of challenges and issues. There are single parents, no parents, poverty of the highest order. There are kids suffering from abuse, disability, learning difficulty.

'Coaching at a professional club is really quite easy because everyone is motivated. The parents want their child to do well, so they are going to be well behaved, on the whole. You don't have the grassroots thing on the Sunday morning where the parents are going wild. There are boundaries in place and they probably know that it's too risky.

'They're probably bunking off work. It could be costing them £100 a week to take their kids to an academy, because they could be travelling all over the country. Boys are training four nights a week. They're drained. Then, in a blink of an eye, someone at the club isn't having them. They're dropped like a sack of spuds.

'The dynamics have changed. When I grew up I played for a really good grassroots club. My parents weren't there watching me every week. Football wasn't on TV every five minutes. Now we've got everyone there: mum, dad, brother, sister, grandma, grandad. By the way, some of the grandparents can be really lively . . .'

One of football's parlour games is to swap horror stories about the orcs who lurk in youth football. Tales abound of tearful teenaged referees fleeing in fear, of parents triggering mass brawls at under-8 tournaments by invading the pitch, and of boys ending up in the local A & E department because they were trampled underfoot, or even assaulted by an adult.

The issue was crystallised by Barrie Funnell, volunteer chairman of the Surrey Youth League, after a weekend in which three games had to be abandoned due to fighting, a parent threatened to stab a referee, a linesman was headbutted and players, egged on by their manager, were only just prevented from smashing up their changing room.

'The level of outright violence, abuse and disrespect has to stop,' he wrote in a letter he asked to be distributed as widely as possible. 'Clubs and everyone involved in trying voluntarily to run children's football need to take back control from thugs and idiots. Personally, I am sick of seeing this happen, week in and week out.

'I have heard all the excuses over the years, seen the blame culture. Take responsibility yourselves, get the police involved where you have to, deal with it there and then. Everyone says it is only the mindless few, and that may be true, but why do I, or anyone else, have to look at this utter contempt for the law, and disrespect for humanity?

'Would you want your name associated with a children's competition that resulted in the death of someone as a consequence of violence? Don't believe it cannot happen. It did to a linesman at a children's match in Holland three or four years ago. If this continues I fear that this may be the result here.'

Even in the cocoon of academy football, Tony McCool has been physically threatened. He was grateful for the corroborative presence of Gerry Francis, the former England captain who has been a long-term assistant to Tony Pulis, when he asked a 14-year-old midfield player at QPR to operate as a centre back as a one-off experiment. The boy refused, went into a tantrum, and was told he would not play at all.

McCool was merely following coaching orthodoxy. He recalled similarly testing the versatility and strength of character of Jay DaSilva, the England under-19 left back, whom he regularly asked to play in a variety of right-sided roles when he was at Luton, before being sold to Chelsea for an initial £40,000 along with his brothers, Rio and Cole. But in this instance, reason was immediately overwhelmed by ignorance and hostility:

'The dad stormed round the pitch and basically wanted to have a fight with me. Rather than have his son do nothing I'd handed him my notebook, and told him to juggle the team, to see how it could fit together. Was I happy with him? Of course not. I just wanted him to do something constructive. The parent lost his mind, threatening me.'

A protective contingency plan, informed by experience in grassroots football, swung into action. McCool reasoned that if he kept his feet facing the pitch, with his arms behind his back, and refused to face the parent it would signal he was not the aggressor. An official complaint, made by the father, that McCool had thrown a water bottle at the boy was dismissed by numerous eyewitnesses, including Francis.

Problems are exacerbated by the promise of financial reward. When the father of another 13-year-old was agitating to be allowed to leave QPR, with the implicit but illegal support of an agent, the intelligence network of academy parents quickly discovered that the young player had been approached by another club. The request was denied, and the family were reminded that the boy had the right to run his contract down.

'There was constant to-ing and fro-ing and bickering, so at the end of the season we agreed to say, you know what, we'll just let him go. When we told the dad, thinking, fair play, that's what he wanted anyway, the guy went absolutely bananas. He started shouting and bawling and grabbed Steve Gallen, the academy manager, on the stairs at the training ground. We genuinely thought he was going to throw him over the balcony. I don't know where his boy is now, who he plays for, if he plays at all. It is the lad I feel sorry for.

'There's not enough control. Players are getting tapped up at six years old. Big clubs are establishing recruitment centres in productive areas like Luton, approaching players and selling them the dream. I go into schools these days, and I'm invariably approached by a lad who says he plays for the local professional club.

'My response is, "That's nice. How many days a week do you train?" "Er, one." I'm not going to put that child down in front of all his friends, but he's not a signed academy player. He is in the development centre. The parents are the same. They want something to boast about. Even if their boy is in an academy, the work hasn't really started.

'As a scholar, have you made it? As a first-year pro, have you made it? You've played ten games in the first team, but have you made it? The best players, the best athletes, the Roy Keanes of this world, will tell you they always want to improve and they never quite achieve. They win a trophy and they think, where's the next one?'

The dilemma is palpable. McCool confided he had just been asked by a friend to advise the family of a 7-year-old, 'who, I've got to say, is the most talented kid I have ever seen'. He had already 'been pulled from pillar to post' by overtures from a variety of clubs. McCool avoided outright recommendations, preferring to analyse the situation dispassionately:

'Let's try and look at it from a pragmatic point of view. You live in Luton. Luton's got a professional football club. The boy is immensely talented. Let's say he progresses further, until he is fourteen. He is going to go to a Chelsea, a Man United, or a Liverpool. Under the current EPPP structure Luton wouldn't be able to stop that anyway. If he's good enough, he'll go.

'So why would you want to drive him round the M25 four times a week? The poor kid's knackered, his schoolwork suffers, he's in the car, stuck in traffic until midnight. I don't work for Luton any more, remember. If you lived in Blackpool, he should sign for Blackpool. To be brutally honest, I don't actually believe he should play for anyone.

'Clubs should not be allowed to contract a boy until he is twelve. He should play grassroots football, play for his school, play in the street. I think that should be part of the development of any player. It's less structured, there's more freedom. I know you get better when you play against better players, but also, just playing with your friends can mean so much. There's a massive moral aspect to this.'

McCool is an admirer of Nick Levett, the FA's Talent Identification Manager, who shares his deeper concerns about the standard of scouting at youth level. Levett has delivered bespoke courses to clubs across the four top divisions, concentrating on the enhancement of such soft skills as relationship-building, communication, and the recognition of unconscious bias.

'A scout at a club I visited said he had just recommended a kid because he reminded him of Alan Smith, the former Leeds United and Manchester United player. So what? Who cares? This lad was ten years old. Why make that comparison? The mindsets will be different. They belong to different generations, different times. They have different DNA, different schooling. They come from different parts of the country. The scout applied his unconscious bias.

'That drives our own decision-making. As a player, if you're a hard-working centre midfielder, you would value the traits of a hard-working centre midfielder. You'd think those traits were more important than the creativity of a tippy-tappy winger that doesn't track back. You have a conflict, a misalignment in your values. It's natural. It drives our prejudices, and drives our decision-making. If people recognise that this bias exists, they will be more effective.'

But football does not operate with neat, philosophical purity. It is a venal world, in which scouts are routinely undervalued. In some, this breeds a mercenary approach.

Cash contaminates, undermines, seduces. McCool's tone hardens:

'I'm a scout and I'm telling you that you're a good player. Why? Because I care about your future, or because if you sign for my academy I will get X amount as a bonus? We all can't do things for free. You can't ring up your mortgage company and say, "Um, I can't pay this month, but just so you know, I have helped develop a boy that could be a player in the future."

'Things don't work like that. Everyone has to make a living. I'm cool with that. But if you put financial reward on the table, in any industry, some people will turn into vultures. They'll trample over anyone, do anything. I've seen it first hand in academies, including with the little kids. Players get signed, and released, for the wrong reasons.

'There was one boy signed after a single training session. I know we all think we are superstar talent-spotters, but I never comment until a boy is two weeks into his trial. He's a bag of nerves. He needs to settle in, deal with the pressure of knowing no one. Let him make a load of mistakes and then, after he has trained six to ten times, I'll let you know.

'It was nothing against this lad, but I couldn't sleep at night knowing he'd been signed. I was close to walking away. My issue is this: that kid and those parents have gone home jumping and punching the air, like, yeah, we've done it. They're cuddling that kid, brilliant, fantastic. But is it real though? Is that player still in the system now? And if he isn't, what detriment did it have on his education? Morally, that's a crime.'

His concern is authentic, vivid. It requires courage to express it in such terms, because the majority of those in youth development prefer to provide private confirmation of the troubling trickle-down effect of the cynicism and brutality of first-team football, rather than raise their heads above the parapet. Careers can be undermined by candour. Power is a potential pollutant at whatever level it is administered.

'You know the football world, the culture of the dressing room. If the first-team manager comes in and decides he's not having a certain player, everyone blanks that player. They turn their back on him. It's not, come in, sit down, you need to know something. You're not going to be part of our plans. We've got three players in the position already, and we believe they are ahead of you. Your contract is costing us too much money. It's, I'm going to turn my back on you and just make you miserable.

'I've seen that happen at senior level. Now it's happening at youth level. The academy manager, head of coaching and the head of recruitment decide, for whatever reason, they don't want a particular kid, or don't think he's got a chance. He's got eleven months left on his contract, so they start blanking him.

'But he plays on the Sunday and tears it up. Inside,

I'm like, yes! Go on, son, prove them wrong. Yet he gets back to the dressing room and no one tells him how well he has done. Everyone thinks they have to stick to the original opinion. There are a lot of good coaches around, but some of them would tear their granny's eyeballs out to get a full-time job in football. The way to do that is to agree with the boss.

'Honestly, the stuff I've seen in academies. Coaches can be vile with the kids, because they think they've got to kiss someone's arse. I've sat in personal development meetings with them, when they discuss the development of the five Cs in a player – confidence, commitment, control, concentration, communication.

'They've got their head down like the school swot, writing furiously in their notebook. They walk down the stairs, and nobody's around now. They see a player and they're like, "Oi, what are you doing? That's rubbish." I said to this one guy, "You should read what you just wrote down in the CPD meeting. The way you are talking to that child is horrendous." '

His voice breaks, in a mixture of incredulity, sadness and contempt. McCool is at pains to stress his respect for the vast majority of his peers yet, emotionally, the dam has burst. Bad experiences manifest themselves, like muggers emerging from a shadowy alleyway. Another episode, on a tour to Belgium, looms large.

'It made me think, what the fuck am I doing? I don't want to be part of this. It was heartbreaking. There was a lad, coming up to sixteen, a left back. It had been deemed that he wasn't going to be signed as a scholar, but I go into these things thinking that every day is a new day and that he might do something that will change their minds.

'We'd spent weeks and weeks and weeks with the club philosophy of playing out from the back. This lad receives the ball from the goalkeeper about five minutes into the game, chops inside, and looks to play a diagonal pass into centre midfield. We're playing a Dutch team, who close down, press. They work hard and they're psychologically powerful, physically strong.

'They can read the game. They've shown him inside, shut the line off because they're very clever off the ball. Our lad is doing what he's been told to do. He's played the ball inside, but they've doubled up on it, knowing where the pass is going. They've robbed it, got a counter-attack, and nearly score. The lad is berated from the sideline. Not that the kid hasn't heard swearing before at school, but pitchside, from the dugout, really?

'Then, out of temper, a coach screams, "Get off the pitch. Get off the pitch! Get off my pitch!" I feel emotional now because the face of that child is right in the forefront of my mind. He has been demolished. There was no acknowledgement, no handshake. You could see that he wanted to cry and he didn't want to show it.

'He made a mistake, but he did what we taught him, so actually we're at fault, not the kid. He walked off down to the corner flag and I couldn't leave him. He couldn't speak to me. He had tears rolling down his face, and I just thought, what the fuck have we become? To be treating so-called elite talent, a maturing young man, in that way . . .'

England, our England. The pretence of the Premier League's youth development strategy, in which players are defined by so-called performance clocks and coaches are turned into clerks by an obsessional desire to harvest self-justifying data, cannot hide the ignorance and intolerance it is supposed to have eradicated. Here is McCool's experience of another European tournament:

'We played Feyenoord, who were coached by Roy Makaay, the great Dutch forward. I think about what he achieved in Spain, and with Bayern Munich, and I am in awe of him. I'm privileged to be standing in the next dugout to him. The biggest thing for me was his behaviour. I never heard one angry word out of him. Not one word.

'Our dugout is carrying on like a typical English pub football team. Quite frankly, we're playing like one. This guy occasionally goes to the edge of the technical area, calls a kid over, and speaks quietly to him along the lines of, "When you get the ball in that situation, maybe have a look there, or there. Do you think you could maybe move there?" All very controlled.

'Our dugout is pumped up, like a drunken crowd at a

greyhound track when the dogs come round the final bend. We're in an elite football environment, shouting and screaming. Do we value knowledge? I see people I want to learn from, people who have pearls of information, let go by clubs because they are seen as a threat to someone who wants all his mates around him. Why do we do that?'

There are good people, striving in unheralded circumstances, trying to find answers to such questions. It is an instructive, affirming experience to visit smaller clubs, less exalted Category Three academies, where first-year professionals are paid £125 a week and coaches like Tony Mee excel in defiance of a system suffocating on stardust and sycophancy.

He moved to Doncaster Rovers in September 2016 for family reasons, after being head of coaching at Rotherham United, academy manager at York City and lead development phase coach at Scunthorpe United. At his level, annual academy budgets are £315,000, a third of which is found by the club. Category One academies swallow anything between £3.5 million and £7 million a year; in return they devour those lower down the football food chain.

Some smaller academies refuse to play more exalted opposition because of their fear of poaching; even if they do fulfil fixtures, many hide their best players, who are given cameo roles as substitutes for the day. Mee, whose softness of tone might not have always manifested itself during twenty-three years as a physical training instructor in the British Army, is more sanguine about such certainties:

'I try and look at it quite pragmatically. If I flip the situation to the grassroots game we try and spirit their best kids away to make our academy stronger. We're telling their coaches they should be proud, with such limited facilities, of developing a kid good enough to go into a pro club. Can we afford, then, to be that sniffy when the Cat One clubs come in and take our players?

'In terms of coaching quality there shouldn't be that significant a difference, because we are pretty much all at the same level in terms of qualifications. But if a Man United comes in and says, "Our facilities are ten times better than yours, our coaches are better than yours and we are Man United," what can you do about it?'

He reads voraciously, studies internationally, and picks the brains of former pros on coach education courses to better understand what drives a successful player. He counsels young coaches 'with no grass on their boots', to use his evocative phrase. They are invariably engrossed by the tale of one of his pupils at Thomas Rotherham College, where he cut his coaching teeth for six years. The boy was 16, and had been rejected by Sheffield Wednesday.

'He was not the best student in the world, a little bit wayward, but a really good footballer. I could see why he had been released, having been in the system, and heard what people thought about size and attitude and everything else that goes with it. I don't suppose he is bothered what I think now, but I will be honest with you. I never saw him as an England player of the future.

'It was the right decision to release him at the time. There was nobody else sniffing around him. He was quick and knew where the back of the net was, but I had a better player than him the year before, a lad called Lee Squires. He was a brilliant kid who got a trial at Rotherham, but broke his wrist at the worst possible time and couldn't play. He didn't make it and is now head coach at a college in the States.'

The football world knows the flight path of Jamie Vardy, Mee's lost boy, from Stocksbridge Steels to Leicester City and the Premier League title. It is unaware of the backstory of Dominic Hart, former captain of Rotherham's under-18s, who is majoring in accountancy and playing for the Northwood University Timberwolves in Michigan. His name is etched on Mee's soul:

'Having to tell Dominic he wasn't getting a pro contract, I actually cried. My assistant manager had to take over because I couldn't do it. I knew how much that contract meant to him. I knew how hard he had tried. He was a superb lad, a great scholar who had come through the club from the under-9s, but ultimately it was probably the right decision.

'People underestimate the humanity of coaching, how arbitrary things can be. It doesn't matter how much analysis we do, how many reports we put into the system, a first-team manager has so little opportunity to look at the under-18s. If our best player happens to have a stinker when he is around that boy has blown his chance.

'I had a lad, Mitchell Austin. His dad was an Australian rugby league player. He'd done a full morning's training and was told at lunchtime he was playing for the reserves against Middlesbrough that afternoon. Unsurprisingly, he didn't have his best game. His future was pretty much decided on that game. He was lost to our system, but made himself a career.'

Austin, a forward, played part-time for Stalybridge Celtic, made nine first-team appearances over two seasons for Cambridge United, and went on loan to Lincoln City, Brackley Town and Southport before he joined Central Coast Mariners in the A League. At 25, he had just been named man of the match for Melbourne Victory in a high-profile friendly against Juventus.

Mee's skill, as part of football's middle management, is to match the pair of part-time coaches who oversee each age group. They tend to be young, technologically literate, and supported by unpaid interns. They spend six hours a week with their players and at least another eight hours, without payment, feeding the Premier League's Performance Management Application.

The PMA is a computerised system designed to evaluate training sessions, and provides a template for six- and twelve-weekly reviews. To employ the jargon, it records outcomes against learning objectives, in the context of a four-corner development model. A player's performance clock archives individual and collective technical development, matches played, sports science support, medical interventions, psychological and social observations and educational progression.

Confused? You will be. The PMA services the EPPP, which demands APP reviews and IAA monitoring. Education is dictated by the QTS, which shapes NVQs and BTECs. The FA promotes DNA and the PGB oversees the professional game. The EPL is becoming increasingly subservient to the PL. Clubs have TBs and AMTs to work in PDP, YDP and FP. Excuse the French, but WTF?

The Elite Player Performance Plan, to pay it the courtesy of its full title, is as self-perpetuating as any civil service chimera. It is supposed to be qualitative, but it demands quantity. The PMA is not standardised, so cannot yield consistent outcomes, yet it is held up to the light as a symbol of collective progress. Be my guest, and savour the subjectivity, simplicity and above all the logic of Mee's approach:

'There's millions of me, coaches who want to make a difference, but career progression is limited. It is the same as being a player. You need a break. It doesn't matter what people on my courses think about my work, or what the kids I have coached think about me. There's no profile. I might have been five foot five inches and eight stone soaking wet when I joined the army at sixteen, but experience of another career has stood me in good stead.

'I am not of that boot camp mentality, but I appreciate elements of military life, like having to take responsibility. I don't think kids in our academies necessarily appreciate what it takes to get to the next level. There is softness there, a fear of pushing them that extra yard, because of the blame culture, the litigation culture.

'I want to stress that if bullying is going on it should be dealt with, as harshly as possible. But at what point are we allowed to make kids uncomfortable? Because it is only by stretching and testing people that you find out whether they have got what they need to survive in the first-team dressing room. The manager wants those who can tough it out, who can take a bit of ribbing without taking things too far.

'You can't measure attitude on a computer. Football can't be an elite development environment, because it is a team sport. If it was a true elite development environment we'd have twelve kids aged between eight and eighteen in our academies. They'd be the absolute top ones in their age group. Of course that will never happen, because we need other boys around them to play the game.

'I'm a great believer in judging players in a match situation. Are they comfortable on the ball? Do they understand the game, the position you are asking them to play in? Do they understand the style of play required? Do they have the right instincts, the correct decision-making processes? Make your decision, as a coach, based on that. And always remember, it is an opinions game whether you are dealing with the England national team or Scunthorpe United under-9s.'

Mee accepts the reality that youth coaches are unlikely to break into the old boys' club of first-team football. McCool is a little more militant in nature, but the pair are kindred spirits, in that they care for art rather than science. Apparatchiks at the Premier League might brand them as outmoded malcontents, but they would, not for the first time, be utterly wrong.

'If you question things you're old school,' reflected McCool, with a thin smile that registered ill-suppressed irritation. 'I've worked in performance analysis for twenty years, and you're calling me old school? I wouldn't survive in that industry if I wasn't susceptible to change. I accept change has got to happen, so I'm not some sort of anarchist by questioning EPPP.

'It has created a lot of jobs, but also created a certain type of person, where it's about me, my career, my future. I will trample over everyone to get there, and if anyone questions that, I'll trample on them, too. I suppose you could say, well, that's just football, but good coaches are walking away from the game.

'This is an industry where experience counts for fuck

all. I'm not saying we should go back to writing the team down on the back of a fag packet, or chucking a bag of balls on to the training pitch, scratching our head and saying, "What the fuck should we do today?" I love the fact that we're planning, that there should be a structure, a syllabus. I get all that.

'But this is like a cult. You see coaches bamboozled by the phrases, caught in the headlights. There are too many perceived elite players. I talked to a grassroots manager who couldn't raise a team for their cup final because six of his players were travelling abroad with a development centre squad. Surely that can't be allowed to happen?'

It is, and it does. No wonder McCool's return to his roots is a bittersweet experience. If padlocks and jobsworths dictate that this generation cannot play, how can we expect our teams to perform at the highest level? The question has undoubted relevance, uncomfortable resonance. It echoes around the National Football Centre, nestling in a 330-acre site set in the Staffordshire countryside.

12

Room with a View

Dan Ashworth punches a security code into a console on the right-hand side of a door on the top floor of the National Football Centre. The password-protected room gives up its secrets quickly, because within three steps the visitor's eye is drawn to a rectangular digital clock, where red numbers are counting down to the World Cup final in Qatar on December 18, 2022.

This clock, according to Greg Clarke, the Football Association's latest blindly opinionated chairman, is 'a joke'. It might be wild, emblematic optimism, yet, since it signals England's avowed ambition to win the global game's greatest prize on that day, it is an inevitable focal point of an office that has the feel of a draft room in the NFL, NBA or Major League Baseball.

The walls are lined with names and thumbnail photographs of England's best young players, arranged into seven age-group squads, from under-15 to under-21. Each section features a fixtures programme and an optimal starting eleven set up in a 4–2–3–1 formation; potential substitutes are arranged around the team, like moons orbiting the mother planet.

This is a visual representation of the talent pool available to the men who occupy eight chairs, tucked under a table on which a gaudy green representation of a football pitch is etched. There are workstations available for the national age-group coaches, and the manager of the senior side. On one, in the corner, rests a replica hand grenade.

This symbolises a running joke launched by Aidy Boothroyd, the under-20 coach, who tosses the toy on to the table whenever he wants to make an incendiary point during post-tournament debriefs, which cover everything from travel arrangements to tactical substitutions. Coaches are encouraged to challenge one another; they, like senior support staff, are also expected to stand before the group and name three young players they believe will make the full England team. FA talent reporters continually assess youth football. Fifty-strong longlists are drawn up for the under-15 and -16 squads; older age groups select from thirty-three players. Ashworth classifies 459 players, from under-15 to under-21 level, as England's elite. One hundred and seventy-five are female and statistics suggest 19 per cent of them will represent the country at senior level. Only

5.28 per cent of the 284 males in the international programme will progress to the senior team.

When I first met Gareth Southgate for the purposes of this book, in late September, he was manager of the under-21s and the responsibility for picking the senior team was less than a week away. Neither he nor Ashworth were aware that the end-of-the-pier show starring Sam Allardyce was about to close over a pint of white wine with undercover journalists.

Our subsequent conversations have enduring relevance, since they concentrate on the issues and philosophies that will shape Southgate's tenure in the most over-exposed job in domestic sport, which is scheduled to last until at least 2020. The odds on him seeing out that contract are prohibitively small; England managers might have three lions on their chest, but they are uncomfortably aware of the metaphorical targets on their backs.

The ugliness of recrimination prompted by recurring failure was typified the morning after England's defeat by Iceland at Euro 2016. The receptionist at St George's Park received abusive phone calls as if she were responsible for the collective nervous breakdown endured by Roy Hodgson and his mentally scarred squad.

Emotionally incontinent criticism, sustained by envy, ignorance, rage and a revealing enjoyment of ritual self-flagellation, amused the rest of the football world and solved nothing, as usual. Yet Something Had To Be

Done. The job landed in the in-tray of Ashworth, who joined the FA in 2013 after a sixteen-year ascent from the lower-league development system.

There is an illuminating flowchart on the wall of his office down the corridor. Entitled, simply, 'Stakeholders', it is the family tree from hell, a maze of acronyms, minor empires and vanity projects. Everyone on the list from fish-eyed FA Council members with a fondness for Wembley hospitality to sleek-suited marketing types who could be selling widgets instead of a tinsel-thin version of national pride has a voice. Together, they form the Chorus of the Damned.

Successive strategic plans written by assorted FA luminaries gather dust on countless shelves, including my own. They form a timeline of good intentions and misaligned visions, from Howard Wilkinson's Charter for Quality, which promoted the concept of an elitist academy system in May 1997, to the Future Game, which set out youth development principles in 2010. Ashworth's England DNA document, compiled with Matt Crocker, his head of player and coach development, riffed on a familiar theme.

Forests were felled to state the obvious, that England had to evolve a unified playing style that was modern, tactically astute and emotionally intelligent. Possession had to be cherished, but combined with penetration and applied by footballers who were not afraid of their own shadows. The DNA document ran to about 40,000 words; I managed to persuade Ashworth to summarise it in precisely 199:

'What do we do when we haven't got the ball? What are the key principles when we do have the ball, or when we are in transition? What are the key principles around set plays? They are the four most important parts of the tactical and technical game. What sort of people do we need? What sort of learners do we need? What sort of leaders do we need? How do we deal with pressure? Why not set the bar as high as we can?

'We have had fifty years of either not qualifying, not getting out of groups or getting knocked out in the early knockout phases of big tournaments. Yet every single time, media and public expectation is, oh no, we will win this one. Then there's an outcry. We didn't get through against Iceland because the players weren't good enough. It was an issue of non-performance under pressure. Are we just going to cross our fingers and hope next time it is going to be OK, or are we going to put building blocks in place with our younger teams? Start with the end product in mind – what sort of men and women do we need?'

The raw material reflects modern life. Wayne Rooney, a hugely beneficial influence on younger players, worries that academy products lack leadership qualities. Everyone is looking for Cristiano Ronaldo's fusion of extraordinary talent and unrelenting perfectionism. To use Carlo Ancelotti's memorable description of the Real Madrid icon, 'his belly is never full'.

Southgate, by his own admission, is as informed by his failures, most notably as an ill-prepared Middlesbrough manager, as he is by his successes, as a player of the highest personal and professional standards, and as a notably empathetic coach. As such, he is an appropriate figurehead for the development system he effectively embodies.

Ashworth's astringency, as a more political animal, is better suited to dealing with the FA's strategic vulnerability in the face of the Premier League's dominance. Southgate is a softer character without being weaker; he is notably unafraid of voicing doubts about the commoditisation of children, who are being transported, with their families, from their communities at the age of 11.

'Every club has got to ask the question, what is it running its academy for? At Middlesbrough, Steve Gibson was willing to give local kids an opportunity of a career in the game. That, in turn, would give the club an identity. Now I accept that might be a little different if you're a bigger club, but if you look at successes in youth development, they involve kids who start at the club nearest their home.

'Having kids myself, is moving a boy because of football something you'd want to do? Move him away from his friends, away from that security? I know people have sometimes to move because of their parents' jobs, and they develop resilience, but if you, the kid, are the reason for the move, that doesn't half pile some pressure on you at a very young age.

'We don't know if a lad in our national under-16s is going to have career in the game, never mind whether he's going to be a senior England player, so how do we know a kid will be a pro at eight, nine, ten, eleven? We can spot a talent, get an idea of the stability of the family, but the path is so complex. Frankly, the reason that is going on is because everyone is frightened to death of losing a player.'

The earnestness by which I was first struck, when he was a Crystal Palace player discussing the pros and cons of his initial ambition to become a sports journalist, has been concentrated by experience. He leans slightly forward to engage in conversation; the tidily trimmed beard and open body language gives him the air of a college lecturer conducting a sociology tutorial.

Southgate cites the example of clubs like Tottenham, Southampton, Middlesbrough and, latterly, Liverpool, who are willing to risk the loss of precocious players because of a more considered, strategic system of financial reward. He would like to see the Elite Player Performance Plan amended, to incorporate a trust fund system.

'Owners and chief executives are all frightened of losing a player, and until people say, "Actually, we might lose him but we're not prepared to break what we do, on you go, good luck with it, let's see where he ends up," the problem will remain. There's no evidence of players being paid more and performing better. In fact I can see the opposite. The best players come through because they have that intrinsic motivation.

'The defining factor in a successful pro is mentality. When a player comes into a club you're assuming he is at a high level technically, but there is something very important about the ability to learn, to keep wanting to learn and improve. It's about dealing with the constant setbacks, the constant need to adapt and adjust.

'If you take the under-21 squad we had in September, twenty out of twenty-three were working with a new manager this season. Five were playing in their first team, and three were going really well. Two weeks later, two of those were out of their first team. You notice the constant flux when they meet up with England. It's a snapshot. You're never going to get the same person through the door.'

Personal development is football's final frontier. There are few additional gains to be made in physical preparation, and psychology is gradually becoming embedded in the performance system. The business of professional sport encourages a more holistic approach to an athlete whose brand value can be commercially decisive. Southgate is on message, in tune with the whole person:

'We've got to be careful we don't dismiss the player who is more difficult to manage, in favour of the player who is easier to look after, the one you can have a more rational conversation with. Talent travels on different routes, and most of these boys are a consequence of where they grew up. Get to know the family, what their individual motivations are, how much they are prepared to suffer to get there, and then you've got an opportunity to work with them.

'Without knowing those things it's scratching the surface really. It's a bit shallow and I'm not sure how much you are affecting them. You are putting sessions on and you're picking them, but you're not really getting to the core. Some of these boys are on huge money but inherently they want to play football. That's their source of frustration. That's why I've spoken to them about relating to the challenge of breaking into a first team.

'I didn't get into the first team at Palace until I was twenty, partly because they went through a season where they got promoted, then a season when they finished third in the league. There was no way Steve Coppell was going to risk a young player. I had a hundred-odd reserve games before I got my chance.

'Sometimes in the reserves we couldn't field a full team, so we'd have lads from Carshalton Athletic to make up the numbers. They were hardened non-league players. We had people like Chris Coleman, Stan Collymore and Steve Claridge, but a lad called Bobby Armitt, who'd been up at six in the morning getting the flowers out at Covent Garden, was our best player. That's the bit the lads in under-23 football don't get now. They are used to lots of things we wouldn't have put up with, workshops, classrooms and flipcharts, but an academy is a fantasy world, isn't it?

'I don't think we talk enough about the hardness of football. It's a shitty, horrible world really. I was a YTS at Palace when five or six lads were called into the office and told they weren't going to go on. The tears . . . flipping heck. It was one of the worst days I can remember because these were lads I played with from Sunday football. I knew what it meant. It drove me on.

'Looking back, Alan Smith, who was my youth coach and later my first-team manager, reminds me of development people like John McDermott, Warren Joyce and Dave Parnaby. They give the kids really good values. They are tough with them, want them to develop as players but know there's another side. They care for what the kid is about.'

Parnaby, Middlesbrough's influential academy director, mentored Southgate when he was working towards his UEFA B coaching qualifications as a senior player. The consensual environment extended to manager Steve McClaren and Bill Beswick, the sports psychologist who assisted him. They took Southgate into their confidence on selection issues, and the type of culture they were seeking to promote.

The challenge evolved from the theoretical to the terrifyingly practical when McClaren left to manage

England. Southgate, his captain, had a year left on his playing contract. He spoke with the club's owner Steve Gibson about his interest in gaining additional coaching experience alongside a new manager, and was entirely unprepared for the subsequent leap of faith:

'Steve wanted Terry Venables, really. He'd been there before. He spoke to Martin O'Neill, but neither of them wanted to take the job. They probably knew what I didn't, in terms of where we were financially. So, I get a call on holiday. Steve asked me to think about being the manager. I knew some of the difficulties, but didn't really know anything about what I was taking on.

'I'm thirty-five, managing in the Premier League. I've never even taken our under-14s, never planned a pre-season. I don't know anything about the development of players, or recruitment. I have an idea of how I want to play but not how that needs to be coached, and the amount of data coming at me is amazing. I'm pretty good with people because that's a skill set I developed as a captain, but I'm on this bizarre pathway of not knowing how to manage a team of staff.

'I've got to thank Steve for having that trust in me. I think he understood I cared about the club. I felt the club's money was his money and I wanted to protect it. Without him, that club is nothing. Dave, from another part of the club, helped to give it an identity. I wanted to bring young players through, a bit too much actually.

'I probably underestimated what was needed to stay

in the league, but we finished twelfth and thirteenth in the first two seasons. We had some very good players, great senior pros like Mark Schwarzer and Mark Viduka, and I had experienced coaches around me, like Steve Harrison and Malcolm Crosby. But the budget meant we had to get recruitment bang on.'

His final appearance as a Middlesbrough player was in the 4–0 loss to Seville in the 2006 UEFA Cup final. He then needed special dispensation from the Premier League to take charge because he lacked the necessary Pro Licence. His final match as Middlesbrough manager was a 2–0 win over Derby County on October 20, 2009, when they were fourth in the Championship following relegation from the Premier League. Gibson explained he had taken the decision weeks earlier, to safeguard the club's best interests.

'I know this sounds a bit wanky, but it is an incredible journey of learning. You learn by your mistakes in life, and in this world those mistakes can finish you. After being sacked you need to go away and think. It was the first time I'd experienced not being in work, and I felt what every man in the street feels in terms of lack of self-worth.

'You feel like you've let your family down. There's no structure to your day, no routine after having been part of something. I didn't have financial worry because I could do bits of media work; it was more that sense of missing a community. I applied for a couple of jobs and didn't get an interview, which was the best thing that could have happened to me.

'I needed to go and live life a bit, have some Christmases away, go skiing, which I couldn't do when I was playing. I wouldn't have done that if I'd been on the managerial treadmill. I had time to think about what I really wanted to do. TV gave me a nice quality of life, but I'm always uncomfortable criticising people for having a go at something, and not being prepared to put my neck on the block to do it.'

Trevor Brooking, who was then the FA's technical director, invited Southgate to shadow him for a year, until he was appointed England under-21 manager in August 2013. It proved to be a unique, elevated internship, which gave him a general's view of what is, to all intents and purposes, a battlefield populated by committee-room politicians and parochial class-warriors.

'That gave me a brilliant insight into every aspect of youth development, from grassroots upwards. I travelled around the county FAs with Nick Levett, seeing how difficult that was. There's the guy who comes up to you and says, "Kids up here are different." Oh, right, are they? Why is that? I experienced everything from skills programmes to being involved with some of the talks with Ged Roddy at the Premier League around EPPP.

'I travelled around the clubs, meeting the academy managers. I got a good look at the national junior teams. It was fantastic for me. I can see how difficult

Dan's job is because of all the strands that have to come together. It's a miracle how any kid becomes a pro because the journey is so individual. There are so many things you have to overcome.'

At 45, Ashworth is six months younger than Southgate. He may be small in stature ('At five foot seven I was never going to be a goalkeeper') but he wields huge influence as a kingmaker, despite the fate of his pivotal supporter, Roy Hodgson. His instinct is to make the FA, an organisation hidebound by bureaucratic tradition and self-interest, more technocratic, outward-facing and partnership-driven.

He has established a People and Team Development department, taken strategic guidance from Lane4, the performance management consultancy established by Olympic swimming champion Adrian Moorhouse, and employed support staff from rugby, cricket, hockey and organisations with Olympic oversight, such as the English Institute of Sport.

Since I once took a sabbatical from sportswriting to help establish the EIS, as deputy to the founding director, Wilma Shakespear, I empathise with Ashworth's aims. There are parallels with the Institute's ambition to create a new culture in Olympic and Paralympic sport through the transfusion of intelligence, insight, passion and creativity provided by young professionals unencumbered by systemic straitjackets and straight-line thinking.

I lasted four years before tiring of the duplicity and inanity of the small-minded mediocrities that sports administration tends to attract. Ashworth is more durable; he understands the principles of power, but has a wider field of vision. He has committed the FA to an annual 'health check' by UK Sport, in which process, progress and efficiency are gauged by measuring more than ninety components.

'UK Sport are ruthless. They do what it takes to win. If you are not on track as a performance director your funding gets pulled. It would be remiss of us, in football, not to look at outstanding sports and organisations. Their landscape might be slightly different, but by taking their example, and tapping and tweaking what we do, we can be more planned and strategic.

'It is not as difficult to operate politically as people make out. I get on well with Ged at the Premier League, and David Wetherall from the Football League. It is about being transparent and open. At some stage we have to leave our egos at the door. Who does what? How does it look? There are lots of stakeholders involved. We won't always agree but we have all got the same success criteria.

'Clubs want young players coming through to play in first teams. Otherwise their academies are not cost-effective. So do we, since in the main that means greater opportunity for English qualified players. Richard Scudamore wants the best and most attractive league in the world. So do we, since players and coaches are challenged every day. I say this with all respect because we are only ten per cent of the player development programme. We have to join it up and make sure it is a parallel process.'

He makes a virtue out of his origins, having been released by Norwich City as a teenaged defender before entering coaching, and working his way up through the academy system at Peterborough United, Cambridge United and West Bromwich Albion. It gives him an insight into the suspicions of clubs, who regard the England setup as a honey pot for impressionable young players. They are wary of players' heads being turned by unsubstantiated reports that the greenbacks are greener elsewhere. Ashworth went some way to assuaging their fears by writing to 1,500 agents, requesting that they not attend training camps or games at St George's Park, but he has a world-weary acceptance of the potential distractions for those on international duty.

'I came straight out of club football to join the FA, so I can understand the frustrations. I have sat on that side of the fence. Boys are at a sensitive stage of their career. I get it, that player X tells player Y what he is on while they are away, but, come on. You're not telling me players, agents and mums and dads don't know what the going rate is. That's not England's fault.'

Ashworth insists there have been 'massive improvements' under EPPP, but the numbers don't lie. By his own admission, from the last snapshot available to him, only 5.8 per cent of the players in Premier League teams were England-qualified academy graduates. There is an urgent need for 'meaningful, challenging playing time' between the ages of 18 and 23.

'Is it B teams, structured loan programmes, under-23 leagues? Is it buying a partner club? At seventeen, eighteen, nineteen we are as good as anyone in Europe. Where we struggle is we don't continue that improvement quicker. In other countries they are in the first team faster, because of money. Young players are cheap. Some will sink, some will swim. Some will have a hundred first-team games by the time they are twenty-one and someone will buy them.'

France have more players in the top five European leagues – in excess of 200 compared to an average of sixty-six English players who get such exposure – than such traditional powerhouses as Germany, Spain and Italy. Ashworth looked into buying into a foreign club while technical director at WBA, and believes others will follow suit 'if B teams, or whatever you are going to call them, are not an option here'.

He argues: 'It is a shame that Manchester City, say, can't do it with Oldham, Bury or Rochdale, who are five minutes around the corner, but from a selfish point of view I don't really mind where these young boys get their development. I'd rather it was in the Premier League, but if it involves playing every week in the

Dutch league or the Football League then great, no problem.

'It is not a perfect system. We are tweaking it, moving it forward. It isn't an impossible task. I wouldn't be sat here if I didn't genuinely believe we have the players and the processes for England to win things, for our clubs to win top European competitions, and for us to produce more England-qualified players and coaches for our top league.'

The rarity value of players complicates progress in more ways than one. Like Southgate, Ashworth supports the introduction of a financially prudent bond scheme to protect the long-term interests of lionised young men whose six-pack swagger is exaggerated by premature wealth and unfiltered flattery. A wage spiral, without the constraining factor of achievement, can be ruinous.

'Maintaining hunger is one of our challenges, because of the money that is available and given to young players who haven't achieved anything. They have fantastic facilities, people picking up everything after them. They have ludicrous contracts at an early age, which are paying for potential rather than output. How do you stop that? If club X aren't going to give it to you, club Y will. We've had some loose conversations, but it almost needs the game to come together and say here is a salary cap, or a bond scheme.

'I also feel the best people in the world are driven by

their passion, no matter how much money they have got. I am lucky enough to work with Wayne Rooney on a regular basis. Does he get paid for playing for England? No. Does he need to play for England? No. Is he there every single time without fail? Yes. Does he want to play in every training session, every single game? Yes. His desire, motivation and commitment to play football on a daily basis, as a multi-millionaire who has played at the top level since sixteen, is absolutely extraordinary.

'We talk about differentiators at Premier League and international level. A primary differentiator is the ability to handle pressure, on and off the pitch. Public scrutiny is part and parcel of the job now, and some can't handle that. What is particularly important in football is having good advice, a good agent, parent, and mentor at your club. We are all human beings and can go off the rails at times, but if you have a good support network it doesn't half help.'

England have won only two knockout ties since Euro 96, against Denmark in 2002 and Ecuador in 2006, so concerns about mental strength are understandable and crucial. Since Ashworth oversees strategic meetings with cricket and rugby union to discuss common problems, it is logical that he and Southgate share the belief of Eddie Jones, England's rugby coach, that psychological resilience is not necessarily innate.

'It's very much trainable,' Jones told the *New York Times*. 'I think everyone's born with a degree of mental toughness. I think it depends on your family life, how you were educated by your parents, what sort of school you went to, but the environment you go into in a team can create a much higher level of mental toughness.

'You never stop learning. The fact is if you think you've stopped learning your career is over. Mental toughness, to me, is your ability to keep doing what you are supposed to be doing regardless of the situation, regardless of whether you're physically or mentally fatigued. Because it hurts. High-level sport is uncomfortable. We try to teach players to be comfortable at being uncomfortable.'

Jones admits he prioritises self-sufficency by actively seeking players from difficult backgrounds, and is wary of the homogenisation of development programmes across the sporting spectrum: 'The reality of elite sport now is that players come through academies and are told what to do. You have to find ways of overcoming that, otherwise you end up with teams that can't make decisions. Players need to stand on their own two feet.'

Southgate spent time in the stocks after having his sudden-death penalty saved by Andreas Köpke in the Euro 96 semi-final shootout against Germany. He was sufficiently self-deprecating, and commercially shrewd, not to wallow in the indignity, but his paper-bag-over-the-head pizza advertisement never quite succeeded in making light of the enduring fear factor that accompanies playing for England. His stream-of-consciousness account of it is telling:

'It's got worse since then. Obviously I experienced it in my first tournament, '96. I'd only been in the England team for nine months so it was an unbelievable sequence. My debut as a sub, my first game, can I get in the squad for the Euros? Yes. Can I get in the starting team? I'm in. Can I stay in the team? Bloody hell, we're winning. I never thought anything about failure. I just thought, well, we're in the semi-final. That's normal, that's what happens . . .'

His laughter is impulsive and inevitably brittle: 'Obviously, then I get hit with a hammer, a thunderbolt. I started to worry, what if I'm the one that makes the mistake? I can't afford another one. In the end I was playing really well with my club, but every time I played for England I was anxious. Glenn [Hoddle] lifted me out of a qualifier at Wembley against Italy, and I thought, well, the worst that can happen has happened.

'I think mental resilience is a consequence of what we go through in our lives, how we respond and recover. Did I have that? I went into Palace as a fourteen-year-old. It was a dogfight of a club. Every day was a war. I've had to deal with injury, what happened to me in '96, being sacked as a manager. I've learned that whatever you go through, you're still standing. I didn't have that at eighteen.

'Everybody is vulnerable really. I didn't realise that

until we played Italy in Rome, in '97. I'd got to the fuck-it point, but I remember after the game Dave Seaman coming in going, "Fucking hell, how nervous were we before the game?" And I thought, fucking hell, Dave Seaman gets nervous? I can't believe that. He's the archetypal calm goalie who's won everything at Arsenal.

'Then I started to look around before games and I'd think, right, OK, they are all feeling the same as me but they're just masking it in different ways. I used to think strikers couldn't be nervous, because what's the worst that could happen? They miss a couple of chances. Whereas if I as a defender make a mistake, it's a goal. But then Mark Viduka talked to me about the pressure to deliver, to score.

'I started to see the bigger picture. I know how insecure everybody is, so why can't I lead this thing? As a manager I know what my players are going through. It takes time to know exactly how they are going to be feeling at any time, and how much they can take, but you can get a pretty good idea of how they might react and the sorts of messages that they might need. You learn when you have to fire into them, and when they need support.

'Clearly, there is still anxiety, from what I saw in the summer. Part of that is the fact the boys aren't really used to playing these big matches with their clubs. We've got some very good young players but they are not battle-hardened. I suppose you've got to ask the question, what are our expectations? The outliers are actually '96, '90 and '66. So until we really start acknowledging where we're at and how much hard work we've got ahead of us, there will be anxiety.'

The thought occurs that a historically dysfunctional system might have inadvertently acquired a powerful symbol of success achieved on existing terms. Southgate's accession to an overwrought, over estimated job will not magically transform the raw material available to him, or remove the temptation to concentrate on the financial rewards in a celebrity-obsessed club game, but the best solutions are shaped in the shadows.

13
Alchemy

It is the ninety-third minute, the point of no return. James Ward-Prowse places the ball precisely in the corner quadrant, with the Nike tick facing upwards, towards him. He takes four steps back at a 45-degree angle, shuffles his feet, and visualises the ball's flight towards the near post. It is aimed, right-footed, just inside the six-yard box.

The routine is well rehearsed and the delivery feels good, though momentum takes Ward-Prowse a stride further forward than normal. The corner is met by Calum Chambers, whose downward header is parried. Pierluigi Gollini, the prone goalkeeper, cannot prevent Jack Stephens volleying the loose ball into the roof of the net.

England's under-21s have beaten Italy 3–2 with the final meaningful kick of the match. Three Southampton players have combined, decisively, on a cold November night in their home stadium, St Mary's, but the achievement is collective, and has greater nuance than the result. The arid promises of the development template for domestic football are beginning to germinate, like seeds on water-infused blotting paper.

A team under the interim direction of Aidy Boothroyd, who was to be ratified as England's under-21 manager on February 3, 2017, defended with occasional incoherence, but they rotated fluidly, worked possession quickly and intelligently. They aligned traditional durability with technical precision and though a fifteen-match unbeaten run would end four days later, in defeat by the same scoreline in France, there was a sense of quiet progress.

Under-21 football is the departure lounge for the executive classes of the international game. Press boxes tend to be sparsely populated, but matches are transmitted live on TV and grounds hum with the kind of pre-pubescent buzz that signals a successful marketing campaign. This particular group, being groomed for the European Championships in Poland in June 2017, are a rewarding case study.

Successful footballers are not made of identical components. There is no magic formula, because alchemy is imprecise. Emerging players come from different backgrounds, use contrasting points of reference and have a broad range of motivating factors, even as they all retain focus on an identical ambition. They are, however, uniformly receptive to new methods and empathetic philosophies.

Ward-Prowse wears the captain's armband with unashamed pride, and transfers it to Chelsea's Nathaniel Chalobah for the following game, on the outskirts of Paris, due to nine changes being made in the starting line-up. The job, and the gesture, is largely symbolic, since the pair are part of a players' leadership group, along with Nathan Redmond, Calum Chambers, Lewis Baker and Will Hughes.

They act as a bridge to management, and frame basic standards of behaviour that must be adhered to, such as mutual respect and punctuality. Coaches, in turn, respond to their input; Gareth Southgate, when he was in charge of the under-21s, acceded to their request to transfer training sessions from the afternoons to mid-morning, so recovery time could be used more effectively. He used the group as an informal barometer of mood and opinion.

This, broadly, reflects the concept of a leaderful team, initially introduced at elite level by Ric Charlesworth, the Renaissance man of modern sport, who has combined political and medical careers with senior coaching positions in men's and women's hockey in both Australia and India. He has also undertaken development roles in New Zealand cricket and Australian rules football. For good measure, his third book, arguing that William Shakespeare had a coach's instinct for the human condition, was written during a year's cultural sabbatical in Italy.

Since good coaches have a magpie's instincts, Clive Woodward purloined his performance principles for the England rugby team, more than a decade before the FA recognised their enduring relevance. Charlesworth explained: 'The leadership group was part of developing a culture for sharing and responsibility. In the end, the players make all the decisions and judgements in the game, and not the coaches. It was about developing people who were assertive, self-starting and problem-solvers.'

So much for the old-school attitude, typified by the former FA educator who suggested empowerment of players would never work at junior level 'because kids would choose jelly and ice cream every day'. There is a maturity of thought in the development process, invariably overlooked during the bovine stampede at senior level to direct doubt or assign blame.

Ward-Prowse, impeccably media-trained, rarely skips a beat in more than an hour spent in the coffee shop on the mezzanine floor of the hotel at St George's Park, where younger age groups mingle in a collegiate atmosphere with the household names of the senior squads. He has evidently inherited an eye for detail from his father John, a barrister whose London practice concentrates on family law.

He is not one of football's hothouse flowers, since his aptitude for the game emerged innocently. At the age of 4 he would kick balloons around the lounge of the family home. He progressed to volleying rolled-up socks, thrown by his parents, into a sofa, which doubled as an imaginary goal. He retains a vivid memory of catching the ball during his first game as a spectator, between Portsmouth and Norwich reserves at Fratton Park, and tossing it to a ballboy. Football meant a bag of sweets, strange sights and stranger sounds.

'Things like that make you smile,' he said. 'You revert back to them in times of happiness. Mum and Dad let me live my life how I wanted. They were supportive, taught me family values, and I ran with it. I was given sound advice and never pressurised. Even now I still have bad times, where I struggle, but that is something for me to go back to, to realise what I am and what I have been through.'

James joined the Southampton academy at 7, and maintained a call-and-response routine with his father until well into adolescence. 'What are we here for?' his father would ask, in a ritual enacted whenever he dropped him off at training. 'Enjoyment' was the obligatory reply, accurate up to a point.

At 12, he was distraught that five other boys were given four-year contracts, leading into what was envisaged as a certain scholarship. In an early indication of the deadly nature of assumption, all were out of the game by the time those contracts expired. Ward-Prowse reacted to the implicit threat by toughening up in unsanctioned supplementary training sessions at

Havant & Waterlooville under manager Tony Mount, a family friend.

He combined middle-class stability and a streetwise mentality and captained Southampton for the first time at 14, in the Dallas Cup, an international youth tournament staged in Texas each spring. At 15 he was playing for the club's under-21s, being readied for the harshness of senior football by coaches Jason Dodd and Martin Hunter, who balanced life lessons with technical tuition and insights into game-management.

Together with Luke Shaw, Calum Chambers and Harrison Reed, he was also fast-tracked academically. Allowed to leave school a year before their GCSE examinations, they spent four days a week studying under a club tutor with the warning that any underachievement in the classroom would jeopardise their football education.

He was given his first-team debut at 16 by Nigel Adkins, who was at St Mary's to see that win over Italy, along with twenty-eight members of the Ward-Prowse family. His maturity, at 22, is striking; he counsels parents of the new intake at Southampton's academy and has returned the favour to Tony Mount by mentoring his son, England under-17 forward Mason Mount, who is cherished by Chelsea.

What are the lessons he seeks to impart? He mentions the eternal truth of the motivational slogan on the wall of the home dressing room at St Mary's – 'Hard work beats talent if talent doesn't work hard' – before expanding on the theme of what it takes to survive.

'Every player faces different scenarios. They have different managers, different coaches, to adapt to and impress. It all stems from that inner drive. You have got to want to get to the level. You can't afford to think about other people. I lost a lot of friends through football with mates not making it. I have seen a lot of people come and go but that is the nature of the game, unfortunately.

'Some lads don't deal with the aggression of being in a man's world. You've just got to brush it off. You've got to be at your best every day, regardless. You have to be a twenty-four-hour professional in all aspects. Eat right, train right, recover right, do it all again. That all contributes to a better game-day, and a longer career. You can't fancy it one week, and not the next.

'There were lots of people better technically than me who didn't pull through because they didn't work as hard as me. I've always worked hard, always believed you get out what you put into it. I want to develop on and off the pitch, and that means thinking about the external stuff, the media work, as well as the tactical, technical and physical elements.

'It is difficult, when you are coming into an academy at seven or eight. No one knows whether you are ready for such a tough environment. At that age a lot of it has to be around enjoyment. Kids can't be expected to concentrate on sleep or nutrition or how they live their lives. They are too young. They might end up as a footballer but it is not until they mature that you'll find out whether they're committed.

'My family gave me a base, a great platform. The club has an ethos of developing people. It is not only about whether a player can zing a fifty-yard ball on to someone's chest. It is about the basics, how you conduct yourself. Jason Dodd and Martin Hunter were key people. They taught me it wasn't nicey-nicey academy football any more. When I got into the first team at sixteen I felt I could deal with it.'

Hero worship has been distilled; Ward-Prowse's devotion to David Beckham has evolved from artless boyhood homage, wearing champagne-coloured Adidas Predators or having a spray-on blond Mohawk applied for special youth tournaments, to the sort of professional respect that cultivates deeply ingrained habits.

Ward-Prowse's free-kick technique owes much to Beckham, who took three more steps backwards, at the same 45-degree angle, and rolled the ball along the inside of his kicking foot, cutting across it to impart additional spin and dip. Ward-Prowse bends the ball in a similar arc to Beckham, and has learned from practising his windmilling arm action, which relaxes the shoulders and tilts the body back slightly, so the ball is launched more effectively off the ground.

Such love is not blind; Ward-Prowse reasons that 'smacking hundreds of balls in training and pulling your groin or hamstring helps no one', so he rations his meaningful set-piece rehearsal to two twenty-minute sessions a week. He weaves a strategically placed bib into the net as a target, and strikes the ball at different angles, at different sides of the goal. He asks a performance analyst to film him, so he can review the drill when it is complete.

'It is a balance of knowing your body, staying sharp, and staying fresh for games. I'm seeing the ball, making sure the technique is right. It gets harder and harder to ensure the consistency level you need in the Premier League. The standard is frightening, ever-changing. Application is a given. You need pace and physicality, because you come up against guys of six foot six who seem six foot wide.

'You need technical ability and mental strength, because managers are demanding more of you. Every one I've had has played the game in a different way. That's helped me because I know how to play a pressing game, how to play a slightly longer game, how to play through teams. You are always at your max, always learning.'

His profile means he can no longer get away with the subterfuge he used on the daily train from Portsmouth, where he and Alex Oxlade-Chamberlain sensibly hid their Southampton tracksuits. He has a considered approach to the financial rewards available to him, and estimates he speaks to his agent, David Manasseh of the Stellar Group, only 'five or six times' a season.

Like several others in the under-21 group, he was struck by the honesty and realism of a presentation by Southgate that summarised his career on two slides. One charted the highs, fifty-seven full England caps and more than 500 senior appearances. The other outlined the lows, his notorious penalty miss at Euro 96, subsequent death threats and his sacking as Middlesbrough manager.

Southgate had been encouraged to do so by Lane4, the performance consultancy: 'In my mind I never won what I wanted to win, so I talked to them about that. I played in big games, but I was pissed off because every time I came with England, the lads from Manchester United and Arsenal were pushing for the title and I wasn't. So, actually, there's a lot that I still want to do. I also showed them all the things that went wrong, all the people that had written me off. I was trying to weave in the struggle, because that is what it is going to be like for them.'

The underlying message, prepare for sunshine and rain, was ideally suited to young players dealing with the uncertainties of emerging from the pupae of modern academies. Revealingly, Ward-Prowse chooses to reinforce the point that management, too, is changing with the game itself:

'Football is different to what it was fifteen years ago. An aggressive tone is normal at half-time when things aren't going well, but I've never seen a manager chucking tea cups around. Managers have their own styles. I don't think I fully appreciated Mauricio Pochettino, because I was very young, but he was class. Everyone loves him, the way he trains, the love he and his staff show you. It is so satisfying working at that intensity. It brings out the best in you.

'Some may play for the money, but I've always believed as long as you concentrate, love the game and work to improve you will get new contracts because the club will want to keep you. Money is an added bonus. It is a crazy journey that you go on, with so many ups and downs, that all you can do is give it your all.'

In the stack-and-rack culture that permeates the Premier League, even that is not always enough. The most extravagant Las Vegas gambler, mind blown on neon, noise and complimentary cocktails, would hesitate to bet on Chelsea's academy producing a regular stream of first-team players. By the time that a first-year scholar, Tariq Uwakwe, made his England under-18 debut in Sweden in October 2016, no fewer than forty-five current academy players at Cobham had represented England between under-15 and -21 levels.

Two of the most prominent are Nathaniel and Trevoh Chalobah. Both have played internationally since the age of 15, and have captained England in their respective age groups. While Trevoh, four years younger, was helping the under-19s qualify for their European Championships in the unlikely setting of Rhyl in November, Nathaniel was on the verge of the most significant breakthrough.

He has a young thoroughbred's bearing, a natural air of authority that is emphasised in callow company. He won his ninety-second youth cap when leading the under-21s in France, but only made his competitive debut for Chelsea seven weeks previously, as a late substitute in the League Cup win at Leicester City. Predictably, he found the experience 'surreal'. He had been introduced to the first-team squad almost six years earlier, as an unused substitute against Newcastle United in the same competition.

Nathaniel was recruited by Chelsea at the age of 10, three years after the Chalobah family came to the UK from Freetown in Sierra Leone and settled in the south London suburb of Gypsy Hill. He had been taken to a trial game between Fulham and Chelsea by his sister, and his talent was so obvious the Stamford Bridge club made an approach to sign him at half-time.

The Chalobah children, three boys and two girls, inherited the athletic genes of their father, a former international tennis player. Nathaniel led the way, relishing playground scrimmages with a small ball, and games with his siblings in the garden. He tried sports as diverse as netball and cross-country running, and played cage football instead of taking the usual route to exposure through a grassroots club.

He admitted to Chelsea's website that 'it was all about street cred. Who could do the most skills, nutmegs, that sort of thing. Could you make your opponent look like a fool?' He was protective of Trevoh and John, his youngest brother, despite being 'scared every time because the other boys were bigger, stronger and older'.

He was involuntarily developing the self-reliance that would enable him to survive, and intermittently thrive, in isolation. He earned six GCSEs, four at A* level, and was sent out on the first of six loan spells soon after signing a professional contract in January 2012, shortly after his seventeenth birthday.

Status at Chelsea is recognised by salary, yet there was still widespread astonishment within development circles at his rumoured wage, £36,000 a week. He was, by his own admission, socially gauche, and took time to adjust to life on his own in an apartment block in Watford, where he underlined his promise by playing a pivotal role in Gianfranco Zola's team, which reached the Championship play-off final.

He struggled over two subsequent seasons, making little impact at Nottingham Forest, Middlesbrough, Burnley and Reading. Southgate, who had personally recommended Chalobah to Sean Dyche at Burnley, reflected: 'They were terrible loans. I had a pop at Nat, because he just didn't get the intensity needed to play, but now the penny has dropped.'

He managed only seven appearances over the course of a further season in Serie A with Napoli, and had to deal with the death of his beloved mother, yet he returned to Chelsea as a more rounded character; he was fluent in Italian and at ease with himself. A combination of tactical maturity, which he identified as the legacy of exposure to the more cerebral, immersive culture of the Italian game, and political expedience, which encouraged new manager Antonio Conte to satisfy fans' yearning for homegrown players, offered a long-awaited opportunity.

Lewis Baker, who scored eye-catching free kicks in those autumn under-21 internationals against Italy and France, was flourishing in exile. He was assertive, expressive, and prolific in his second season on loan to Vitesse Arnhem in the Eredivisie. There was a focus lacking in previous loan spells at Sheffield Wednesday and MK Dons; in essence, he had also grown into himself as a footballer and a young man.

Southgate admitted: 'It looked like he was heading down a bad pathway, but he has really impressed me over the past year. It is a combination of things, living in Holland, having to grow up and adapt to a different style of football. He plays every week, scores goals from midfield, and is technically great because he's genuinely two-footed. It has all come together because he has had to go away and fend for himself.'

Baker's discovery was relatively conventional, even if his father Audley's sporting heritage, as a six-time world powerlifting champion, was atypical. Chelsea beat six other clubs, including Arsenal, Aston Villa and QPR, to sign him as a 9-year-old from Luton Town, who received £8,000 for the year he spent in their Centre of Excellence. All he needed was game time.

Nathan Redmond, by contrast, had played more than 200 senior matches, for Birmingham City, Norwich City and Southampton, by his twenty-second birthday. He developed his touch and incisive movement in street football but was doubly distinctive, in that all his formative role models, from his mother Michelle to his cousin Sacha and his first coach at a grassroots club, were female.

His mother's influence is perhaps best explained by her Twitter biography, which reads: 'Master of the Redmond household. Mother to Nathan, Niall, Tiah & our angel Tilly in the heavens. Scorpion by birth, sarcastic by nature.' She juggled three jobs to keep the family together in Sheldon, east Birmingham, and imposed the highest personal standards on her children.

She refused to allow Nathan to take up a scholarship at Birmingham until he had earned his GCSEs in English, Maths and Science. She was similarly dogmatic in her opposition to her son seizing the chance to sign for Arsenal or Manchester City at the age of 17, because she believed he would be marginally involved at first-team level. Her reward for insisting on a longer-term approach to career advancement was to see him score for Norwich at Wembley in the 2015 Championship play-off, an experience which prompted her to confess, 'I nearly wet myself.'

He had been a boisterous youth, who relished pick-up games of basketball, and early indications of a creative mindset were not restricted to his success as a drama student. His solution to every boy's nightmare, the loss of a front door key when no one would be at home to allow access at the end of the school day, was to make himself a sandwich he didn't like, and place the key between two slices of bread. His reasoning, that he was less likely to misplace a sandwich box, was the product of conspicuously tangential thinking.

His mother encouraged a 'no fear' mentality, but it takes time for some young players to appreciate the seriousness of the profession. Redmond, at 22, would never dream of giggling on the substitutes' bench while his team were being relegated, as he did at 17 when Birmingham lost at Tottenham on the last day of the 2010–11 season. He and teammate Jordon Mutch shared a joke before they realised the risk, and lowered their heads to avoid cameramen, seeking stock images of mortification.

He had been impeccably coached at under-21 level by Richard Beale, who has also been responsible for the emergence of Jack Butland and Demarai Gray, and discovered adversity can be used to advantage. Relegation led to the release of thirteen players, freeing room for him to flourish under new manager Chris Hughton; he made thirty-seven first-team appearances and was named the club's young player of the year.

Norwich, progressive and lacking big-city pressure, proved to be an ideal transitional club before an £11 million transfer to Southampton in the summer of 2016. Redmond, named England under-21 Player of the Year, knew he needed independence, though his mother still administered cooking lessons over FaceTime on his smartphone.

There is a sense of a brotherhood evolving, unseen and under-appreciated, at international level. Redmond, a relative veteran, is so close to Nathaniel Chalobah that his sister Tiah sends the Chelsea midfield player sweets. The England teammates share a slogan: 'Enjoy the life, enjoy the journey.' To underline the point, an FA TV clip captured them literally dancing in their seats on the aeroplane taking them to the match in France.

Southgate had done his job well, on a basic human level. Redmond, too, has a vivid recollection of that presentation: 'He completely opened up to all of us. It was like: "This is what you're going to get. I understand where you're coming from. I've been this, I've done that." That was one of the conversations that really got the lads. They felt like they could really open up to him. But he was also saying: "If you're not ready for this, this is not the life for you."'

Football's popular mythology has the gifted boy

retreating to a bedroom that resembles a shrine to his heroes, in order to dream the impossible dream. Passion for the game, a love of its legends, is taken as read. Some, though, cannot claim to be altar-boy perfect in their devotion. Will Hughes, who made his first England under-21 appearance for fifteen months against Italy, following an anterior cruciate ligament injury, has twice flirted with walking away from football.

From the age of 8 to 14 he was a 'serious' tennis player, a sport he believes 'taught me individual responsibility'. He had entered Nottingham Forest's academy at 9, but was semi-detached in his commitment, and drifted away after his under-12 season. It was then that his mother took a life-defining initiative. She wrote to more than 100 charities, explaining her status as a single parent, seeking funding for Will's education.

He moved to Repton, a public school set in a swathe of rural Derbyshire. He could play football on twelve pristine pitches, and was invited to try out another twenty-five sports. His progress was gauged against such alumni as C. B. Fry, the Corinthian all-rounder, Harold Abrahams, inspiration for *Chariots of Fire*, and Bunny Austin, the gentlemanly tennis player who preceded Fred Perry. No pressure, kid.

Hughes played football for the school, a tradition begun in 1893, and turned out for local club Mickleover Jubilee with his friends. He was alienated at 15, when his two favourite coaches at Derby County's academy left the club, yet when he accepted a scholarship a year later he realised the game provided an outlet for the frantic competitiveness that once led him to throw the Monopoly board across the room when he was in danger of losing.

Long-term injury tested the moral foundation established by his mentor Nigel Clough, who advised him 'not to get sucked into the bubble of football', and recalibrated his value system. He learned Spanish to broaden his horizons, adding weight to A levels gained in Business Studies and Politics.

Duncan Watmore, who scored a sublime chipped goal in the defeat in France, is another outlier in England's under-21 group. Rejected at 12 by Manchester United and rediscovered by Sunderland, playing non-league football for Altrincham at 17, he has a first-class honours degree in economics and business management. Only one other Premier League footballer, former Leeds United and Bradford City defender David Wetherall in 1992, has achieved such academic distinction. 'A great kid,' observes Southgate. 'A coach's dream.'

His mother Georgina is a rector, serving three churches in the Tarporley parish in Cheshire. His father Ian, a former managing director of Accenture, held senior civil service positions within Downing Street under three prime ministers, and endured nine months as chief executive of the Football Association before despairing of the chimp's-tea-party politics that bedevils the domestic game.

We meet, appropriately enough, in the library at the Academy of Light, where blue plastic scholars' folders are stacked on rectangular tables. Duncan speaks quickly, at up to 194 words per minute compared to the average of 120, but in a considered, engaged manner that reflects a balanced upbringing.

'You put enough pressure on yourself, so you don't need your parents adding to that. When we were released by United, in the February, some families stormed out and refused to return but Mum and Dad were adamant that if I was going to leave, I would do it in the right way. I'd enjoyed six years at the club I supported, so the least I could do was stay, train and play for another three months.

'I didn't necessarily think of myself as the next big thing, but you've got to find a new identity as a person, because even though you're young, everyone has a label. I was known as the "Kid at United". I was proud of that. It had been all football, football, football, but now I could concentrate on my education, play rugby and cricket, do athletics. It made me a more rounded person.

'I've been very lucky. I've managed to make it without sacrificing everything. Those years in which I was free, at secondary school really, are the years when you make your best friends, play your sports, go out at the weekend. You can't do that if you take academy life seriously, which you have to do these days.

'When you get into the first team it is a different culture. People have made their way there in different ways. My route back was a little weird, but everyone is different, in terms of background and personality. It takes a while, but I've noticed that as you get older, the regimentation becomes less obvious.'

He played junior football for Hale Barns, and progressed to Altrincham's first team, training three nights a week, along the way to securing a place at Manchester University. Alternative education was undertaken at places like Colwyn Bay, where he remembers, fondly, 'the ultimate scrap'. His pace regularly took him behind the home defence, but he struggled to stay upright on a glutinous surface despite switching from his normal moulded boots to studs. His manager was apoplectic, the opposition vengeful. They won 1–0 but 'it was basically a fight'.

Watmore wears a survivor's smile: 'You learn a hell of a lot. It's men's football. Academy football is kids, there's no escaping that. By definition you're going to have to be more physical, smarter in how you play. Another big thing, which maybe gets played down, is the pitches. Academies have the best pitches in the country, and it makes such a difference. You've got to learn a completely different game.

'If you can pass the ball and trust your first touch,

you play one-touch football. You can't do that on most of the non-league grounds I played on. You had to be a lot cleverer about how you went about it. When you are on a muddy, overgrown pitch, hearing everything from fans who lose it because they're angry or a little drunk, you learn different ways of playing.

'It is not necessarily the most fun but though the standard is miles worse than you think you are capable of playing, you pick up so much. At Sunderland a lot of the lads are sent on loan to places like Boston or Gateshead, because you get a false idea of the game by just spending it on the perfect pitches, at the perfect academy, with great coaches. As a player you should definitely take advantage of that, but you need to appreciate the other side of things.'

Life lessons multiplied at university, initially regarded as a platform for a career in management consultancy. Watmore lived in halls and avoided the traditional Pot Noodle diet by using his football income to buy chicken and salmon, but only knew how to stir-fry. He 'didn't realise the taboos' of the game, so threw himself into the student's lifestyle before it began to affect his performances.

The rewards, and the complications, of cutting back were crystallised by his first TV appearance, in an FA Cup replay for Altrincham against Burton Albion. His preparation that day involved lectures in macro-economics and maths statistics, but the adrenaline rush of broader scrutiny and the buzz of a capacity crowd refined his ambition to become a full-time pro.

Sunderland signed him in May 2014 and he transferred to Newcastle University, where, despite renting a flat close to the business school, he physically attended only 8 per cent of his lectures in the last two years of his degree course. He compensated by accessing online tutorials and studying textbooks during the late afternoon and evenings, and at weekends.

'Everything changed. Football was full-time, six days a week and I'd never done gym sessions before. I didn't know how to squat, for example, and the rest of the guys were perfect physical specimens who'd had strength-and-conditioning coaches since they were fifteen or sixteen. You get a lot of banter, a nice word for it, but if you're called a geek, or whatever, it is good-hearted.

'Kevin Ball and Robbie Stockdale, my under-21 head coaches, were fantastic with me throughout my degree because they understood what I was trying to do. Every now and again they'd give me a day off to catch up on my lectures. In general, though, uni never realised how serious football was, and I don't think football realised how serious the degree was.'

His bemusement at the stranger's double-take that signals recognition in city streets is evidence of a more worldly approach to celebrity. He argues that footballers have greater natural intelligence than they are given credit for, since instant decisions, taken under pressure, require a measure of intellectual maturity.

'I've picked up so much from senior players. They just know the game. They are so switched on about where to go, how to be, what kind of decision to make. That is such a higher level of thinking than people can fathom. People think it's just about kicking a football around, but there's so much intelligence in football that people don't realise. The word I'd use to describe it is recognition.

'I'm getting better at it, but I've got a long way to go. In my position I need to recognise when to dribble, when to take us up the pitch, when to calm us down, keep the ball, when to press off the ball, when to sit in, get our shape, get our breather. I need to recognise the type of players we are playing against; are they quick, are they strong, do you want to put them on one foot or the other? That's game intelligence. It's about recognising the situation, the opposition, the circumstance, the way we're playing, the confidence of the group, the fans, everything.

'The biggest life-changer for me was living on my own, not knowing many people, and having to get my mind into the football and just deal with it. When I was younger I didn't realise the sacrifice it would take not seeing friends, and acting professionally 24/7. This is not one of those jobs where you can go in and think, I'll have an off day today, I'll just chill.

'I've learned about the intensity of the group dynamic,

how everyone deals with stress, especially being in the relegation zone over the past couple of years. The fans obviously deserve better, and it doesn't help anyone by responding to pressure by taking it out on one another in the changing room. If you start falling apart as a group you'll fall apart on the pitch.'

David Moyes is Watmore's sixth manager in three years; the battle for individual recognition and the threat of rejection is constant. Careers change in an instant; Watmore heard the anterior cruciate ligaments in his left knee snap in a challenge with Christian Fuchs in the eighty-fifth minute of a 2–1 home win over Leicester City on December 3, 2016.

The pain was grotesque and immediate. The mentally debilitating process of physical rehabilitation takes the injured player into dark places that Watmore sought, typically, to illuminate by reading motivational literature. In a perverse way, it helps that he has shared the fears of his peers, and felt the mortification of those whose savaged pride prompted them to slip away, without a proper farewell, when the worst news came, and they were rejected.

'I've seen many more drop out of the game than stay in, which is pretty scary. The ones who were released here were all quality lads. You see their talent on a daily basis, and you see others with the same talent go on to make it. Small things make the difference: work ethic, luck, opportunity, injury. You need the right time to impress the manager, the right manager for your style of play.

'You've got to have faith, but it can be devastating if others don't have faith in you. It is so cut-throat. Sam Allardyce had faith in me, but I am still learning about the mental side of the game. There are times you need to switch off, because it can consume you. It is so easy to over-think things.

'For most kids, football happens too early. I got the best of both worlds. I got to enjoy my life as a teenager in a stress-free environment. There's no right or wrong way, but I would advise anyone in an academy to keep the balance of having friends and family outside football. Sometimes you can get carried away about making it as a footballer. You've got tunnel vision and suddenly, one day, they don't want you any more. You will look back, and regret the power of the dream.'

14
Ballers

Millwall's training ground on Calmont Road, in the semi-detached suburban sprawl of Bromley, is an unprepossessing place. It is warm and welcoming, but short on the sort of creature comforts to which the day's triallist had become accustomed, as an FA Youth Cup winner and age-group international. He was in the right place, at the right time, with the wrong attitude.

The pitch furthest from the changing rooms had been nipped by winter. It wasn't really suited to the bladed, high-socked boots he wore. Yet they were new, worth £280 on the open market outside the sinecure of his kit contract, and looked sharp. They fitted his assessment of his eminence, which blithely ignored the fact his career was in jeopardy.

His teammates for the day had admired the boots in the changing room, but were dressed for work. The triallist, informed he had no future at his Premier League club, couldn't get enough purchase on the hard, firm ground and after ten minutes of slipping and sliding, was offered alternative footwear, so that he had a better chance of doing himself justice. His refusal, motivated by a perceived loss of face, sealed his fate.

'Nah, the kid's not for me,' said manager Neil Harris, who as a legendary figure at a proud blue-collar club knew the value of a workhorse over a show pony. Millwall have a productive youth system and an outstanding academy manager in Scott Fitzgerald, but there is no time, and even less inclination, to preen in League One. Players with academy pedigree may be permitted the occasional forty-yard diagonal pass, as a genuflection to football's finer arts, but they are expected to dig in and hit the channel when nothing obvious is on.

The triallist was quietly replaced at half-time, and at the time of writing, hasn't found a Football League club. In the emoticon-fuelled fantasy of his Twitter account, he remains a baller, a scion of the Snowflake Generation. Like many of his post-millennial peers his sense of entitlement is matched by his mental fragility and his capacity to take offence.

Other demographers refer to them as Generation Z, the first technologically driven generation, whose insecurity is masked by their assertiveness on social media. Born either side of the millennium, they are also known as the Founders, the Plurals, or the Homeland Generation. At Tottenham Hotspur they are referred to as the

Speedy Boarders, a group which prioritises instant gratification at the expense of such quaint, old-fashioned notions as diligence and merit.

Football, inevitably, magnifies and distorts such attitudes. Marketing executives confirm boot launches need to be carefully calibrated, because contracted players are hyper-sensitive about being given the latest models as soon as they are available. Woe betide the representative whose baller is beaten in the race to show them off on Snapchat or Instagram.

Boots are bling, so seductive that even in such a haven of common sense as Tottenham's academy, the scholars' lockers are used as display cabinets. Empty boxes are piled high for all to see since they signify the seniority of a player's boot deal; those players with an annual stash of six or more boot boxes are deemed to be true ballers.

John McDermott, Tottenham's Head of Coaching and Player Development, smiles at the pretension, and calls a succession of players from his under-18 squad into a small, sparsely furnished office in the dressing room area to give a human dimension to his philosophy. The boys have an initial adolescent awkwardness in front of me, a stranger, but are impressively earnest.

Jaden Brown, a defender capped by England at under-16 and -17 levels, bashfully confirms the boot-box culture. Japhet Tanganga, a right-sided central defender who is another international regular, speaks thoughtfully about social distractions and the perils of estate life in his formative neighbourhood, Hackney.

Jack Roles, whose Lampardesque knack of arriving late in the penalty area from midfield will result in his contributing seventeen goals in twenty-two games before Christmas, explains the relentlessness of agents, seeking his signature. He remains unrepresented since he accepts they will be of little use unless and until he wins his second professional contract; McDermott's policy, increasingly difficult to sustain in an overheated market, is that first-year pros receive a standard annual wage of £38,000.

Nigel Gibbs, Tottenham's principal under-18 coach until he joined Swansea City as Paul Clement's assistant just before Christmas, reflected: 'John's moral compass doesn't move. There are no egos, no agents here. There's a purity about John in terms of it all being about a player's development. We don't buy players in. It doesn't matter who they are. When they are here there are consequences for their actions.'

To illustrate the point, McDermott recounted the story of one of his England under-18 internationals, who made the schoolboy error of hiring an acquaintance's home for a house party. Such extravagant gestures, difficult to reconcile with a scholar's monthly wage of £380, are quick to reach his ear, since Spurs' culture at youth level demands grounded, self-contained individuals.

The reprimand was thoughtful, and effective, since the

aspiring pro was ordered to work with the groundsmen at the training ground for a month. It was not intended to belittle and intimidate but to educate; the player learned from the professionalism of the grounds crew, the pride they took in their relatively poorly paid work. It was a reminder of the privileges he had taken for granted.

McDermott is deeply impressive, impeccably motivated, yet politically vulnerable because of his ill-concealed disdain for the bureaucratic aspects of the Elite Player Performance Plan. Spurs, a club with a creative, cohesive youth strategy that engages Mauricio Pochettino, the first-team manager, were marked down in their annual audit because their academy coaches have the lowest usage of the computerised Performance Management Application. The authorities chose to ignore the inconvenient fact that Tottenham's first team is studded with players those same coaches have shaped and encouraged.

As a self-confessed purist, disciplined by his economics degree, McDermott believes English football is suffering from a form of gout, a rich man's ailment. He is inured to so-called Pedestal Parents, who tend to be over-indulgent and overbearing, second-guessing coaches while disregarding the dangers of being beguiled by the highest bidder for their son's services.

This leads to difficulties at international level, where players' cliques can form on geographic or financial lines. Tottenham's teenagers, on football's minimum wage, share a dressing room with teammates who can be earning up to £10,000 a week. McDermott is uneasy with what he calls the 'bromance' of selection at younger age groups for England, since experience informs him that the majority of those gilded players will be out of the game by the time they are 22.

He believes in the veracity of the 800-game rule, which calculates that a senior player's career will be sectioned into 200 outstanding performances, 400 diligent performances and 200 shockers. His intention, to breed the strength of character to survive setbacks and inconsistency, is inherently complicated by what he describes as 'Disneyland' training complexes.

Young players are examined minutely, from saliva tests to agility exercises, but data-driven certainties do not take into account human nature, or the idiosyncrasies of physical maturation. Harry Kane may be lauded, on T-shirts and in song, by Spurs fans as 'one of our own' but as an immature 14-year-old, the youngest in his age group, he was close to being disowned.

The in-house jokes about his lack of speed, physical definition and agility, which was 30 per cent lower than his peers, have even reached England manager Gareth Southgate, who sees him as central to his plans: 'Harry?' he asked with a chuckle. 'A very stable family background, but loads of loans, and didn't look a particularly good athlete at a young age, if I'm being extremely kind . . .'

McDermott's creativity and trust in intuition is shared by Pochettino, whose management team reflects the breadth and subtlety of his approach. The Argentine has classic leadership traits: he is warm yet ruthless, emotionally intelligent without compromising his sense of authority. Jesús Pérez, his assistant, is a sports scientist, who coached in Spain and was fitness consultant to the Saudi Arabian national team before joining Pochettino at Espanyol and Southampton.

His analytical approach is balanced by Toni Jiménez, the goalkeeping coach, who won three senior caps and an Olympic gold medal for Spain. He is an extrovert, who employs the rapid, rough-and-ready humour to which footballers traditionally respond. The management group filter and contextualise; they also have an implacable faith in the vivacity of youth.

McDermott gives two examples of Pochettino's methodology. The first concerns Nabil Bentaleb, the Algerian defensive midfield player who was playing street football in Birmingham when he joined Tottenham's academy. The underlying reasons for his season-long loan at Schalke 04, which is expected to end in a £17 million transfer in the summer of 2017, were contained in this apparently throwaway comment by the manager: 'when your face is not smiling, your feet are not smiling'.

The second involves another verbal aside, designed to benefit Shayon Harrison, a left-footed striker who made his competitive first-team debut against Liverpool in the League Cup in October 2016 and spent the second half of the season on loan at Yeovil. Following his involvement in a training session with the senior squad, Pochettino told McDermott that Harrison was 'lazy', deliberately loud enough for the player to hear.

Events unfolded as the manager intended: the player asked McDermott, a more familiar figure, for feedback. He was asked to reflect on Pochettino's frame of reference; he has worked with Diego Maradona, the embodiment of impulsive genius, and sees, on a daily basis, the dedication that drives Harry Kane to dismiss the doubters. Harrison wasn't lazy by normal standards, but the observation invited him to examine whether he could give more of himself to his work.

The presence of agents at development matches at Tottenham's training ground is tolerated rather than encouraged. The most prominent are identified by their restless eyes, fractured conversations and personalised number plates, found on black Range Rovers and white BMW saloons. Scouts are corralled between the left-hand corner flag and one of the goals.

Parents are the most fascinating creatures in this human zoo. At Spurs they congregate around a silver-grey vintage Citroën burger van, and spread along one touchline on the main pitch. Eavesdropping on their conversations is, frankly, compelling since they drip with ill-disguised desperation, institutionalised fear, and instinctive suspicion.

On this particular morning, the visiting parents, family groups with pushchairs and siblings in tow, were enraptured by the usual mixture of prejudice and unconfirmed rumour. One knot was scandalised by a supposed £250,000 payment to an academy player of dubious provenance; another cluster were murmuring darkly about over-training leading to a sudden spate of stress injuries. A third gaggle merrily bitched about a goalkeeper whose sliced clearances rarely ended in the same postcode twice.

Their interest was piqued by the sudden presence of a familiar figure in a dark suit, fawn gabardine raincoat, and Tottenham club tie. David Pleat was taking in the under-18s on his way to another afternoon's scouting session, at Leyton Orient. Prominent agents, like Sky Andrew, danced attendance; Pleat acknowledged their presence professionally but seemed glad to be distracted by the intervention of a bustling, stocky man in a flat cap.

'Mr Pleat. You are a great man. Sir, could you kindly help us again? They will listen to you.' It transpired his admirer was the father of Jacques Maghoma, the Democratic Republic of Congo midfield player whom Pleat recommended to Burton following his release by Spurs in 2009. His career has subsequently flourished at Sheffield Wednesday and Birmingham City. Another son, Paris, was progressing well in Tottenham's under-16 team.

A third son, Christian, was approaching his nineteenth birthday and had a critical decision to make. A tall central defender, with a languid demeanour and the obligatory diamond-studded earring, he had been offered a six-month loan at Newport County, bottom of League Two. Pleat, conscious that he had not started a competitive match in a previous loan spell at Yeovil, advised him to take it, on the proviso he would be guaranteed game time. The proposed deal subsequently fell through.

The timing and nature of a young player's loan is critical if he is to make the step from the tea dance of under-23 football to the guerrilla warfare of the men's game. Pleat is intrigued by the philosophy of Jürgen Klopp, who tolerates strikers and defenders taking their lumps in the lower leagues, up to a point, but prefers to develop midfield players internally and is working towards the centralised education of young players, through shared training facilities.

To those of us of a certain vintage, and to a national radio audience accustomed to his insight and erudition as a co-commentator, it comes as a surprise to realise that Pleat is 72, the same age at which the manager to whom he is inextricably linked, Graham Taylor, passed away in January 2017. Yet his influence, as an adviser to Tottenham chairman Daniel Levy, primarily in assessing players between the ages of 18 and 21, has endured in the twelve years since his spell as Tottenham's Director of Football ended.

His thirty-year association with Spurs includes four

separate spells as manager, but he does not always get his own way. Levy accepted his advice to invest £5 million in Dele Alli, yet demurred when Pleat urged him to investigate the possibility of signing Duncan Watmore from Sunderland. 'He has what I call progressive pace,' Pleat reflected, eyes narrowing as if summoning the spirit of the ginger-haired winger. 'We know he is intelligent. He's had the perfect apprenticeship, scores goals, and puts the full back on his heels. He'd be perfect to bring on steadily.'

He cautioned against signing Will Hughes from Derby because he felt he lacked a change of pace, and the three 18-year-olds he identified as the best in their age group at the start of 2016 had enjoyed mixed fortunes. Rico Henry, a full back developed by Walsall, struggled to establish himself at Brentford; by contrast Sunderland's Jordan Pickford emerged as a senior England goalkeeper of the future and Tammy Abraham's goal-splurge on loan at Bristol City in the Championship testified to talent too often ossified in Chelsea's academy.

Pleat, a former England schoolboy international, was once Nottingham Forest's youngest player. He made his debut thirty-three days after his seventeenth birthday. The first team trained in the car park at the City Ground the day before matches in the old First Division; beer barrels were used as goalposts in intra-squad matches between four seven-a-side teams.

There were no sports scientists urging caution because the numbers suggested players were in the red zone of potential fatigue. Knees were grazed, knocks were accepted as an occupational hazard. This is not romantic self-deception, an anthem to a post-war, pre-space-travel generation. Pleat merely asks for greater respect for balance:

'Uneven surfaces improve your control, but the modern grass, or 3 and 4G, pitches allow a player to learn how to be controlled and restrained in the challenge. Why not accept the merits of both? Ron Greenwood was right. This is still a simple game, in which successful, balanced teams do the right things quickly and accurately. We have become too regimented, too rigid. It's a form of follow-my-leader. I can't remember the last time I saw an academy team playing their way, instead of the way they are told they should be playing.

'Leicester City won the Premier League because they did something differently. They were happy to concede possession, funnel back and counter. When I watched them I often used to visualise Cloughie shouting at his son Nigel to get back to the halfway line, knowing the damage they were able to do on the break through Bowyer and Robertson. Going back further to 1962, Ipswich Town played a deep-lying outside left, thirty-four-year-old Jimmy Leadbetter, and two strikers, Ray Crawford and Ted Phillips. By the time the rest realised what was going on, the season was halfway through and Sir Alf Ramsey had effectively won the league title.'

This is no ramble through football's version of the Natural History Museum. Pleat embraces modernity on his, and its, own terms. He would cap young players' salaries, employ more welfare staff, and allow no boy younger than 12 to join an academy. He believes clubs should prove their commitment to development by offering four-year contracts, essentially extended scholarships, to their most promising 14-year-olds.

'They might get more coaching time these days, but they're too young. Their minds have to develop. I see so many young players do something well in a match, immediately turning to the bench, seeking the approval of the coach. It's frightening that they've not been able to acquire enough confidence to relax and play. We don't realise there are a lot of anxious, nervous boys out there. It's very difficult for them.

'Money is a massive problem, because that fear of failure can sometimes spur you on. I remember my first job as a manager. We had our first child, with another on the way. I had nothing but football. That meant I had to put my heart and soul into the game, give it all my time. When players out of the team are insulated by money they simply can't be as hungry as they should be.

'There are so many factors in a boy making it. The right environment and pastoral care are very important. Injuries affected my pace as a player, but I don't think I failed just because of that. I lacked a mentor, a sympathetic coach, a proper man to guide me. I see loads of little kids on Saturday mornings. They're tiny. They're not ready. I see parents who have no idea. Then the agent comes along, gets into them, and the boy is on the wrong road.'

Pleat was alarmed by an early experience of football's dark arts, when he was told an agent paid another agent £10,000 to acquire the rights to promote a teenaged player he mistakenly believed had a chance of forging a professional career. Another dubious alliance involved a chief scout whose best youngsters used mysteriously to join a rival club represented by his partner in a property deal.

Poaching of players between the ages of 16 and 18 has become so endemic that Tottenham's principled stand on their pay scale for emerging players leaves them vulnerable to predatory competitors. Marcus Edwards, the 17-year-old attacking midfield player injudiciously likened to Lionel Messi by Pochettino when he gave him a first-team debut at Gillingham in the autumn of 2016, was stalked by several clubs during a six-month dispute that preceded his first professional contract.

Tottenham are understood to have considered reporting Chelsea to the Premier League for an alleged illegal approach to Nya Kirby, an England under-16 international who was also linked to Manchester United and Liverpool when Spurs were informed he wished to leave at the end of the 2015–16 season. He played for Chelsea in the summer, before a proposed move was scrapped, and underwent a trial with Arsenal before signing for Crystal Palace.

Andrew Mills became the UK's first FIFA-licensed agent in 1993, when the system at least maintained the pretence of incorporating the professional safeguards effectively abandoned when individuals were given the opportunity to register as deregulated intermediaries for £500. He still runs the Treble B Management company, but a parallel career in football administration and recruitment has merely emphasised his disaffection with the youth game.

A lean, expressive man, who speaks with his hands, he sits in a hotel bar, close to Chelsea's training ground at Cobham in Surrey, as a survivor in a brutal trade. Yet his reference point, from a human perspective, is of himself as a teenager crying in his mother's car outside the Richardson Evans leisure centre, beside the A3 in south-west London, following his release by Wimbledon.

His melancholy is affecting: 'They told me I didn't need to come back, and I had to ask myself some questions: "What am I now? How do I fit in? How am I going to tell my mates at school?" There was no mechanism of transition even then, when the dream wasn't as big, fluffy and champagne-fuelled as it is today.

'At what point does football become a job? When you're eight, ten, twelve? I see these boys around here in their Chelsea kit and I know they are being treated differently at school. They're superstars. But I also know that for every positive element that attaches to them, there's a negative.

'What we've done in professional football is to over-complicate every layer of their development so they don't know what to do when they come out of academies without a job. They have very little ability to self-generate the internal strength it takes to actually get to the sharp end of this career. The academy system has softened them. We've taken that resilience away from them.'

To reinforce the point, he spoke of a boy he had just been asked to mentor by a friend. A former age-group captain at a Premier League academy, he was approached on his release by six individuals claiming to be established agents, on the strength of a single YouTube clip of him scoring a twenty-five-yard free kick. Mills was disgusted by their reckless opportunism:

'I'd never heard of a single one of these agents. I'd never heard of the companies they said they'd worked for. I don't believe they were agents. I believe they travel around youth games, trying to attach themselves to the best kid for a slice of the action. Football has created that environment. The boy is now on the phone to me every day, asking, "Where do I go? What do I do?" He's a lovely lad but he has lost his ability to make something happen for himself. He's been used to a protective environment, first parentally, and then through the academy, where he's been told only positives, right up until the significant negative of, thanks, but no thanks.'

Mills understood the nature of the problem when he watched the boy's last game for his club. A typically callow end-of-season team containing boys playing one or two years up were beaten 6–1 after trailing 5–0 at half-time. The debrief was delusional, since the coach chose not to acknowledge the magnitude of the failure.

'As I wandered over to see this lad, the coach put his hand on his shoulder and said to him, "Different class today, son. You did really well out there. I thought you bossed the midfield." Then he walked off. This is not a dig at him, because I think coaches are told in their manual they have to find a positive, but, in my vocabulary, that team had just been dicked.

'Now, there were some positives, because in my mind they did well to draw the second half, but that wasn't the point. I turned to the parents and said, "This is where we're either going to fall in, or fall out." The lad didn't boss the midfield. If he's not sat there gutted, maybe even disgusted, then there's something wrong. You don't want it enough and you're never going to want it enough. The system, the industry, lets these boys down.'

Yet what about the agent, the speculator who can walk away from the wreckage with a lightness of stride that compensates for a marginal lightness in the wallet? What responsibility does he, or she, have for the broken boy for whom help never arrives? Mills laughs mordantly at the implicit innocence of the challenge.

'I've never been asked bluntly about it before. The truth is, agents have zero responsibility. Unless they are that way inclined, and have an interest in the human element, that won't change. The agency business is, in its most basic form, the jungle. You eat what you kill. Football has kept the agency business in that position, because of an offhand approach to it.

'There are hundreds, thousands, of these intermediaries. Only the top ten will make real money, and I will have issues about how some of them behave. I think any of my players would happily speak to me now. As an agent I was bothered by what happened to the boys whose one big deal had gone, and their agents suddenly weren't there.

'I had a call yesterday from a boy at PSV Eindhoven, who is coming back from a significant injury and wants to come to this country. He's reviewing his agent's advice over the past three years and wondering if the agent was acting in his best interests. He had some responsibility to ask himself those questions before. There are so many layers to the miseducation of these boys, and the misguidance quite often starts at home.

'Clubs should, unless there are exceptional circumstances, allow young players to see through a minimum development period with the club. If, say, you take a thirteen-year-old he should have a minimum of five years. You shouldn't be able to get rid of him as a fourteen-year-old. Get rid of the scout that saw him as a thirteen-year-old instead. But football has no interest in that, because there is no benefit to anyone other than the boys.

'I hate to say it, but academy players, all players for that matter, are products. Football doesn't give them the ability to look you in the eye and have a conversation. FIFA don't want to know about good and bad agents because they've worked out there's not a simple set of rules they can put in place that can police the industry. The easiest thing for them to do is reverse out and say to the FA, "You do it." The FA have done the same thing, because, well, why wouldn't they? They're being led by FIFA. They have looked at it, tried to do it, said, "Well, actually, this is too complicated."'

His pessimism seemed pertinent in the FA's winter palace at St George's Park, where they held their annual Talent ID Conference in early December. The star turn was Stuart Worden, an occasional playwright and theatre director who, for twenty-two years, has been principal of the BRIT School, a creative oasis situated 600 yards from Selhurst Park that has produced stellar musicians, actors, fashion designers and electronic-games entrepreneurs.

Together with five dancers from the school, he outlined a compelling vision of nurturing creative young adults, imbued with originality, responsibility and ambition. He spoke of breaking free of the shackles of formal education, which values science above art. He recognised the legitimacy of comparisons to football's development system, but his version of an academy was 'a home for people to express themselves, to feel connected'.

Spot the difference, people.

'Don't do community projects because they get you on *Match of the Day* 2,' he urged his audience of coaches, scouts and club officials, as he discussed a link to a local hospice, through which pupils at the BRIT School work with terminally ill patients on a range of creative projects from radio shows to drama assignments. He had no intention of demeaning his host's efforts, since he was still entranced by the fact he had awoken that morning in a hotel room bearing the name of Sir Bobby Robson, a family idol.

He understood the difficulties, because they mirror those in many creative industries, and accepts the BRIT School's status gives him an additional layer of protection, since he has legislative authority to ban agents from contacting pupils until they have completed their GCSEs. He used the singer Katie Melua as an example; musical impresario Mike Batt was forced to wait six months before she could record her first album for him. The appropriately entitled *Call Off the Search* sold three million copies.

The critical difference involves the talent drain; unlike football's penal drop-out rates, around 70 per cent of BRIT School pupils are still working in the arts seven years after graduation. Their process is demanding, with eight-week assessments designed to build resistance to criticism, but more organic, less cluttered with commercialism and discord:

'We need to question talent, but also value it. We don't have a set theory about it, but we assess it on a hunch. Our end game is sustaining the lives of our pupils, and fear is a terrible thing to give a teenager. Everyone says, "Put them under pressure." Rubbish. Get on there and give it some.

'These facilities are extraordinary but I have to say that reducing the number of people in young footballers' lives would be a good thing. There are a lot of voices in their ears, because an industry is being built around them. Our dancers, for instance, have two or three teachers to respond to. They don't have to listen to the whole world.'

There is nothing remotely impertinent about suggesting the football world should listen to him.

15

Feeding Frenzy

Failure has a name, a face, a passport to everywhere and nowhere. At 13, Freddy Adu was going to be the best footballer on the planet. At 17, he briefly piqued the interest of Sir Alex Ferguson at Manchester United. At 27, a veteran of thirteen clubs in eight countries across three continents, he makes most of his money by organising stag weekends in Las Vegas.

He is football's version of the bogeyman, a victim somehow manipulated into an ogre. His fate, as a recklessly hyped young player who fell to earth when the world was supposedly at his feet, is woven into mythology as a warning to others. Eat your greens, boys, or your dreams will die in such outposts as Jagodina in Serbia, Rize in Turkey, or Kuopio in Finland.

Others may take Adu's name in vain, but pupils in year nine at St Ninian's High School in Kirkintilloch have selective hearing. They are enraptured by Karamoko

Dembele, their celebrity classmate. He is 13. He looks 10, plays for Celtic with sinuous grace against young men of 20, and according to those top-of-the-head, back-of-the-envelope calculations that come with the territory is on the verge of becoming a pubescent millionaire.

Dembele, Lambeth-born of Ivorian descent, moved to Govan in Glasgow with his family, aged 5. Like Adu, he has an early boot deal with Nike. Industry sources suggest any contract will be structured to spectacularly reward advancement; the sum of £100,000 for each of his first fifteen first-team appearances is mentioned, though with the usual caveat that such estimates tend to have the credibility of bookmakers' reports of their losses to a once-in-a-lifetime punt.

Barcelona may have demurred, because of their wariness of FIFA's cross-border recruitment restrictions, but Manchester City and Chelsea – football's topsy-turvy version of billionaire art collectors who obsessively buy up Old Masters for their private collections – are among those clubs looking for the upside in an association with a boy who has risen to prominence with stunning speed.

In September 2016, Dembele's performance in the St Kevin's Boys Academy Cup went viral on YouTube; comically small, he engaged the opposition in a pantomimic chase with the ball at his feet. In October, Celtic invited global attention by playing him in an under-20 match against Hearts. It was hard to reconcile the warning of Chris McCart, the club's head of youth, that 'it is crucial that we do not push him too far, too soon', with the subsequent feeding frenzy.

In November, Dembele was hailed by the Scottish tabloids as a 'Tartan Teen', a national treasure. Stewart Regan, chief executive of the Scottish FA, vowed to 'fight tooth and nail' to maintain his allegiance to Scotland, who gave him an under-16 debut in a 2–2 draw with Wales in the Victory Shield. Dembele also attended an England under-15 training camp, announcing on Instagram that he had been selected for a friendly against Turkey in December.

The haste with which the post was deleted suggested options were being kept open, but he duly made his debut in a 5–2 win at St George's Park. His pursuit by England was inevitable, since his birthplace fulfilled a rather obvious criterion. Dan Ashworth, the FA's technical director, is an unapologetic advocate of a recruitment strategy which takes into account family history, residential qualifications, and even refugee status:

'I am a recruiter by trade. That was my job at my previous club. Each individual case is different, but it is our duty to explore them all. It is a parallel process. Wales, Ireland and Scotland do it. They maybe don't have our pool of players and have to be creative. We, in England, do it in cricket, rugby and athletics. FIFA put the rules down for every country to follow. Why should we not follow them?

'Look at Diego Costa, a Brazilian-born player who

plays for Spain. Look at the Turks and Poles who play for Germany. It would be remiss of us not to look at every option. We have been a little bit lazy, looking only within England. Why not look at expat communities in the USA, for example? I don't get how we can be criticised for that. We will and we have unearthed one or two gems. Every other nation and every other sport is doing the same thing.'

In that vein, England were also pursuing Ben Woodburn, who fulfilled a schoolboy fantasy in a League Cup quarter-final against Leeds United by volleying a close-range goal at the Kop end to become Liverpool's youngest scorer. He captained Wales at under-17 level, and starred in an under-19 win against England in the late autumn, yet was born in the border town of Chester and qualified for Wales only through his maternal grandfather.

He represented a good bet. His mother Alison sought normality, successfully lobbying Liverpool to allow him to stay at the family home in the Cheshire village of Tarporley rather than moving in with house parents closer to the academy site in Kirby. The club hired a driver to take him to school, and ferry him to and from training.

Ashworth can't be blamed for the dispassionate application of logic, since it is a professional duty, but a quiet voice whispered caution. I had seen the Dembele movie before, and the script was difficult to digest. The main characters were a Somalian refugee and the taxi driver sitting across the table from me in a cabbie's café, appropriately situated in London's Smithfield meat market.

Sonny Pike had it all at 14. His legs were insured for £1 million. He starred in McDonald's advertisements, featured in Coca-Cola promotions and had a clothing deal with Paul Smith. By 17 he was suicidal, a rag doll tossed between five agents and other random opportunists. His relationship with his father was fractured beyond repair as his family life disintegrated.

Now, at 33, he has acquired the stability that eluded him during a truncated childhood, pockmarked by trials at clubs as diverse as Ajax and Grimsby Town. His smartphone carries photos of his infant son Beau and his 7-year-old daughter Freya, who accompanied him on a fun run in aid of the British Heart Foundation. Rather than an enforced diet of football, he is replenished by boxing. He reveres the fighters' bravery and feels at home in the earthiness of the East End's bear pit, York Hall.

He devoted three years to acquiring 'the Knowledge', and spends six days a week behind the wheel. He has the cabbie's twin obsessions – the iniquity of Uber and the brain-deadening relentlessness of the urban crawl – and slips into character as someone closer to child star Mickey Rooney than Wayne Rooney, who can loosely be described as a footballing contemporary.

His bitterness with his father, a builder portrayed as the ringmaster in a tawdry circus, is regurgitated in quiet, urgent sentences that run into one another, like a tumbling tug-of-war team. He seeks advice from me on a potential book project and seems resigned to his telephone number remaining in the contact lists of TV producers who freeze him in time as a curly-haired imp who could make a football float.

He worries about the sedentary nature of his job, the slight swell around his waist that signals impending middle age. His eyes are heavily rimmed, but bright when he speaks of a newly developed ambition to visit academies, to tell his story for the common good. 'I want to look forward,' he says, acutely aware that media interest in the Dembele case will drag him back.

Sky Sports were at the front of the queue: 'Karamoko is very talented but as I experienced myself, it can go from being a good thing to a bad thing pretty quickly. Once you get to the money side of things and people start earning, it can go very wrong. I'd imagine his parents have already had lots of new friends presenting themselves. They have to realise how all the focus, attention and distractions could mix up their son's feelings and affect his game. It's a lot for a kid of that age to take on.'

The former refugee, Islam Feruz, is only 21, but has a slight fleshiness around the face and shares Pike's world-weary caution. Comparisons with Dembele are a little more raw, but he freely admits, 'I had my head turned at fifteen,' when he joined Chelsea following the death of his mentor at Celtic, Tommy Burns, who had helped prevent the family being deported when he was 12.

His mother Aisha insisted that she, Islam's stepfather and three sisters claimed asylum in the UK after fleeing to Yemen from the Somalian conflict, but other sources suggested they lived in Tanzania. The family lived in a flat near Chelsea's Cobham training ground but despite his progress being monitored by a small army of scouts, his potential, as a fast forward with close skills, remained unfulfilled.

As it was four years since I had last seen him play, I asked some of those scouts for a read on his character: one referred to him as 'Billy Big Bollocks', while others spoke sympathetically of a quiet young man, a misguided victim of premature publicity. What was incontestable was that his career had meandered, worryingly.

He made a solitary substitute's appearance on loan to OFI Crete, lasted two days with Krylia Sovetov in the formerly closed Russian city of Samara, and returned home twenty-four hours after joining FC Aktobe in the Kazakhstan Premier League. He spent a total of sixteen minutes playing on loan for Blackpool, whose manager at the time, Lee Clark, was unamused by Islam's suggestion on social media that 'this team take more kick-offs than corners'.

The sense of drift and disarray was emphasised when a court summons was issued in June 2016 for his arrest when he failed to answer driving charges arising from a cruise through the Gorbals in his £80,000 Porsche. He pleaded guilty to driving without insurance, while disqualified, in a case heard at Glasgow's Justice of the Peace Court on February 1, 2017. Having made a solitary start in the first half of a season-long loan at Excel Mouscron, he had entered the year with a new adviser, David Wilson, Chelsea's scout in Scandinavia, and a vow to prove his maturity.

Chelsea gave him the chance to do so by recalling him from Belgium and sending him on another loan, to Swindon Town in League One, where, together with two other academy products, Charlie Colkett and Fankaty Dabo, he would come under the influence of the club's director of football Tim Sherwood, a noted promoter of young players.

Islam's admission that he should have stayed longer at Celtic underscored comparisons with Dembele: 'It all just seemed to happen at once and hit me overnight. There was so much publicity. It's hard to cope when you are so young. It's easy to put your faith in other people and it becomes easy to lose focus on football. People will now want to get involved with him and, no doubt, promise plenty. People will try to sweet-talk him.'

Ashworth, too, sees the bigger picture: 'We've all got a responsibility, the governing body, the clubs, the media, the parents as well. If you are a young boy or girl, put on a pedestal as a saviour who is going to earn millions of pounds for the family; blimey, that is pressure.

It is easy to point the finger at the clubs, but everyone goes into this knowing in the cold light of the day it is unlikely the player will get there.'

Manchester City warded off competition from Arsenal, Chelsea and Liverpool by paying an initial £175,000 for 13-year-old Southend United defender Finley Burns in January 2017. Phil Brown, Southend's first-team manager, was merely stating the obvious when he described the deal as 'an absolute punt' yet the names and improbable backstories, each with their own showreel on YouTube, kept coming.

Rashed Al-Hajjawi, a Palestinian born in Norway, signed for Juventus at the age of 10. Mustafa Kapı was launched into the market as a 14-year-old, through a first-team debut for Galatasaray. Liberian-born, Edmonton-raised striker Alphonso Davies was pursued by Manchester United after breaking into the MSL at 15 with Vancouver Whitecaps. Across Glasgow, at Rangers, the promise of 15-year-old Billy Gilmour had seven Premier League clubs, led by Chelsea, poised to start bidding at £1 million.

Another 13-year-old, Hannibal Mejri from FC Paris, had been snapped up by Adidas. A midfield player with David Luiz corkscrew curls, he is due to remain at the French national institute at Clairefontaine until June 2018, but has already had a trial at Arsenal. The usual suspects, Manchester City, Manchester United, Chelsea and Liverpool, have also registered their interest.

His father Lofti, a former Tunisian Second Division player, has spoken of his ambition that Hannibal will become a lawyer or doctor rather than a footballer 'with a chickpea in his head'. He told *Le Parisien*: 'Football is an execrable world. This environment is full of incompetent and dishonest people. Our duty is to protect our child.'

It is a myth to refer to hidden gems, secret starlets. Though Jude Bellingham, yet another 13-year-old, was below the mainstream media radar at Birmingham City, his name was spoken of with something close to awe in certain football circles. The biggest clubs sought unsuccessfully to entice him, and his family, with the guarantee of a life-changing two-year professional contract, to commence on his seventeenth birthday.

Agents, some inexperienced so-called 'plant pots' but most of them sufficiently established to know better, stalked him on social media. He was even approached on Instagram by a Premier League star, seeking contact details on behalf of his representatives. All were rebuffed by his father, a man of firm principles and far-sighted priorities.

The duty of care in such a febrile atmosphere was shared by Kristjaan Speakman, who became the youngest academy manager in England, at 32, when he was promoted to the post by Birmingham City in 2011. His relationship with the Bellingham family, fostered over six years, is based on mutual trust, common respect and a holistic approach to the boy's welfare.

Speakman is direct and to the point: 'Jude embodies everything that is good and bad about youth development. He is an outstandingly nice boy whose mum and dad have done a fantastic job with him. People are materialistic and want to commoditise him, but they [his parents] will never allow that to happen. He's a child. Let him be crap, let him be brilliant, but just let him play.

'Football is starting to forget why people get up in the morning. As coaches we want to get out there on the field, and get the balls out. The fans love a local boy playing for their team. The boy wants to play for his local club, and, one day, for England. I know this sounds corny, but that is Jude's dream. Money is trying to supersede that dream. We are trying to share it.

'There are too many people in the game who think you will come running when they offer lots of money. I can understand the temptation for some parents to take life-changing amounts, and my relationship with Jude's parents has to be authentic, so we can express and communicate what is best for him.

'There is a small team of people working their socks off to try and protect him from everything that is going on around him. As a club, and as individuals, we have certain principles and values, so for a senior player, one of his heroes, to text him directly on behalf of his agent is unfair, unrealistic and manipulative.'

One independent agent, not involved in Jude's

case – and, to be clear, not making a direct comparison with it – gave an insight into the nature of the frenzy. He discovered, to his cost, the perils of association with a prodigy when, after spending several years nurturing two schoolboys until they were on the fringe of their Premier League teams, he was powerless to prevent them being spirited away by another agent.

He had no means of redress since, under FIFA rules, players can pursue a deal using whatever representative they wish, regardless of whether they had signed a contract with anyone else. Members of the extended family are often involved in the deceit; it has been known for players to play off up to eight agents against one another in search of the most lucrative deal:

'It is more cut-throat than ever, because there is no support from FIFA and the FA. They've basically made the decision to allow everyone to do whatever they want. Agents use the loophole about commercial representation under sixteen to build a relationship with parents. Then they start to mess with their heads, "He's got his boots, so he is well on the way to being a pro."

'Parents speak to each other. For most, their first thought is the money, so they are very easily led. The young boy does what his mum and dad tell him. Big agencies take up to ten boys from the same club, knowing all they need is for one of those ten to pop up in the first team. Where's the mentoring? Where's the guidance?

'The agent doesn't know if the parent is talking to

another agent behind his back. Is that right? Of course not, but the temptation is to make a few quid knowing most of these lads will never be seen again. The clubs play their part. They big people up, making them feel good. They fawn over a player, but when the time comes to say goodbye they'll be given a DVD or put on a circular. It's a nonsense.

'The good agent shares a vision, sets out a pathway, knowing that if it is followed it will benefit him in the long run. It is about managing expectations, looking for market value while giving the family an idea of how it can go, good or bad. At fourteen you are only just beginning to see a picture of what a player could be. The system is killing the kids. It's sad to see. The only innocent one in the whole process is usually the boy who just wants to play football.'

The shamelessness of the process is still startling. A senior figure at a Premier League club confided that he was approached at an airport by a close relative of an England international, quietly testing the market for a move. He was promised first refusal, just as he had been when the player was 15, and the family were looking to launch his professional career with a seven-figure contract.

The relative's indifference, when reminded that he had reneged on that apparently forgotten promise, after using the club's interest to trigger an auction, was telling. He evidently felt he didn't need to care, since he was a seller in a seller's market. Cash outweighed courtesy and common decency. There were mouths to feed, lifestyles to fund. The player needed to pay for the chaotic communal playground of a villa overlooking the Caribbean.

Just as little care is devoted to the truth, scant attention is paid to the complexity and humanity of a boy's development. Jude Bellingham was being described, on the grapevine, as the 'New Wayne Rooney', a lazy piece of headline-seizing shorthand that was, in a football context, ill-considered and borderline illiterate.

Jude is known internally as 'Project 22', since Speakman and his coaching staff are seeking to develop him in the modern idiom, as a player who can play in a variety of roles – namely as a number four, eight or ten. He has already trained with the first team and Speakman is looking beyond the perceived probability of him supplanting Trevor Francis, who was 16 years and 139 days old when he made his debut, as the club's youngest player.

'When, in say five years' time, he is in the first team he has got to have all the component parts. He has to have the clear head to play as a four, the box-to-box qualities of an eight, and the cleverness and creativity of a ten. He needs the challenge of taking on substantially different roles. Combine those qualities, and you have the project, to produce a world-class player.'

Speakman's emotionally intelligent approach involves chaperoning boys to big matches and honing social skills through restaurant visits. Should a player have a boot deal, he asks the parents to maintain the benign deception they paid for them. The fact that eighteen academy graduates have made the first team since 2010 is statistically impressive, even without taking into account supplementary case studies such as Demarai Gray.

He sent a simple text to Speakman – 'I got picked at 20' – on January 4, 2016, when Leicester City activated the £3.7 million release clause in his contract and signed him from Birmingham. The message provided cryptic confirmation that a private prediction, shared between coach and player, had come to pass. Gray made his debut for Leicester at Tottenham in the FA Cup six days later, and within five months had a Premier League winners' medal. He cites England under-21 teammate Nathan Redmond as a key influence and is a regular visitor to Birmingham on his days off.

'He feels like he is coming home,' Speakman says, with an endearing sense of pride. 'Coaches say they have a relationship with a player, but that has to mean more than taking a session. I have known Demarai since he was an under-9. He was a bit of a silver medallist, not quite in the top group, but I can say, hand on heart, that I saw him as a Premier League player at fourteen.

'We knew what he would look like at twenty. He was a great kid, with all the athletic components he needed. He was a late developer, with a June birthday, but he loved learning. He had a single mum, but the family structure was strong. She kept him grounded. I knew so much about him I could see where he was going.

'Players don't mind an uncomfortable journey provided they know how, why and where they are going. Outside, people looked at what he couldn't do. They said he couldn't run, and wasn't particularly quick. But we loaded him with belief. We developed almost a parental relationship so we could be constructively critical. We had a capacity to hit the reset button and get on with a new day.'

As head coach of England's under-15 squad, Kevin Betsy will be a complementary figure in Bellingham's development. He has played in every division, from the Premier League to the Conference, but has had a strong sense of vocation ever since he worked in McDonald's, 'flipping burgers', before Woking sold him to Fulham at the age of 18.

At 38, having been recognised for the excellence of his coaching at Fulham's academy, he exudes energy and an intelligence tempered by realism. He has augmented the lessons of his fifteen-year playing career, distilling the principles of an eclectic range of coaches and managers that includes John McGovern, Paul Hart, Jean Tigana, Christian Damiano, Steve Wigley, Steve Parkin, Kevin Keegan and John Gorman. Self-education has continued across Europe, with particular focus on study visits to Barcelona, Bayern Munich and Ajax:

'As a pro, you get lazy. You finish your career and you

think, right, I'll be a coach now, but it's a different ball game. So, for me, it was about understanding the profession, learning the trade from the under-9s all the way up to where I felt I needed to get to. I was respectful of the trade. Coaching is an art. You're a teacher. You're not a dictator.

'You have to know the person. Your first connection needs to be with the boy, so you understand him in the greatest of detail. I ask what his background is like, where does he live, how does he train, does he see his family, what's his history, his heritage. Until I know that, I can't coach him to maximise his potential. Once I do, I can start tapping into the psychological aspect of the role and develop the player.

'You have to try your best to educate the parents. Some come from a tough background. I've been a player. I've been on the other side. I know how it feels when they ask whether they should stay local and wait for the money, or take it when it is available. I try to teach long term. Get the money at twenty-two, twenty-three, when they've played a hundred league games, rather than at sixteen. It's a bigger reward, for better development.

'I understand the pathway because I played at every level. I gained experience with different managers, different styles of football. My perspective is one of a late developer. I was really small, still a dot in football terms at fifteen or sixteen. It wasn't until I reached eighteen that I grew into my body. It means when I'm analysing players, I'm always more patient.'

He believes EPPP has seen a step change in the sophistication of youth development, but appreciates the value of old-school attitudes, such as Paul Hart's insistence on shin pads being worn during combative training sessions. For context, he rummages through the memory on his smartphone, and produces a photograph of a minibus in a car park filled with luxury first-team coaches.

'This was us, at the Premier League finals when I was with Fulham's under-16s. Players from other teams were a bit sniggery. Our lads were a little self-conscious about arriving in the minibus, but that set the tone of my team talks. It's not about how you dress, what haircut you've got, what earring you've got, what boots you've got, what bus you turn up in. It's about what you do on the grass, how you conduct yourself around the place. That's all that matters. We won the tournament.

'The traditional loan system stress-tests players, through games and experiences. Travelling on a bus that's not great, up north, League Two, maybe no pre-match meal, playing under lights on an average pitch. I was no different. I took things for granted that I shouldn't. At Fulham in the Premier League I was in the bubble, so when Steve Parkin wanted to take me to Rochdale I said no.

'Six months later he was at Barnsley. He called me again. I said yes. It was the best experience of my life because I was playing football, in front of a crowd. In the end, I sacrificed my contract at Fulham. I had two years left but I wanted to go and play and learn my trade. It was a great decision. In a football context, on the grass, you can be pure, you can be free.

'Off the pitch it is more difficult. We've needed to police the agents, because players were getting tapped up in what is a public arena. It is not necessary. It is not right. We are trying to create a learning environment, an environment of excellence. We have a duty of care to do our best for our kids, to provide them with a setting that is safe and comfortable.'

Inevitably, given the conflicting priorities of club and country, there is an ambassadorial element to his job. He visits academies to establish connections with club coaches on a personal and professional level, supplementing a full-time FA education officer who liaises on academic issues. Players with disciplinary problems at school are not considered for international selection.

There can be difficulties with players on relocation packages, who take time to adjust to a different city and a new peer group. Betsy speaks of players 'taking ownership' of their development, a buzz phrase which in essence means committing to their craft, but is aware of the sensitivities of boys whose sporting eminence can breed envy and resentment.

'In my experience players love one-to-ones. They love relationships. They want to be talked to. Perhaps we haven't been giving them the autonomy to speak, to have a voice, to come up with new ideas. They're the ones on the pitch. They see it, they feel it. They are very clever human beings. As coaches we think we know everything, or at least we used to. We don't.'

My mind wandered back to a Saturday morning in September 2016, in which the lawnmower drone of low-flying light aircraft, struggling in strong crosswinds, provided a suitably surreal soundtrack to one of the strangest matches of the season. The scoreline, a 6–0 defeat for a side containing aspiring scholars, was both simplistic and deceptive.

It is no exaggeration to suggest they were extremely fortunate to avoid a double-figure humiliation, but the result was utterly unimportant, since life had taken precedence and put football into true perspective. Across the pitch, backstories coalesced and mutated. Coaches, with their tactics boards and copybook compassion, were powerless in the face of physical and psychological immaturity.

One boy had what can only be described as an extended toddler-tantrum, angrily half-volleying the ball at his own goalkeeper from just inside his own half in what could easily have been interpreted as a deliberate attempt to score an own goal. He was all smiles after being substituted at half-time, when a sports psychologist joined a semi circle of support staff. The pressure on him to excel had eased, even though his performance would ensure his eventual release.

Elsewhere, a defender prone to periodically bursting

into tears was being watched by his seriously ill father. A midfield player, slovenly in possession and sullen in nature, was merely recreating the mood that drove his schoolteachers to distraction. The most assertive player, who at least attempted to galvanise the team after half-time, was channelling the diligence and determination he brought to his role as a carer to younger siblings in a fragmented family.

A Spanish striker, starved of service at the conclusion of a week's trial, never stood a chance. His plight paled alongside that of the most promising player in the group, who was absent, mourning the murder of his best friend. When he returned he did well enough to be retained, but he was to lose another friend to gang-related violence later in the year.

Coaches attempt to create emotional bonds with fragile young men, but they are also hostages to fortune. I will carry with me the smile of that wannabe malcontent, as he idly kicked a ball around with unused substitutes behind the home dugout. It took weeks to emerge, but his rationale for his behaviour was perverse, stark and bleakly comprehensible.

In his scrambled brain, he apparently reasoned that he could have tried his best and been found wanting, anyway. Now the pressure was off. He embraced failure, relished its release. I shuddered to think of the price he might pay, in years to come, in the dark, pre-dawn moments of self-reproach.

16

Work Hard, Dream Big

Complimentary chocolate bars turned to ash in the mouths of fifty-one scouts, eagerly availing themselves of Wycombe Wanderers' hospitality in the Honours Lounge at Adams Park. The team sheet contained the barely digestible news that Ryan Sessegnon, the primary reason for many a visit on this misty Monday night, was on the bench for England under-19s against Bulgaria.

There were distractions in the form of Tottenham's diminutive Marcus Edwards and Trent Alexander-Arnold, an athletic right back being fast-tracked by Liverpool. Looking to the longer term, Chelsea's Dujon Sterling, quick, strong and at ease playing in an unfamiliar role on the right of a front three supporting the main striker, confirmed his ability to impose himself on important occasions. His ninety-second-minute header secured a fortunate 2–1 win.

Tom Davies, born on the day David Beckham was sent off as England lost to Argentina on penalties at the 1998 World Cup in France, had a nineties haircut and a sixties habit of playing with his socks rolled down. Ronald Koeman, who was introducing him to Everton's first team with increasing confidence, was taken by his tenacity and his capacity to pass incisively, but some observers wondered whether his fractional lack of pace would preclude a career at the highest level.

It was the sort of match in which momentary inferences of weakness, and inflections of mood, meant more than they perhaps should. Eyebrows were raised and opinions hardened, for instance, when Manchester City's central defender Cameron Humphreys appeared to flinch and turn his head fractionally away from contact during an aerial duel.

In an episode that seemed to support doubts about the delicate nature of some young players, Aston Villa winger André Green collapsed extravagantly under minimal challenge. He clutched a fluorescent-booted foot, which was left to hang limply as, describing a windmilling action with his index fingers, he demanded his substitution.

In truth, he did not appear to be a candidate for emergency surgery immediately after the match, when he signed autographs at the tunnel entrance without discernible discomfort. The rationale of his evident reticence was simple to follow, even if it offended old-school sensibilities. Since Villa were about to appoint yet another new first-team manager, Steve Bruce, the last thing he needed was to pick up an injury on international duty.

The compensation in his dying beetle impression, for the men clustered at the back of the smaller stand, was that his departure paved the way for Sessegnon's appearance. I'd been promised by Mel Johnson, sage of the scouts' tea room, that the Fulham defender would make me 'purr', and though he played out of position he changed the tempo and shape of the game.

Normally a left back, he began wide on the left of the three, where his pace, close control and aggression allowed him to dominate the opposition full back. His instinctive appreciation of space, and capacity to see and supply deft angled passes through a slightly square defence, also marked him out as a potential playmaker.

The youngest member of the team, he was only 16. He joined Fulham with his twin brother Steven at the age of 8, and became the first player born in the twenty-first century to score a senior goal, in his second Championship appearance for the club, a 2–2 draw with Cardiff in August 2016. In terms of market value, he was being compared to Patrick Roberts, the winger Fulham sold to Manchester City for £12 million at the age of 18 in July 2015.

Little wonder, then, that Mike Rigg, Fulham's sporting director, and his head of talent identification and recruitment, Malcolm Elias, one of the formative figures in Gareth Bale's development at Southampton, were on point, protecting their investment. The stature of the scouts sitting around them, and the presence of representatives from RB Leipzig, the new force in the Bundesliga, suggested the chase was on.

Chelsea sent Mark Ridgway, their area scouting co-ordinator, Manchester United their youth specialist, John Lambert. Liverpool's chief scout, Barry Hunter, was in the same row as Alan Watson, Manchester City's UK scouting and recruitment manager. There were familiar faces from Arsenal, Leicester City and another dozen Premier League clubs. Some, like Middlesbrough's Lee Adam, understood their place in the financial pecking order and pragmatically preferred to study a robust Bulgarian team for signs of unheralded promise.

Foretelling the future is, of course, a perilous business. If it were simply a matter of the consistent application of natural talent, Zeli Ismail would have had a greater chance of fulfilling the prediction of his former academy manager at Wolves, and becoming football's first £100 million player. Instead he was enduring a dispiriting sequence of twelve successive defeats at Bury, where he was attempting to revive a faltering career.

Neil Smillie, a former Wycombe Wanderers manager back on eerily familiar territory that evening, knows more than most about the intricacies of development. His seven-club playing career began at Crystal Palace and included an FA Cup final appearance for Brighton & Hove Albion in 1983; he managed Gillingham, and became Nike's head of talent identification in 1999, soon after being sacked by Wycombe.

His role is to detect and deliver the best young players, so they can contribute to what is widely acknowledged as a marketing masterclass, fusing money and modernity so that a pair of football boots becomes a personal statement. The sums involved in endorsement deals might have changed – 'offering five grand to a boy on thirty thousand a week isn't going to register' – but the essence of his job, recognising attributes and projecting their evolution, is constant.

He requires diplomatic skills to deal with parental demands, which are becoming markedly more extreme, and has that scout's knack of subtly judging the correct level of information to share. When we were introduced by Johnson, close to the boardroom in which he was dismissed in another life, he engaged easily and quickly asked me to name the young players who had impressed me most during my research.

A slow smile broke across his face, as warming as a winter sunrise, when I mentioned Jude Bellingham at Birmingham City. He positively beamed when I spoke of the astonishingly mature leadership qualities of Tommy Doyle at Manchester City, and the quickness of Jadon Sancho's brain and feet, as a right-footed left winger.

'Ah, Jadon can be anything he wants to be,' he said, recommending I take a look at another member of the England under-17 squad which, together with the under-20s, is regarded as the best group in terms of depth, quality and potential. Manchester United's Angel Gomes, born in London when his Portuguese father Gil was playing non-league football at the end of a career that peaked at the 1991 mini World Cup, was showing signs that he might develop into the best number ten of his generation.

His name was being mentioned alongside that of Marcus Rashford in the echo chamber of football gossip but, as Smillie wryly remarked, a lot of people at United doubted Rashford's ability to train on when he first saw him 'as a twelve-year-old dot'. The strength of Rashford's family unit, critical when Manchester City attempted to recruit him at 14, was an enduring lesson.

Given the speed of his ascent, it is sobering to realise Rashford's natural peer group remains the under-19s. Gareth Southgate admits he has to be aware of the dynamics of promoting players from age-group football to the senior squad because 'the social bit, sitting with people you don't know at dinner, makes it difficult to feel natural. If you don't feel natural it makes it really hard to train and play as well as you might, because you feel people are watching everything you do.'

Of the England squad beaten 3–2 by Germany in the quarter-final of the under-17 World Cup in Mexico in

2011, only Raheem Sterling has a full cap. That provides a benchmark for the 'Class of 2016', which startled the football world by defeating Germany 8–1 to win the Croatia Cup in early October.

Gomes and Sancho scored within eight minutes, a platform built upon by further first-half goals by Phil Foden of Manchester City and Chelsea's George McEachran, younger brother of Josh, the midfield player who has come to symbolise the too-much-too-soon generation. Liverpool's Rhian Brewster scored twice before the rout was completed by Chelsea's Callum Hudson-Odoi and Reading's Danny Loader, who was one of six second-half substitutes.

As a player from a Championship club, Loader was the exception that, in an increasingly elitist youth system, proves an expensively applied rule. Manchester City provided four of the starting side against Germany, Chelsea three. Analysis by the YouthHawk website, of the allegiances of players called up for England across six age groups in August and September 2016, confirmed the trend.

Chelsea provided twenty players, Manchester City fourteen. Arsenal's total of sixteen included seven selected for the under-16s, whose international assimilation programme – designed to offer experiences of different cultures, climates and conditions – accelerated later in the year with two friendlies in Brazil, a win and a loss. Tottenham and Everton supplied ten each but

Liverpool and Southampton only three apiece, two fewer than Fulham, Manchester United and Wolves.

Arsenal's Reiss Nelson, who signed his first professional contract on December 10, 2016, his seventeenth birthday, typifies a player in transition. His potential had been confirmed in the summer's European under-17 championships, when he scored nine times in ten games. Nimble, skilful and dexterous, but prone to occasionally overplaying, he benefitted from the physical and mental demands of regular training sessions with the first-team squad.

Intriguingly, Barcelona scouts, monitoring his progress, suggested he would be employed at full back in their system because of his athleticism. His education, enhanced by first-hand evidence of the ability of senior players to think quickly, move intelligently and take the right decision under pressure, has encompassed coaching duties at Arsenal's Hale End academy, which he joined at the age of 7 after being spotted playing for Moonshot, a junior club in Catford.

It is a delicate process. Kevin Betsy's workshop sessions with the younger age groups are primarily visual, and scenario-based: 'Even though it's in retrospect, they need to see things. "OK, why did I move it there, why didn't I do that? If we're trying to break the block, why not overload it in the middle?" You let them see, test, and if they fail, you have to correct them, give them advice. They're not coaches, they're football players, but you have to give them an understanding.

'We talk about what teamwork looks like, but what does that mean? It's all phrases, but if you don't show people, they don't know what's right. It might be a video clip of you shaking hands with an opponent after the game, or even a player not doing it. You know, you've lost a game and the camera is still rolling. Three or four won't shake hands with the referee or the opposition and just go in, down the tunnel.

'So the next time you've got a meeting, you don't lambast anyone, but you subtly put messages to them about what's right and what's wrong. It's about respect. Wearing that badge, it's a duty of care to the next generation. Your status is already elevated because you're playing in the England shirt and you've got to present yourself in the manner that is respectful of that.'

The danger of over-indulgence is marked, and there were signs of inconsistency at another under-19 international, a 1–1 draw with Holland at Telford United, earlier in the season. Though technical director Dan Ashworth was in a crowd swelled by schoolchildren on half-term, lack of FA staff meant that a well-meaning functionary from the host club was left to announce that players and management were unavailable for post-match interviews because 'they have to eat'.

Since the teams had staged a penalty shootout, won 8–7 by England, to try to recreate match-day pressure, it seemed puzzling, to say the least, that they were shielded from the sort of scrutiny to which they will be subjected, whether they like it or not, as their careers progress. Their world contains greater perils than a scribbler with a sense of curiosity.

Karim Fatih is the founder of A Better Perspective, a self-styled gambling and integrity consultancy that works with educational staff at such clubs as Watford, West Ham, Brighton, Charlton and Derby. A former professional gambler who 'returned to the real world' because he missed 'contact with other human beings', he believes young footballers are being targeted due to their premature wealth.

Though casinos cannot legally admit clients under 18, he alleges academy scholars are bombarded with marketing material promising up to £1,000 in free chips as introductory VIP offers. He highlights the disproportionate numbers of athletes being treated at the Sporting Chance Clinic for gambling addiction, some 70 per cent of all entrants.

A 2014 survey of almost 350 footballers and cricketers concluded that around 6 per cent merited the description 'problem gamblers', more than three times the rate in the wider population. The majority of these were senior players, but Graeme Law, a former York City player who researched gambling in football for his PhD, tells of an 18-year-old player jeopardising his first-team place by playing distractedly after losing £2,000 on the bus to an away game.

Fatih counsels academy players on the seductive

culture of betting and reflects, 'I see a lot of boys under twenty-one who are hardened gamblers. They think they know it all, but actually they know so little.' He blames the 'search for the buzz that playing gives them', and draws attention to the detachment inherent in the youth system:

'The spirit of the group tends to be in inverse proportion to the quality of facilities. I see boys and staff working their nuts off in a normal environment. There's not the rigour elsewhere, in the equivalent of a seven-star hotel. I see teenagers who are excellently educated, very polite, but there is very little going on behind their eyes. The word that springs to mind is "robotic". It seems they are on a treadmill. They do everything unquestioningly.'

Southgate is aware of the balance to be struck between individuality and conformity, especially in the older age groups. England's under-20s, preparing for the 2017 World Cup in South Korea, have a players' leadership group that coalesces around Bristol City's French-developed central defender Taylor Moore and Newcastle United goalkeeper Freddie Woodman. Southgate sees independence of thought as 'a natural evolution of how they work'.

Ashworth expands the point: 'Each team sets their mantra. What does it mean to come and represent England? What are we looking to achieve? What will we accept and what will we not accept? It is not about a prehistoric code of conduct, do this and do that. They have to set out what they want. They have to love coming here. They have got to be desperate to come back, devastated if they are not picked. We are trying to instil that pride of playing for your country.'

The manifestation of that pride, the visualisation of a shared ambition, is an A4 laminated sheet, taped to the bathroom mirrors of each member of England's under-20 squad whenever they are together. A product of their leadership group, it features a photograph of their ultimate prize, the mini World Cup, and a simple list of pledges of professionalism. It may sound twee, but it works.

'The picture of the cup is there because every morning we wake up and have to see it,' Moore explained. 'It reminds us we are capable of winning it. The rest is basics. Telling people they are not doing things right if it is going to help the team. Cleaning the changing rooms, putting kit around the right way before handing it back to the kit man. Arriving five minutes early for every meeting, every mealtime. Getting into the routine of doing stuff in a correct manner. Small details, but every little helps.'

Moore is blond and tall, angular and eager. His voice has similar inflections to that of Southgate; it is a soft, sensible monotone that hints at maturity beyond his years. His childhood exile in France might have been parentally driven, but in an era in which very few senior professionals have the courage to leave the feather-bedded lifestyle of the Premier League, his example is instructive.

Having already been spotted by West Ham, he moved to Le Touquet at the age of 7, when his parents Barry and Julia sought to combine a business opportunity with enhanced quality of life in an elegant coastal resort. 'Chucked into a French school not speaking a word of the language', with his younger brother Keaton, he used football to aid his assimilation.

Racing Club de Lens, the region's powerhouse, first attempted to recruit him from junior club AS Etaples at the age of 11. Since the club was ninety minutes away, and acceptance of an academy place was dependent on moving to a boarding school closely associated with Lens, he asked for a year's grace before entering into such a demanding environment.

'You're twelve. You arrive there with a suitcase even bigger than you, and have got to get used to things. It is scary, but at the same time very exciting. Yes, you are leaving home, leaving your parents, but you are going to be with your teammates 24/7, playing football every day. There are some tough kids, from tough backgrounds, but togetherness builds.'

Like many French clubs, Lens recruit heavily from the African diaspora around Paris. Academy regime is strict; lessons are taken from 8 a.m. to 4 p.m., when the boys make a fifteen-minute journey to the training ground. They eat, spend an hour on school homework, and then train for up to two hours. Lights are out, back at the boarding school by 9.30. They are allowed to use their phones for only an hour a day.

'The coaches are demanding. Though they want to turn us into the best pros possible, they sometimes forget we are human beings as well. They don't think about the fact we are twelve or thirteen and have not been home for four weeks. Sometimes you need that little bit of freedom and encouragement. There's a lot to deal with.

'You are living with thirty-five other boys, and having to be careful about what gets stolen from the changing rooms. You get judged by what you do rather than by who you are. That massively helped me grow up, more than people think. I love my family, but you feel independent. You are in an adult world. It hardens you.'

That so-called pre-formation stage is completed at 16, when survivors of the system are housed in the club's training complex, and start to study for their baccalaureate at a new school. The lifestyle is marginally more relaxed, since good habits are deemed to have already been instilled. Players are expected to be responsible for their actions, and are conditioned to unforced demonstrations of respect.

They stand whenever a stranger enters the dressing room. In public areas, such as a hotel lobby, they are expected to shake hands with everyone they encounter, 'whether that is three people, or a hundred'. Professional contracts are awarded sparingly, a practice which ironically plays into the hands of predatory English clubs.

'One, maybe two or three in the same generation will sign a professional contract. They put everything in place for you, but it is up to you whether you really want it or not. Desire is a big factor. A lot of young boys now think it is all going to come easy. When it gets tough they really don't know what to do. They don't make the right choices sometimes.

'You do wonder, what if I had a normal life? You watch your mates doing normal things and have to know what you want. You tell yourself, in a few years it will be worth it. That's where I consider myself stronger than most of the boys I came through the system with. I had less of a comfort zone.

'I am not going to knock the English system but there is a lot more money here than in any other European country. Sometimes there is so much, we don't know what to do with it. That could be a good thing or a bad thing, I don't know, but there is definitely lot more reward without achievement.'

Moore made his first-team debut at 17, in front of 50,000 spectators drawn by the Derby du Nord against Lille on May 3, 2015. Lens' relegation from Ligue 1 was already assured, and he played out of position at right back. Apart from a moment of panic when he realised he had to take throw-ins, a disconcertingly new experience, he set up the goal in a 3–1 defeat and acquitted himself well. Yet the club was in turmoil, created by major shareholder Hafiz Mammadov, an Azerbaijani businessman, and the mood was sour.

He grew up fast: 'In a senior dressing room, when stuff is going wrong, you see people – managers, coaches and players – panic. Some are coming to the end of their careers, and don't know what is around the corner for them. You sense a certain fear. Though it is a team game, everyone realises it is every man for himself.'

Called up by England, he featured in the winning team in the 2014 European under-17 championship in Malta, where Holland were beaten on penalties in the final. The nucleus of that group has progressed through the international system, but the lack of conformity in their club careers since then is symptomatic of an age at which, according to Southgate, 'they are starting to get the reality of a first-team manager telling them what's needed to get in his team'.

Patrick Roberts discovered that even scoring against his parent club, for Celtic against Manchester City in the Champions League, is not enough to pierce Pep Guardiola's carapace of professional reserve. Josh Onomah, who first trained with Tottenham's first team at 14, was marking time after his breakthrough season in 2015–16.

Joe Gomez, one of those quietly mentioned in the England coaches' room as having the requisite qualities to evolve into a senior international, was rebuilding his career at Liverpool following a thirteen-month absence in which his recovery from a torn ACL was complicated by the diagnosis of tendinopathy in his Achilles.

Southampton's Josh Sims was named man of the match in his Premier League debut, but Adam Armstrong had been sent to Barnsley to pay his dues in the Championship by Rafa Benítez, his manager at Newcastle. Dominic Solanke, his England strike partner, was embroiled in protracted contract negotiations with Chelsea, complicated by incorrect reports that he had demanded a long-term contract worth £50,000 a week.

Solanke's dilemma, of seeking supposed market value in terms of his earnings at the expense of first-team exposure, had wider implications. His case rested on his worth as a bargaining chip to a club which farmed thirty-eight players out on loan in the first half of the 2016–17 season, and used the academy as the sort of counter-productive, cost-efficient profit centre inadvertently encouraged by UEFA's Financial Fair Play strategy.

The theory, that clubs should not be penalised for investment in community schemes, infrastructure projects and youth development, appears reasonable enough. But in reality, it gives them carte blanche to sign far more young players than they will ever need; some will be hawked in a secondary market that resembles a supercharged car-boot sale.

Winners' medals from the FA Youth Cup are of

marginal compensation to a generation at risk of concussion from repeated contact with the glass ceiling that tends to descend at Chelsea on or around a player's eighteenth birthday. Solanke, who benefitted from a second phase of development at Vitesse Arnhem, faced a career-defining decision without being given confidence or context by his employers. It seemed likely that he would opt to leave at the end of the season, with any transfer fee being decided by the arcane Professional Football Compensation Committee.

For some, like Chelsea's Izzy Brown, rehabilitating at Rotherham before progressing to Huddersfield Town following a disappointing season in the Netherlands, exile highlights immaturity. In others, it broadens horizons, contracts the field of vision so that distractions are marginalised. Mandela Egbo, another product of Steadman Scott's Afewee project in Brixton, required patience and diligence at Borussia Mönchengladbach; when Tafari Moore, the dreadlocked Arsenal full back, approached his namesake Taylor for advice about moving on loan to Utrecht, the response was unequivocal:

'I told him, "It will do you a world of good. Not only will you come out of it a better player, but you will come out as a better man." Taff was very excited. The boys are very curious, and I suppose I helped the group in a way when I arrived. I was the different one, not the special one, and thought it might be difficult to settle, but we wanted to learn from each other.

'French coaches work on repetition. It is very controlled. I was expecting the English game to be less technical, but the boys were really good, showing high technique at speed and intensity. I know there is this perception of a washbag mentality, and results can make it easier to look at young players and say this or that is wrong, but I've found most of the boys have their heads firmly on their shoulders.'

The critical difference between Moore and the majority of his peers is that his experience of a cruel, claustrophobic first-team environment is vivid, rather than hypothetical. His return to England in August 2016, to join a young Bristol City squad assembled by a young manager, Lee Johnson, was a direct result of upheaval typically associated with the senior game.

He failed to feel the love from Alain Casanova, the former Toulouse manager, who replaced Antoine Kombouaré at the end of a fractious season, in which Lens finished sixth in Ligue 2 and Moore became vulnerable to political positioning. Moore was judged harshly during the new man's summer stocktake, when he was absent, captaining England at the European under-19 championships in Germany.

'I got caught in a bit of a trap between negative mentalities. The new coach came in and within five days he said, "Listen, I don't want you here. I don't need you. You've been away at the Euros and I don't like your attitude." It was hard, having spent eight years at the club, giving blood, sweat and tears, having him tell me, "You are out."

'It was unexpected on one level, but looking back over my last year there I was caught up in so much jealousy and negativity from people who once wanted me to succeed. There was a change, an incredible envy. My parents got it as well. I'm lucky I have a stable family. It was getting out of hand. Some of the things that were said, and done, were just ridiculous.

'I had gone from being the next big thing at Lens, to the one that no one really wanted. I began to ask myself, what have I done wrong? I'm captain of England, playing well, training well, and working hard. They started leaving me out of the squad for silly little details, a bad pass in training or a recovery run they said wasn't good enough. The coach came for me, in front of the whole team. After a while the politics became too much to live with.'

Moore's next trial, after his return to England, was to be sent on loan to Bury for the second half of the season, but few successful footballers are frightened fawns. The fortitude of Hull City's Moses Odubajo, another England under-20 graduate, was second nature to him. The pain and uncertainty of two serious knee injuries in three months paled alongside that endured when his mother Esther, a nurse, died from malaria when he was aged 13. He and his older brother Tom hid their plight from social services, and survived on Tom's monthly salary of £300 as a scholar at Barnet's academy.

Yet many young players, thrown into a maelstrom of insecurity and inconsistency, fail for want of a credible mentor. Freddie Woodman has found his in Steve Black, a conditioning coach and motivational speaker hailed as 'a second father' by rugby legend Jonny Wilkinson and as 'a spiritual guide' by Joey Barton.

Garrulous, engaging and keenly observant, Black can best be described as a People Whisperer. A proponent of *kaizen*, the Japanese philosophy of continual improvement, he works informally, often scribbling furiously on a notepad as he draws out the personality traits and charts the value systems of his subjects.

His sessions with Woodman are as likely to be held in a garden centre's coffee shop as a gymnasium. He relishes the instinctive curiosity and relentless work ethic of the young goalkeeper, who has Southgate as a godfather because of the England manager's enduring friendship with his father Andy. The tone of their relationship was set at their first meeting, when Woodman was 16.

'What do you want to do?' Black asked.

'I want people to regard me as one of the best goalkeepers in the world.'

'I'm with you one hundred per cent, son.'

Woodman is energised by the memory; unlike some of his age, he is unabashed by his idealism, comfortable with the scale of his ambition. He has the conviction of the convert, a freedom of expression which hints at the distinctive character of those attracted to goalkeeping's perverse mixture of isolation and centrality:

'I pick people's brains, pepper them with questions. I

like to do extra, on and off the pitch. I'd looked at sports psychology, but didn't find anything I felt I needed to make me mentally stronger. Then I met Blackie. He is simply the best at what he does, even if it is sometimes difficult to explain exactly what he does.

'It's weird, so different. I had a six-month spell when we didn't work together. I didn't go off the rails or anything, but I was definitely not as focused. Without him, I felt vulnerable. Then we got back together and broke down my career goals. My mindset changed, so that I felt unstoppable. Nothing was going to get in my way. It is me on the pitch, but Blackie's voice is in my head.'

Black encourages him to dissect his matches into five-minute segments, to guard against the magnification of mistakes. A mental device to consign any errors into the past as soon as practically possible, it is designed to reflect the exposed nature of the job. Significantly, when we spoke, Woodman brought up the example of West Ham's Darren Randolph, who had redeemed a handling error, which allowed Liverpool to equalise at Anfield the previous evening, with a world-class save to protect a point.

He has the additional advantage of being able to filter the experiences of his father, who moved from Newcastle to become Alan Pardew's goalkeeping coach at Crystal Palace, the club where he began a playing career that spanned twelve clubs. Father and son have only recently confessed to conspiring in Freddie's truancy from primary school, so he could see Andy train at Oxford United.

'I was about eight. Mum thought I'd been dropped off at school, but I'd be in the car begging Dad to take me training instead. I used to sit by the goal, with a ball at my feet, and watch him. Seeing the players, hearing the banter, had an impact on me like no other. From that moment on I wanted to be in a football environment.'

He used to join in sessions as a teenager, when his father was starting his coaching career at Charlton; their professional relationship deepened when they were at Newcastle together. Freddie never forgot the desolation in his father's voice when he described a brief period out of the game, selling photocopiers to keep the family finances ticking over.

The young keeper spent two months on loan at Crawley in 2015, 'loving the pressure of Saturday–Tuesday–Saturday, where the result really matters'. Rafa Benítez, preparing for an immediate return to the Premier League with Newcastle, delivered on his promise to provide similar experience by sending him on loan to Kilmarnock in the second half of the 2016–17 season. This enabled him to complement lessons from 'people who live and die for the job'.

Woodman cites Yohan Cabaye, Andros Townsend, Matt Ritchie and, above all, Tim Krul as key influences. The goalkeepers, from separate generations but identically motivated, would spend long hours on distant pitches at the training ground, honing their reflexes and deconstructing their craft. The lessons would continue in the analysis room.

'Tim basically became my coach. He handed out bollockings, but praised me when he thought I deserved it. We would watch my matches together, analyse the good and the bad. He's back in Holland now, but we still speak all the time.' He cherishes one particular text message, congratulating him for England's win in the 2014 European under-17 championships.

'You'd better get your bags packed,' it read: Krul, who was at the World Cup with the Dutch squad at the time, had paid for two sets of flights, match tickets and accommodation in Brazil. Freddie, thrilled by the respect implicit in the generosity of the gesture, took his father to watch Holland come from behind to beat Australia 3–2 in Porto Alegre.

Andy, who became manager of Whitehawk in the National League South in February 2017, is a huge influence, but Freddie describes his grandfather, Leslie Bates, as his 'hero'. The intimacy of their relationship, based upon familial love and a respect bordering on awe, compresses the generations and touches on the themes of courage, resilience and fellowship England coaches are seeking to use in creating a stronger sense of identity in representative football.

Leslie's service as a sailor on a minesweeper engaged

in the D-Day landings in 1944 acquired life and texture when his grandson visited the beach at Arromanches, where Allied troops and warships had come under murderous fire from German artillery, with the England under-19 squad in 2015. Freddie sent Leslie a photograph of the scene, and was suddenly struck by the fact he was the same age, 19, as his grandfather when he went to war.

Leslie's medals, which he has given to Freddie, are a reminder of the sacrifices made by men who grew up too quickly and died too young. Football cannot match the intensity of the memories those medals generate but it demands maturity, rarely a smooth and consistent process. Woodman and Moore share leadership qualities but their distinctive responses to an identical question, about the advice they would offer a young boy incubating the dream of following in their footsteps, were enlightening.

Moore's scars were revealingly raw: 'I have learned you have to be a team player, be respectful of those around you, but you have to put yourself before anyone else. You can't trust what people say, whether it is teammates or managers. You've got to be so careful of the difference between what people say and what people do.

'A lot of stuff at clubs happens behind closed doors. Keep thinking, keep working, keep learning. Everyone's pathway is different and in football anything can happen tomorrow. You never know what is coming. Be on your toes, alert to everything, and don't let your dream slip away because of a bad attitude.'

Woodman's sense of privilege endures: 'We're in danger of taking enjoyment out of the game. I'm determined that won't happen to me. I'm stringing my boots up every day, training on the best pitches at one of the biggest clubs in England. If you'd have told me that was going to happen when I was ten I would have cried. It's amazing.'

He smiled. We both knew the relevance of the message that accompanies every autograph he signs: 'Work Hard, Dream Big.'

17
Men at Work

THE REAL WORLD OF PROFESSIONAL FOOTBALL (OR, 11 RULES OF SURVIVAL)

1: Football is not fair – get used to it.

2: The football world gives nothing about your self-esteem. Coaches and pros expect you to achieve something in the game before you pat yourself on the back.

3: You will not earn a fortune on your first professional contract. You only get the money when you play for the first team.

4: If you thought your teachers were rough – just wait until you cross the manager.

5: Keeping the changing room tidy, being a ball boy, collecting balls bibs and cones, is NOT beneath you. Just welcome the opportunity to be in a professional footballer's environment. Relish every moment.

6: When you mess up on the pitch it is not your teammates' or your coaches' fault. Don't throw a dummy out and sulk. Learn from your mistake.
7: Schools may have done away with winners and losers, but football hasn't. Football is competitive, so make sure you are a winner.
8: There's no such things as winter breaks, or Christmas and Easter holidays in football. There are no half terms either. Do you want to be a footballer or go on holiday?
9: FIFA and Football Manager are electronic games. They are not real life. Living in the real football world is demanding and sometimes it does not go well. Handle it. Do not get caught up in the world of fantasy and make-believe.
10: Once you cross the line, no one will care that you have a sore throat.
11: Before you talk a good game, make sure you can play one.

The signs are tacked on to the thin walls of a cluster of whitewashed outbuildings in which the needs of academy players, senior professionals and their respective coaches are met by a rudimentary gymnasium, a small kitchen and an overworked tumble dryer. There are few frills on football's factory floor, and it seems appropriate that Mick Harford heads the welcoming committee.

Luton Town's chief recruiting officer carries the scars of his former life, as a centre forward with the instincts of a cage fighter. His fearsome reputation is not entirely undeserved, but he is good company and has a native intelligence that doesn't support the enforcer stereotype. We exchange gossip as Paul Hart, the primary reason for my visit, finishes a phone call. To my shame, I dredge up the most clichéd question in the book.

'Any kids coming through?'

Harford nods slowly: 'Two or three good 'uns.'

If anything, he is guilty of underselling the club he has also served as player, coach, manager and director of football. A Luton team containing nine academy products won 2–1 at League One Gillingham; seven homegrown players featured in a 2–0 defeat of a hybrid West Bromwich Albion side at Kenilworth Road.

Their reward, since the victories were in the ill-conceived, disastrously received Checkatrade Trophy, was a maximum £15,000 fine for supposedly fielding under-strength teams. A grievous blow when every penny counts, such retribution shredded the credibility of the Football League and its chief executive, Shaun Harvey.

Compounded by fines imposed on a further eleven clubs, it was a revealing example of corporate obstinacy, hypocrisy and sycophancy. Not even a concerted lobbying campaign by the Premier League, which sought a competitive outlet for their academies against League One and Two teams, could sustain the disingenuous notion that a competition boycotted by supporters was fulfilling its stated objective of promoting young talent.

The refusal of Arsenal, Liverpool, Manchester United, Manchester City and Tottenham Hotspur to compete accentuated the Football League's subservience, and highlighted a strange contempt for the strategic independence and financial welfare of its member clubs. Once again, politics had polluted the development process.

Chelsea, whose belatedly confirmed presence smacked of tokenism and expedience, were allowed to start their fixtures two weeks later than the rest. A young developmental team was eliminated in the group stages, leaving Adi Viveash, their academy's head of coaching, to contextualise the compensatory benefits of failure:

'The competition has been a real eye-opener for players as to where they are,' he said, after a 3–2 defeat at Exeter City. 'A lot of them think they are in certain positions where they should be playing, but are they good enough for league football? There's the question mark. I'm saying to them, "Are we playing at being a player or do we really want to be a player?" '

Hart could at least relate to the tone of that challenge, issued by a diligent tutor to a callow group of aspiring professionals whose first car is invariably a customised Range Rover, judging by the automotive beauty pageant at Chelsea's training ground. His principal role at Luton is to assist Nathan Jones in his first managerial job at a club whose youth policy owes more to economic necessity than philosophical purity, but, at 63, he has a world-weary grasp of realpolitik:

'The Premier League wants the best players, playing against each other for the biggest clubs. They don't give a monkey's about anything else. No one can question them. They rule. The Football League is in their grip and the FA haven't got a voice, but the league that is going to develop future England teams is the Championship.'

Hart has managed seven clubs, been caretaker manager at another two, and established acclaimed youth development programmes at Leeds United, Nottingham Forest and Charlton Athletic. Leeds used seven of his academy products, Harry Kewell, Jonathan Woodgate, Ian Harte, Alan Smith, Gary Kelly, Paul Robinson and Stephen McPhail, in reaching the Champions League semi-final in 2001; he nurtured England internationals Michael Dawson and Jermaine Jenas at Forest.

Those sceptical about his continuing relevance will dismiss such achievements as ancient history. Football is prone to the myopia of modernity and the pretension of progress, but the big, broad-shouldered man, wedged behind a small desk on which last night's polystyrene coffee cup lingers, has a lifetime's experience to offer in his defence.

His bloodlines are authentic. Father Johnny scored sixty-seven goals as an inside forward for Manchester City between 1947 and 1960, broke his leg a week before he was due to appear in the 1955 FA Cup final, and succeeded Malcolm Allison as the club's manager for six months in 1973 before retiring due to pancreatic problems.

He was a shy man, who preferred the private rituals of coaching to the front-of-house exposure of management. He saw pessimism as a parental duty when his son attempted to combine football with A-level studies, and pointed out the potential perils of a playing career that eventually extended to 567 appearances as a centre half over eighteen seasons.

'Dad was right,' Paul says, his voice moderated by reminiscence. 'I was not particularly brave, not particularly quick. I just had this inner desire. I took a risk and ignored everything else. This was a time when you found out you had been released by looking on the noticeboard. That was it. There was no consoling arm around the shoulder. It was, "Nah, not good enough."

'I went on trial to ten or eleven clubs, and got knocked back before Stockport County gave me my chance. I didn't think I was a strong person until I coped with that. Rejection has stayed with me. You never become immune to breaking that news, as a coach. All you can do is deliver it with as much honesty as you can. There's no question that whatever front the kid puts on, he is devastated.

'My father told me to keep my mouth shut, and my eyes and ears open. If anyone wants to discuss anything with you, good or bad, you listen and say thank you very much. I was a subservient type of pro, in the first team at Stockport at seventeen. My nose was broken six times before I was eighteen. I wouldn't wish that on anybody, but it was the type of environment that did me well. It grounded me from minute one.'

He comes from a generation that remembers the sting of corporal punishment, the welt left by a teacher's strap across a penitent's backside. He now works in a world of learning objectives, HR protocols and structured permissiveness. Coaching is a tightrope walk across a dangerously slack line slung between the old and the new.

'I have been hung on the peg by a teammate, slapped on the face when we were on the pitch. I never complained. I thought, yeah, you are right. I made a right pig's ear of that. I didn't do it again. Part of the strength of my development style is enabling a player to overcome criticism, or cope with a dressing room environment.

'I can tell you exactly what you need to do if you are good enough, but when you deliver the truth you are seen as some sort of ogre. We're dealing with a different breed, so the critique, good or bad, is always followed by a "but" or an "if". I have consciously tried to appear an ordinary bloke who works hard, and wherever I've been I have dealt in the basics, humility and respect.

'We had some disasters further down the line at Leeds. Woodgate went off the rails a bit, but he was intrinsically a nice boy who got in with the wrong crowd. They were a good group, lads who pushed the boundaries but knew right from wrong. They were taught how to play first-team football. That's what is missing today.

'England players being taken home in limos is not the problem. I sat on a PFA committee fighting for freedom of contract, so I believe players have the right to be paid whatever is in the club's budget. Wealth is a part of life, but I worry that players are not respectful of that wealth. There is no need to flaunt it. Don't ram it down people's throats.

'We have lost the common touch I try to engender. Too many average players are earning too much. Some seventeen-year-olds are being paid huge sums. It is alarming, all about shaking off the competition. If the boy comes on and makes the first team, great, but if he doesn't it is a drop in the ocean to Premier League clubs.

'We are all fighting to keep players at this level because we know the big white shark is out there ready to hunt them down. Instead of asking themselves what is best for their sons, parents are quite obviously being influenced by money. I tell them to be careful because if they make the wrong choice, that's the last we will see of their boy for five years.

'Those temptations are not going to go away. Parents get to know things before people in my position through agents and, I hate to say, illegal approaches. All you can do as a coach is promise you and your staff will do all you can to provide the quickest possible route into the first team. Touch wood, that has been a promise I have been able to keep.'

He believes in the vocational elements of youth coaching, 'the simple joy of throwing the jumpers down or seeing boys move onwards and upwards'. Yet such idealism is balanced by an insight into the quiet desperation of lower-league life, where there are few paper trails and development funds are anecdotally vulnerable to plunder. He fears for the probity of the system.

'I can't get my head around how flimsy it all looks. I would say to any club that can't commit fully to driving an academy, "Don't do it. Cut it all out. Do yourself a favour and do the kids a favour." There have been so many clubs who don't fund the academy properly. Budgets are meant to be ring-fenced but I don't believe that. People take the money, and siphon it off for the first team.

'Youth development has been made very complicated by EPPP. That created around 700 jobs, which means somewhere down the line you are not getting the best. You are perpetuating averageness. I know I am going to get slammed for this, but in the old system of Football Combination and Central League you got knocked around by senior players and learned your trade.

'I believe in elite principles and practices, but can you go to an under-21 league game and know that a particular boy could cope with the rigours of a Football League season? I'm not sure you could. The challenge of development is to get through your life as a pro. You've got to be tough, ready to do the dirty bits.

'I have a big thing about heading the ball. No one teaches that any more. I teach the basics, the theory of the three-game turnaround. Everyone can play badly, but what do you do in the game after that? You're hurt, so you make sure the first thing you do is done properly. If you are a centre half: win the first header. If you are a centre forward: win the first header, get hold of it, pass and spin.

'If you get the ball keep it, pass it to the same colour shirt. Do you feel better? Yeah, good. That's how you build a game. Do the simple things. Go back to basics. Third game you are back on blob. You never get dropped. It is not the manager who gives you confidence. It is you. I always ask my players, "Who picks the team?" "Ah you, gaffer." "No. You do. Players pick teams." '

And the best coaches make better individuals, who have longer careers, more satisfying lives. They do so through contradictory qualities, idealism and scepticism, applied consistently. The game needs the emotional checks and balances provided by its tribal elders, men like Hart and Steve Heighway, whose return to Liverpool at the age of 69, in a consultancy role at its Kirkby academy, was a restatement of the club's identity.

'My mantra is engage, confront, challenge and inspire,' Heighway told Chris Bascombe in a typically thoughtful interview for the *Daily Telegraph*. 'My career has been about helping young people. I was tough with them, incredibly tough with them at times. I could be confrontational with them. Not one of them has held it against me. That's what makes me proud. That's my style. It's how I work.

'I hate the phrase "old school" but a lot of the ideas of the past are still relevant. In the rush to be modern, don't kick the baby out with the bathwater and discard everything. Being new and modern is about adding to what has worked before. Not everything in the 60s, 70s, 80s was irrelevant. Not everything can be about technical evaluation. There is more to it. Who you are and what you are is about more than what you can do.

'What drives a player? That's what makes the best stand out from other technically good footballers. You can't measure that. You can't use science or data to identify that. Physicality, mental strength, personality – those are what you're looking for to go with the talent. If you don't have that you will be found out. What I don't understand is the amount of form filling those running the game want from coaches now, everyone asked to record and write about it all. Coaches want to be on the grass watching and working with players. You can't superscript football.'

To borrow from legendary US basketball coach John Wooden, who regarded coaching as a cerebral undertaking, a life force rather than the foundation of a game plan, 'it takes time to create excellence. If it could be done more quickly, more people would do it.' The process is based on personal influence, small cells of individuals united by principle and best practice.

When the system works well, knowledge cascades, as refreshing as a mountain stream. Experience spreads, like spilled ink on blotting paper. Inspiration is a starburst of enthusiasm. Heighway is correct: academic strictures and prescribed structures imposed on the youth development system in England will never replace the spark of human contact.

Jürgen Klopp's great strength at Liverpool is to recognise the club's living legacy, and align it to current thinking. The ethos of Bill Shankly is more than mildewed nostalgia; his values have an enduring relevance beyond folklore or whimsy. Similarly, Steven Gerrard's coaching apprenticeship, which started at Liverpool's academy in February 2017, is an extension of the relationship he formed with Heighway as a young player.

Complementary modernity is embodied by Pepijn Lijnders, who has moved from Liverpool's under-16s to a newly created role overseeing a so-called Talent Group, which is being integrated into the first-team environment each Tuesday. The Dutch development coach, initially recruited by Brendan Rodgers after twelve seasons spent with PSV Eindhoven and Porto, explained the overarching philosophy to Jonathan Northcroft of the *Sunday Times*:

'There's a saying that talent needs models, it doesn't need criticism. I really believe in that. So at the moment we bring Trent [Alexander-Arnold], Ovie [Ejaria] and Ben [Woodburn] up and they can watch Adam Lallana, the way he prepares himself in the physio room, the way he prepares himself before the training session, how he puts his shin pads on, how he treats his boots – everything. All these small things, these unwritten things, for young players to learn from their models is so important.

'That's before you even speak about the pitch: how Phil [Coutinho] controls the ball and turns away, how Hendo [Jordan Henderson] is the playmaker from out the back, the motor. And in training they see how Sadio [Mané] is creating space for himself before he receives the ball. That is one of his biggest strengths, so he plays one v ones in the areas we want him to.

'It's a one-club mentality. With our vision, with our future, with our ideal. The ideal means what makes us specific, what makes us recognisable. Indirectly we try to represent the fans. We want to represent their passion. That's why we choose this playing style, because it all has to link together: the manager, the coaches, the players, the staff, the academy boys, the fans. That all has to come together, and over time you can compete.'

Academy director Alex Inglethorpe, who learned under John McDermott at Tottenham, sought to ensure quality time for his coaches by cutting player numbers, from 245 to around 170. He, too, imposed a £40,000 salary limit on first-year professionals. He found his metier after managing Exeter City, and has proved that the best young coaches, with the brightest minds, do not necessarily need to be drawn to the soap-operatic intensity of first-team football.

Karl Robinson seems wedded to that culture: following a six-year tenure, he was out of work for less than a month after being sacked in October 2016 by MK Dons, who six years previously had made him the Football League's youngest manager, at 29. Braving the dysfunctionality of Charlton Athletic, a club embroiled in a guerrilla war between supporters and an absentee owner, appeared rash.

Yet there was instructive method in his perceived madness. His reputation as an outstanding development coach immediately prompted Chelsea to entrust him with the further education of Jay DaSilva, who had outgrown under-23 football. It triggered the thought that, ultimately, his skill set will be best suited to a senior development role, either with England or a major Premier League club.

Heighway's influence on him has been fundamental, personally and professionally. Robinson was one of a small group of young coaches nurtured by him at the Liverpool academy, a grounding subsequently enhanced by assisting Sam Allardyce at Blackburn Rovers and following Paul Ince to Milton Keynes. His reverence towards the old Liverpool winger, who had been coaching, unpaid, in Florida before his return to Merseyside, is striking:

'Do you know my best piece of advice? Let them play. I vividly remember one of Steve's sessions. He didn't want any cones. He put two jumpers down as goalposts. What he got was unpredictability, freedom of expression. What he created was a natural English footballer. Now we are robotic. This has to be here, that has to be there. Coaches are told, "These are the boxes you have to tick." Well, fuck your boxes.

'Every kid needs a different development plan, so why categorise everything? Each boy is different physically, psychologically, technically, tactically. I don't want criteria, a curriculum of how a player should be developed. That should be torn up and thrown in the bin. Do I believe in the X factor? One hundred per cent.

'When I was coaching at Liverpool's academy it was obvious to me, from a very young age, that Jordan Rossiter was going to be a professional footballer. It was obvious that Cameron Brannagan and Ryan Kemp were going to play somewhere. Jon Flanagan? Obvious.

'Why does one make it when another of equal talent fails? Self-belief, support mechanisms, lack of external pressure, but Steve also used to talk to me about the best having a poorly developed sense of fear. That's the crux of it. Do we encourage fear, massage it? No, we eradicate it, while maintaining the mentality that you want to be the best, every single day of your life. Very few have that trait.

'Fear creates anxiety, anxiety creates tension and tension creates mistakes. Our job is to manage that internal process, to train the mind so a player can replicate something without thinking. Why does Steven Gerrard score from nearly thirty-five yards in the last minute of a cup final? Why does David Beckham put that free kick against Greece in the top corner in the last minute at Old Trafford? Why do the greatest players produce the greatest moments at the most pivotal times?

'Because they have seen it, and trained it. Biomechanically, they know they can achieve it. Their technique stays the same in the most fearful of moments. Some players develop that technique faithfully on the training ground, but they cannot reproduce it because they tense up under scrutiny. Golf sets us an example.

'If I stood on the first tee at St Andrews for a game between you and me I could hit a drive two hundred and sixty-four yards, dead straight. If I had two thousand people watching me, with millions more on TV, I guarantee you it is going straight right. Fear would lead to me tensing up, somewhere on my backswing. Tension would wreck my technique and ultimately create the mistake.'

Pressure is minimised by poetry and physics: 'Steve used to liken striking a ball to a boxer throwing a punch. It wasn't thrown through his fist. It was thrown with his heart and his head, which allowed the shoulder, the elbow, the extension of the wrist and forearm, and, finally, the fist, to channel the power.

'When I am teaching someone to strike a ball I talk about hip movement, biomechanical merit, how high the heel must go, about the positioning of the knee over the ball. The questions are constant. What about my standing foot? Where should that point? If I open it up more, will it give me more movement through my legs to cut the ball, just like in golf?

'If I want to turn the ball end-over-end, how much does my left hip rotate, as I am a left-footed player? How can I give it that last bit of depth so the pass drops into the target's feet? How am I going to drive the ball? How am I going to step in, hit the top of the ball, punch down through it to create that movement? I've not even spoken about the angle of the foot yet.

'I am intense about coaching. I covet every aspect of it. I am a young manager, a young coach, but I have old-school and new-school values. My job is to fill my players' toolbox. Their job is to pick the right tool, ninety-nine point nine per cent of the time.'

Robinson's additional responsibility, unspoken but unarguable, is to augment the sort of self-help networks around which education can flourish. His most underrated achievement at Milton Keynes was to oversee the establishment of a cohesive coaching structure from the under-9s to the first team. He could not have done so without the drive, expertise and innovative spirit of Dan Micciche, the Dons' head of academy coaching.

The son of Italian immigrants, Micciche grew up

watching AC Milan and Napoli, but became a Juventus fan when he was captivated by Roberto Baggio at the 1990 World Cup. He celebrated cultural difference, relishing Serie A's patience and control as a release from traditional Anglo-Saxon aggression, and embraced the work ethic of a large, close family.

He dared to be different at youth level with MK Dons, creating a short-notice fixture list based on feel and flexibility, rather than the rigidity of a pre set programme. His experimentation involved shortening pitches, to challenge technique and imagination through the compression of space. Rather than relying on facile age-group victories, he scheduled physically demanding practice matches against men's amateur teams. His subsequent appointment as head coach of the England under-16 squad signalled a welcome expansion of the FA's thinking.

Micciche's coaching process involves splitting the pitch into lanes, which provide visual reference points and encourage positional understanding. Players are given trigger words to memorise and are asked to 'play on different lines and find pockets of space'. Each individual is given three areas, linked to their strengths, to work on during a match.

Improvisation is approved, within the context of what Micche terms a' '6–6–6' strategy. This involves winning the ball back cleanly within six seconds, attacking with a minimum of six players and progressing the ball over the half way line within six passes.

Unsurprisingly, he describes his coaching style as 'extremely flexible and instinctive'.

He has had distinctive tutors. John Cartwright, his first academy manager at Crystal Palace, has been slaughtering sacred cows since the seventies, when his Palace team won the FA Youth Cup in successive seasons, and his England under-18 team won the European championship.

Now 76, Cartwright has not noticeably mellowed in retirement. He still believes English football is blighted by insubstantial coaching, lack of respect for individual skill, and the elevation of players above their true worth. He decries the influence of 'football academics' and 'crash-bang-wallop fightball' produced by an over-emphasis on results. He castigates the system as a 'confused, blind, and utterly distorted shambles'.

Predictably, Micciche is a catalytic presence in the England coaches' room, where the dilemma of dealing with the 'baller' outlook of what Aidy Boothroyd terms 'the merchandise generation' is a constant factor in the plan–do–review performance management system that operates across the age groups.

Gareth Southgate confirms: 'We have debates about whether we are indulging the academy mentality. Some groups don't want to do things without the ball; one of the conversations recently concerned a really talented boy who wouldn't get picked for a first team because he doesn't do enough without the ball.

'Dan's view is that we won't produce a Ronaldo or a Messi if that is our mentality. We don't create that type of player because we worry too much about lads doing this, that or the other. I get that a little bit, but my argument would be, well, he's not going to play in a Premier League first team unless he runs his socks off.

'I want players to express themselves massively. I want to have a picture of what is in their mind because it fascinates me. We've got to find a way into these boys because they have great technical ability. Can we make it work for them? It is our duty to try, but if they don't have the other bits they're not going to have a career in the game anyway. If we're not hammering home that message we are doing them a disservice.'

Southgate's innate decency is shared by Micciche's other major influence, Chris Ramsey, who coached Gerrard, Ashley Cole, Ledley King, Jonathan Woodgate and Jermaine Jenas at international youth level before spending a decade at Tottenham Hotspur. In his latest guise as QPR's technical director, Ramsey blames clubs for 'taking hunger out of the individual' by 'paying kids end-product money when they have yet to produce'.

He believes an avaricious culture leads to young players 'being burned out more mentally and emotionally than physically'. Conversely, too many 'very early choices' made about children recruited as young as 7 results in 'kids being unnecessarily washed up'. Poaching, and associated underhand behaviour, is the inevitable by-product of a system in which owners promote self-interest over the collective good.

As he expands on his philosophy, Ramsey exudes a familiar combination of concern and compassion, cynicism and a keenly developed conscience. He has managed consistently to work around human frailty, in all its forms, without losing sight of the fragility of the boys who fall within his sphere of influence. It is not a comforting scenario:

'Agents have spoiled the game by giving economically challenged parents false hope. You can't always condemn them for taking what is offered, because if you are a single parent in a run-down flat with two or three kids, who is told, we will give you a car or a house, it difficult to say, "Turn them down," because they are understandably thinking about the rest of the family.

'As a football fraternity, we haven't looked at our players as children. They are treated as commodities, which is what they are, to be brutally honest. We have to ensure they have some sort of childhood to round them off as people. They get identified as a footballer. They don't get to mix with their peer group outside the game.

'Think about it. They define themselves through the formative years of their lives as good or bad people, depending on how well or how badly they have played. They are expected to deliver a consistently high level of performance over ten years, which any pro will tell you is close to impossible. They are not mini-adults. No wonder some of them go out of the game without laying a glove on it.

'Think about the kid who is brought into the club at seven, and released at eighteen. All those years, training four nights a week, playing matches that he's told matter. All that time in the car, probably with an over-zealous dad in their ear. Their siblings are dragged along, experiencing a football season without being a footballer. There's no escape. Again, is it any wonder some of them simply come to the end of their energies?

'I played in the era when clubs had the upper hand. I was on £80 a week when I made my debut for Brighton in the old First Division in 1981, where we won our last four games to stay up. I was eighteen. I was given a pair of boots and a pair of training boots, and had to negotiate a new contract with my chairman, Mike Bamber, and my manager, Alan Mullery.

'I didn't know what to ask for, so I went for £150 a week. Nowadays kids are secured on silly amounts that give them the sort of comfort which creates apathy, or a sense that the game owes them a living. We are giving teenagers ten, twenty, even thirty grand a week. Give that to a grown man and he is probably going off the rails, let alone a kid who is forming his personality.

'Parental education is so important. As a father, I like to feel I have empathy for children, and I coach in the manner I expect my son to be spoken to. There are times when you have to be harsh, but it is a matter of striking the correct balance. The problem is that so many parents are so desperate for their boy to sign they allow so many horrible things to happen.

'For example's sake, parents walk into the end-of-season review meeting, complaining that their boy has been bullied. They accuse the coach of berating the kid, singling him out for criticism. I take every complaint seriously, especially when it is made in the right way, but why have they waited so long if the abuse has been consistent and obvious?

'They wouldn't allow that in any other walk of life. If that was at school they'd be going mad. They'd be steaming in there. Why have they allowed it in this situation? They have only allowed it because it is football and they can see the gravy at the end if their boy makes it. They have been desensitised by the game.'

Again, it is impossible not be struck by the sense of sadness, underpinned by anger. The venality and vitriol of the senior game is a running sore, an open wound which seeps into youth football. It is a virulent form of infection against which Robinson also struggles. His tone is similarly thoughtful, and tinged by exasperation:

'We have some of the best kids in the world, but the pathway has been narrowed by external influence. Agents make our boys more expensive, so if you are a chairman, what are you going to do? Take an English boy of nineteen for X million, or a cheaper foreign player? What will be the business model that shapes the game in years to come?

'We know agents are going to be part of this industry for the rest of our lives. There are some really good ones out there, who really care, but there are some cowboys. The ones who are not chasing the pound notes, who wait, develop, support and underpin their player, usually make more money in the long run. We need to protect the kids from those who drag them around, move them on as early as possible, and push, push, push.

'I know of certain parents, at clubs at which I have worked, saying, "What is in it for me?" on being told their son is being offered a contract. The true role of a parent is sacrificing your life for your kids, like my dad did for me and like I would for my daughter. Now people are sacrificing their kids' lives in pursuit of personal wealth.

'Do you want to know what my problem is with the whole thing? I love seeing kids come through. I love it. I hate the shit that swirls around it. I hate the people who want to be deceitful. The bit where I stand on the grass with young players, shouting at them, supporting them, is what I am interested in. I'll be ruthless with them. I'll be a friend to them. I'll love them, manage them, be a psychologist for them. I simply can't stand the money, the lies, the horrible side of the game.'

His admonition lingers in the air, as pungent as

cordite across a battlefield. Before it is too late, it is time to visit Teesside, and meet an unassuming man blessed with the serenity of a shepherd and the sensitivity of a psychotherapist.

18

Portrait of an Artist

The screensaver on Dave Parnaby's computer is an image of innocence, a photograph of a baby boy sitting beside a football. He permits himself a grandfather's indulgence and studies it intently, as if feeding off the joy and release it represents. 'Little Mason is a gift,' he says quietly, with a warmth which pervades a large, functional office dominated by an old-fashioned boardroom table.

Middlesbrough's academy director has paused briefly during the course of yet another 'first in, last out' day. He had a late night, scouting at Scunthorpe, and must accommodate a coach education meeting before a long afternoon dealing with the Premier League's Action Plan. He has a new recruit to welcome in the evening, and rises impulsively to snatch five minutes' renewal in the sports hall at the end of an airy, well-lit corridor.

'Poke your head around the door, and tell me what

you see,' he says, conspiratorially. A group of young boys, under-9s at a guess, are on their toes, playing a five-a-side match that flows seamlessly, enthusiastically, occasionally chaotically. 'Did you notice there were no coaches? Not needed. They just love it, don't they?'

It seems impossible to reconcile the pleasure creasing a pale, open face, which retains hints of his own youth with the news contained in a six-paragraph club statement that, at the age of 62, he will retire in mid-March 2017 as soon as his replacement, Craig Little, is in post. Yet when Mason Parnaby came into the world on January 4, 2016, Dave's world changed, too.

Mason was born to Stuart, a former England under-21 international who flourished under his father at Middlesbrough's academy, and his wife Paula. The couple had been expecting their first child in January 2014, but three days after doctors were unable to detect a heartbeat thirty-six weeks into the pregnancy, Poppy Isabella Elizabeth Parnaby was stillborn, weighing 5lb 13.5oz.

On average, seventeen more families in the UK will endure neonatal bereavement today. They will feel uniquely distressed, numb and, in too many cases, insufferably lonely. Paula is patron of 4Louis, a family-run charity that seeks to support stricken parents by supplying hospitals with 'cuddle cots' and memory boxes.

The Parnaby family's memory box, lemon with a pink ribbon, contains such unbearably poignant items as an imprint of Poppy's hands and feet in clay, a curl box for a lock of her thick, dark hair, and an acknowledgement-of-life certificate. A glass angel signifies a sleeping baby. They are prized possessions, a permanent reminder of life's preciousness.

'We had a tragic time,' Dave reflects, his eyelids seeming to sag under the weight of recollection. 'We lost Poppy and, after everything, welcomed little Mason. I have two more fantastic grandchildren in Texas and I'd like to have enough time in my life to enjoy them all. I love this place, but I'm going out on my own terms. It is nothing against the game; as the saying goes, great game, shit industry. I do believe I am very, very lucky to have found this club.'

And they, in turn, are fortunate to have had him, as the founding father of a productive, universally admired academy that reflects his inclusive personality. One of the touchstone comments of John Wooden, whose books can be found alongside those of another inspiration, the educationalist Sir Ken Robinson, in a bookcase close to the window in Parnaby's office, seems particularly apposite: 'A good teacher or coach must not only understand others, but himself or herself as well.'

Parnaby's childhood ambition to be a professional sportsman, by his own admission more realistic in cricket than football, was tested to destruction at the age of 25, when he scored twice from midfield playing for Rotherham reserves against Barnsley. Ian Porterfield, the Rotherham manager, called the following day, offering a year's contract.

Heart met head. Teaching offered security. His wife Jean was pregnant with their first child Ian, a former professional golfer who now works for Callaway in the United States. They had just bought a house. Despite Jean urging him to follow his dream, regardless of domestic responsibilities, he turned the offer down.

He played for Middlesbrough in the Northern Intermediate League, went on trial to Stoke City with a 16-year-old Paul Bracewell, and turned out at centre half for Gateshead in the Conference. He remained engrossed by the game, and his aptitude for engagement and education marked him out as a natural coach.

His life was fashioned by a new set of circumstances and unheralded individuals whose influence was imposed imperceptibly in rowdy classrooms, draughty sports halls and on wind-whipped playing fields. They were PE teachers, formidable characters given greater substance by secondary careers as accomplished athletes.

Stan Stoker played rugby union as a full back for Gosforth, when they were a power in the land in the seventies. He also played cricket for Dorset and his native Durham in the Minor Counties Championship as a right-handed batsman and right-armed medium fast bowler who profited from swing and dip. He remained Parnaby's advocate and adviser until his death, aged 71, in October 2015.

Keith Robson was Parnaby's first head of department at Longfield School in Darlington. He had a rugby background, but specialised in gymnastics. Parnaby marvelled at the unforced authority of both men, the discipline they imposed with such ease that standards of behaviour became second nature. Forty years on, their protégé remains reverential:

'I used to watch Stan at work. He was so relaxed and easy. Keith's standards were so high, and his discipline was so good. Everything was carefully planned. He took registers before lessons. He would be dressed all in white, immaculately clean from head to toe. He taught me how to teach, the organisation of a class, how to speak.

'The art of teaching is small details. Who is looking at you? Who is picking their arse? Who is picking their nose? Who is looking into the distance? I always say, give the coach the respect of looking at him. You might not be listening but at least you look like you are listening to him. Do you get your points across? Can you deliver a hard message subtly to a fifteen-year-old boy?

'I learned about dealing with parents. Honesty: that is the answer. Me mam always said, you are what you are. I'm pleased people think I have me mam's blood. My dad was a twisty old bugger, a miner all his life. Me mam gave a lot, she still does, even though she is on dialysis these days. You have to tell the truth. You can't fabricate, promise something you can't deliver.'

The most important lessons never lose their relevance. Parnaby will speak from the heart later that evening, when, together with Barry Watson, the academy's head of education and welfare, he welcomes one of the new academy intake, disgorged from minibuses to train during school holidays at the club's Rockcliffe Park complex. His message to the boy and his parents is scoured by two decades' worth of common sense:

'You come into my office at the age of nine, and I register you. This isn't a fun activity. It is a professional sport. Somewhere down the line you may or may not progress. I can't tell you that you won't be sitting here at ten, and we're releasing you. You could be here at fourteen, and we're giving you a two-year extension. You might be twenty-six and have come to the end of your third professional contract, and we're in the office crying and cuddling because you've come to the end of your journey.

'My favourite saying is, "Enjoy the journey." Make sure you are sticking in at school and you achieve what you can achieve. You parents have to support that. We will do as much as possible to develop your child into a good player and a good person. His well-being, social outlook and education are at the top of our agenda.'

Boundaries, topographical and moral, might have been bulldozed elsewhere because of the Premier League's global land grab, but Middlesbrough's academy remains true to an embattled community. Parnaby has recruited consistently and exclusively from a thirty-five-mile radius; he has been allowed to prioritise identity and local pride.

Middlesbrough, he says, 'is a tough, tough town'. There is a sense of abandonment by the southern elite: local steelworks have closed, unemployment is rising and as the population is shifting and the coke furnaces cool, the talent pool available to the football club is shrinking. Social issues – inordinately high rates of cancer, infant mortality and supply of class A drugs – bedevil the region.

No institution or individual is immune from change. The club's spiritual link to the town remains strong, and will be protected while Steve Gibson, the steel-worker's son who is by common consent one of football's most passionate and far-sighted owners, remains in charge. Yet the global nature of senior recruitment is beginning to filter down into the professional development phase, between the ages of 16 and 18, where 'Boro feature players from Austria and Brazil.

Football is evolving, data-obsessed and centrally driven. Middlesbrough's academy might have supplied fifty-two first-team players, but it was placed under special measures by the Premier League because investment in it was perceived to be below the level required by the Elite Player Performance Plan. Since criticisms included a lack of GPS monitoring equipment for every player, Parnaby had every right to regard the auditor's verdict as an insult to the intelligence and informality of his approach.

'I spent twenty-two years in teaching and when I came here in 1998 I told Keith Lamb, the chief executive, that if he was looking for someone to manage the budget he had the wrong man. I have a good relationship with Ged Roddy at the Premier League, but I don't live in a measurement, target-setting culture. I deal with my gut, my heart, my background, my relationships.

'I sense a sea change. My door is open 24/7 but I get really, really worried when, because of EPPP, and the Action Plan we need to follow to achieve our licence for the next three years, I get stuck in this office and I'm not in the corridors, in the sports hall or down on the pitches. You should be seen by everyone and not hidden in this closet. I'm conscious of being a figurehead; parents should be quite happy to approach you, and the kids should be able to say hello.

'It's difficult. Any organisation that you work under, be it the Premier League, Football League or Middlesbrough Football Club, has to change with the times. But we always concentrate on the boys themselves. They are better technically, because of repetitive practice and greater access to them, but can the surrounding area supply enough of them?

'When I first started, Steve said he wanted Middlesbrough's academy to give the children of Teesside the opportunity to become professional sportsmen, and we've stuck with that. From a youth development point of view, competition in recruitment has become significant. I haven't lost a player to a predator club in nineteen years, but I sense more pressure building as the years go by.

'You've got to believe in what you're doing, but maybe we will unearth someone that will be, for want of a better word, stalked. I've got to question myself: if I was placed in another environment, that's bigger, richer, with all those possibilities of recruitment at my fingertips, how would I react? Where would my moral ground be?

'I have always stood by the rules and regulations. They are there to be adhered to, not got around or broken. It is not hard to keep your recruitment staff ethically sound. You just say, well, these things are not happening. Whenever they come to me with a possibility of a player, I ask about background research and go through a checklist with Wendy, my administrator, just to make sure everything is being followed correctly.'

Since the major North-east clubs are officially classified as geographically isolated, the relationships between them are delicate and different. When he took the job, Parnaby called a meeting at Maiden Castle in Durham with Alan Irvine and Ian Branfoot, his counterparts at Newcastle United and Sunderland respectively at the time. Their 'no poaching' agreement endures.

'We have to work really hard to find talent, but the

reality is a boy could be with us on Tuesday, at Sunderland on Wednesday and Newcastle on Thursday. At that meeting we agreed competition was fair, until the point a boy registered. I promised not to make any form of approach to a parent, agent or player, and that if I got wind somebody was trying to send one of their players to me, I would ring their club directly.

'Touch wood, that agreement still exists between Ged McNamee, at Sunderland, and Joe Joyce at Newcastle. We have a healthy respect for each other. I would almost class us as friends, because we've done the job so long now, together. We understand that if, say, Newcastle release a player, and we think we've got this magic wand, we'll have a trial of him. And, vice versa, a boy we released a year ago is doing quite nicely at Sunderland.

'Have they got a magic wand? I don't know. There are so many aspects to a player's development, social maturity, mental maturity. Pennies drop, things fall into place at different times in their lives. Ron Bone, who is seventy-four now, but still works as my recruitment adviser, is my barometer. He talks about potential and patience. Our job is to identify the potential. And then you've got to be really patient.'

Soon after our conversation, in late November 2016, another domino fell. Sunderland announced that McNamee, who had overseen the development of such prominent players as Jordan Henderson, Jordan Pickford and Duncan Watmore, was leaving the club after twenty years as part of an academy restructure. It was a signal of more ruthless, less accommodating behaviour, and begged the question of what the game will lose when such men, of high virtue and long experience, walk away.

Perhaps we should enjoy Parnaby's principles before they fade into history, as tantalising and mysterious as an entombed inscription on papyrus:

'I couldn't care a toss about agents or predator clubs. I haven't got the time or energy to worry about them. It doesn't matter if you put barriers up, and try to exclude them from your training ground. If they want to operate, they'll operate. When I hear about the shenanigans of money, contracts and agents in the North-west, London and the Midlands I reckon we are geographically advantaged, rather than disadvantaged.

'I contest the agents all the time. If I get a whisper of somebody approaching one of our boys, before the first of January of his sixteenth year, I challenge them because, as I understand it, it is illegal. We had one boy who had been with us since the age of nine. I wanted to offer him a scholarship, and called the parents, asking them to come and see me.

'Half an hour later, my phone went. It was a number I didn't recognise. This person said, "I am with the family." I'd never spoken to him in my life. "Which one? Who are you? First of all, I don't know you. I am not going to give you any information. I am allowed to offer a scholarship any time after the first of January of a boy's fourteenth year, and I have decided to do it now. I am not going to talk to you about it. I'd have a think about what you're doing."

'That's my stance with all of them, but too many clubs are fearful of losing a player rather than testing the agent. If any parents want to walk out and speak to one that is their choice, but don't come back to me. I don't have the pressures at board level that others have to deal with. I've never been asked about where the next one is coming from. They're interested, but Ron's credo of potential and patience sits as well upstairs as it does down here.

'There's an understanding of what youth development is all about. There's a lot of talk about players getting £5k a week – and the rest – elsewhere but our first professional contract ranges from £400 to £550 a week. We are really pleased when a boy gets an England call, because we value the Three Lions, but some of them come back and are never the same again, because they have shared a room with a Chelsea boy or a Man City boy.

'I do not know what their wage scales are, but I do remember Lee Congerton sitting in on his first meeting with us as Sunderland's technical director. His background was Liverpool, Chelsea, Hamburg. He was quite astounded by our first professional contracts, amazed by how we'd kept the lid on it, kept it controlled.

'Who is right or wrong? Management is about standing by your principles and convictions. Some academies are a business within an organisation. We know who we're talking about. Do they have to operate like that? I don't know. My concern is that the talent within them would be better across the game, rather than sitting at one, two, three or four clubs. Is that healthy for English football? Is that producing better equipped players for England, as EPPP is set out to do?'

The questions hang as heavily in the air as his swiftly sidelined solution to the overstocking of the system, first proposed seventeen years ago at a meeting of Premier League clubs at Loughborough University, which had the pretension, formality and backstage manoeuvring of a United Nations summit.

Parnaby suggested a two-tier system. Below the age of 12, boys should be registered on a coaching rather than playing basis, enabling them to represent their schools and play with their friends. Once they reached secondary school, the best would be filtered into a competitive academy-based games programme. The FA and Premier League, he insisted, had a dual responsibility to tend the grassroots of the game, where parental and behavioural problems fester.

'The coaching registration was a new concept, almost like a sorting office, where once the under-12s came along you narrowed the base so there was a smaller group to work with. You've given them five years to develop, they've had decent coaching at the clubs, but they've integrated with their friends before they come on board.

'I was new to it all, a bit wet behind the ears, and nobody grasped the nettle. Why? The only thing I can think of is fear of losing that special seven-year-old, or ten-year-old. There has always been the challenge that there are too many players in the system. We've talked about combining age groups, nines and tens, elevens and twelves, but the rule book dictates.'

EPPP limits choice and innovation. Parnaby is a friend and ally of John McDermott at Tottenham, who sought, unsuccessfully, to withdraw from PL2, the under-23 league, and institute a less formal programme of practice matches at home and abroad. Though conscious of disquiet at such regimentation, Double Pass, the EPPP auditors, who operate from the Brussels suburb of Dilbeek, refer to their role as 'strategic optimisation'.

The company is run by Hugo Schoukens, a former banker who progressed, from 1992 to 1999, from being a part-time youth coach to Anderlecht's academy director. Seeking a thesis topic at the Vlekho business school in Brussels, he was approached to develop a football version of a software programme designed to evaluate gymnastics academies by Jo Van Hoecke, a professor at Vrije University in the Belgian capital.

This thesis formed the basis of his MBA in Sports

Management at Leicester University, and was rolled out by the Belgian Football Federation. Schoukens and Van Hoecke founded Double Pass in November 2004, and once Vrije University had been compensated for their intellectual property rights, the company rapidly expanded their reach.

They began working in the German development system in 2005, linked up with the Premier League in 2012 after being recommended by Bundesliga officials, and operate similar models in the United States and Japan. Clubs are evaluated on a so-called eight-dimensional approach, incorporating such 'critical success factors' as strategic and financial planning, talent identification and development, organisational structure and decision-making ability.

Double Pass demand a huge amount of operational data, aligned to what is generally a four-day study visit. Clubs are judged on specific objectives, ranging from coaching standards, social support, communications strategies, infrastructure programmes and facility management. Though neutral and objective, conclusions are invariably controversial.

Middlesbrough were harshly judged, even though their 160-acre training complex, set in the village of Hurworth, near Darlington, was substantially upgraded in 2012, when it was used for Olympic preparations. It has been good enough for the All Blacks, but not, apparently, for disciples of a strategy based loosely on the marginal-gains model employed, most prominently, by British Cycling.

Parnaby offers a cogent case for the defence: 'It was quite clearly stated to me that we hadn't operated with a GPS unit for every player. We hadn't upgraded our indoor and outdoor areas, hadn't employed a full-time psychologist, and didn't have sufficient or appropriate performance analysis to a level of those we were being judged against, or with, in the cluster method.

'What we have invested in is in the kids. We have put time and energy into making sure they are OK, that the parents understand what we're trying to do. We have not lost a player over nineteen years. I am not saying we are the best, I never would, but does that not give you some indication that we have a decent environment here?

'The scientific approach dictates that GPS units should be used by every single boy within the professional development phase. In our case it's something like forty-four boys. Who processes that data? How is it used? Does every boy use that data? I'm being sarcastic here, but does anyone know the average number of sprints for a left-sided centre back under twenty-three? I don't think I've ever looked at any of it like that.

'There's nothing wrong with good housekeeping. Administrative and facility development can only be good. But, to my mind, it has become too scientific. Everything has to be accounted for and measured. If you've got a philosophy, how do you measure your philosophy? If you've got a curriculum, how do you measure your curriculum? If you've got a playing philosophy, how do you measure that? You've got targets to set for each department in the academy. What are your progress targets? How do you measure it?

'I don't come from that background. I don't speak that language. Mine is more about emotions and people, relationships with parents and between players and coaches. There are lots of informal chats around the building, up to and including the chairman and CEO, that you can't actually record or measure. In our report we got lots of plaudits about our informal, everyday operation, but we were criticised that we don't formalise things enough.'

That glaring contradiction was emphasised by the success of the annual Premier League coaches' conference at Rockliffe Park, held over three days in May 2016. The irony of the event featuring the national under-14 final, in which Middlesbrough defeated Chelsea 1–0, was compounded by praise for the texture of the club's thinking, and the all-encompassing nature of the welcome. Parnaby's pride was tangible:

'We stripped it back, warts and all, and invited the whole country to come here. We peeled back all the layers and let them see everything. The plaudits we got were fantastic. Basically, it captured what we are about, the coaching philosophy, playing philosophy, how we educate children. We shared everything, didn't hide anything. It was a fantastic credit to all the staff, who were brave enough to expose themselves to scrutiny.

'Whenever I am asked about the academy I speak of a whole host of people. It is my job to make sure they are not undervalued. From a remuneration point of view, that's a difficult jigsaw puzzle to put together. I have to make sure the recruitment department and the army of scouts at 40p a mile are appraised and patted on the back in the same way as the under-23 coach who's just getting promoted to the Premier League.'

The academy had six full-time members of staff at its inception; it now employs twenty-four. The three senior squads – first team, under-23 and under-18 – are on site every day. Younger age groups from under-11 to -16 train in a hybrid system on Tuesdays, Wednesdays and Thursdays. Two new classrooms, lowered into the complex by a crane, house an expanded performance analysis department. The car park situation, though relieved by space at an adjoining school, is dire.

Middlesbrough can reclaim the modest wages of young professionals, but have one of the lowest youth development budgets in the Premier League. The subtext of its expansion from £2.3 million to a little less than £3 million is that even Gibson and his board will be tempted to demand a reward on inflated investment. That prospect is a more pressing form of accountability than any player audit.

Parnaby is no Luddite. He welcomed the unanimity

of a ninety-two-club meeting at Chester Racecourse late in 2016, which agreed to academy managers undergoing a mandatory two-year foundation-degree course, funded over three years through the Premier League's learning programme. Yet there is a sense he is getting out at the right time:

'I couldn't define the role of an academy manager. It is impossible because it is so diverse. You have to deal with a full spectrum of backgrounds and influences. I know this is the way we are headed, and it was good at last to see the Premier League, Football League and Football Association sing from the same hymn sheet, but does a degree equip you to deal with little Johnny's dad who is shouting from the rooftops?

'Parents are more knowledgeable about their rights, because we have given them so much information down the years. I am always trying to reassure my coaches: "You are professionally trained. You have to be tactful in your response but when they challenge you on what you are delivering you have to be strong enough to stand and say, actually I am an expert in this. I have been professionally trained. You wouldn't go into a classroom and tell a teacher how to teach."

'I've tried to put a salary structure together, to value the lead coach for the under-9s and -10s the same as his equivalent with the -15s and -16s. I'm thinking about the really testing years for development, at thirteen and fourteen, when you've got to deal with puberty, self-esteem, growth maturation. Have we got the know-how, the gut instinct, the eye, the experience within the building to get it right?

'Steve Gibson says football has become a science not an art. He paid me the biggest compliment by telling me, "I do believe you are an artist." That is really nice. That's what I do. Can I define myself, quantify why we have been successful? If you went round the staff I'm not sure what they'd say. I'm pretty good with people, pretty crap with management and structures. Hard work, long hours, enthusiastic staff, a balance, a humility about us.

'All the top, top performers and coaches have that. I spent a day with the All Blacks. They wouldn't let anyone unload their bags from the bus. We talk about mavericks, but they wouldn't suffer them. No dickheads in the dressing room. They haven't got time for high maintenance, because you end up spending eighty per cent on managing that, and only twenty per cent on pushing people along.'

One of the most famous coaching maxims involves being tough on talent. A process more subtle than it is grandstanding or intimidating: it requires a teacher's deftness of touch and a priest's depth of commitment. Parnaby's inspiration, Sir Ken Robinson, speaks of finding your element, a place in which passion can be expressed and explored without restraint or remorse.

Parnaby understands: 'Something happens when I

am around this place, something that feels really good. Does that make sense? It could be when Ben Gibson comes to me and asks what I think. It could be when I'm watching the first team, and Stewie Downing cuts in from the right and smashes it into the top corner with his left, just like he did in the under-17 play-offs, all those years ago.

'I was in my element last week. I had the under-23 leftovers, a couple of first-team players, and some promoted under-18s. I prepared the session, went out, and knew I was in a different place. Something chemically happens in your body at that moment. As Sir Ken says, "You love talent so much you will never work again."

'I ask the kids whether they are in their element and they think I am mad. I tell them they were in their element when they were ten, when they used to get out of Dad's car and run in here. Now they get out of the minibus of a morning and they trudge in with their toilet bag underneath their arm. Another bloody day at Middlesbrough Football Club. I ask them, "Why is that? Is it just your age? Is it where you're at in your life? Or is it us? Are we not providing the stimulus you had at ten years old?"

'As a coach, there are times in the dressing room when you know you have pitched it right. Roy Keane said on the Pro Licence course that Alex Ferguson never failed to press his buttons, either before a game, at half-time or at the end. Even that is getting prescribed. "What is your match-day preparation? What is your match-day plan?" Let me deal with my emotions. Let me deal with the boys' emotions.'

Another of Robinson's notions, that 'life is your talents discovered', filters through the brain as Parnaby sees me to the glass double-doors before saying his farewells. He has the busy man's knack of appearing unhurried, unflustered, and has obviously been at work in my sub conscious. I wound down, after a five-hour drive home, by watching a TEDx talk given by Robinson in his native Liverpool.

A sanguine, meditative figure who leaned on a stick and sketched a stellar cast of characters from the Beatles to the Dalai Lama, the educationalist reached the following conclusion: 'We live in a virtual world, a world of ideas and thoughts and feelings and theories and possibilities. It is about the old maxim that nothing is as powerful as an idea whose time has come, and nothing is as influential as a life well lived.'

Dave Parnaby's football life has been well lived. Don't listen to those who tell you that his time, his ideas, have come, and gone.

19

Tropical Fish in Shark Bay

The abuse consisted largely of mindless mockery, vicious in its tone and consistency. The dominant coach had a tight circle of allies – including support staff, a veteran first-team player and a senior club administrator – who appeared to conspire to varying degrees in the creation of a climate of fear. Contempt was collective, but individuals would endure selective humiliation in front of their peers.

Its effect was cumulative, devastating. One foreign teenager ran away. Another promising player suffered from clinical depression and gave up the game. Good staff, including other academy coaches, did what they could to help, although they felt powerless; a sympathetic video analyst advised yet another victim, a second year scholar to feign homesickness if he could not bring himself to report for training.

The coach had played top-level football when the

money was modest and the fame was local rather than global. He was protected by his status as a trusted servant of a club of great virtue and tradition, but reminded of his perceived ill fortune each time he drove into the training ground in the sort of family saloon used by time-serving double-glazing salesmen.

His high-mileage Vauxhall was conspicuous in a cluster of high-performance four-by-fours. He could show the kids his medals, but their youth and prospective wealth taunted him. He knew he was winding down his career, because he had been demoted from the first team to the role of development coach by a manager who arrived with his own backroom staff.

He came from a generation in which bullying apprentices was standard practice, part of a supposed toughening-up process. He wielded great power over his charges, since he dictated selection policy and influenced the loan programme. His infamous behaviour eventually persuaded the father of one prospect to act. Unlike most parents, he was an educated observer, since he had coached and managed semi-professionally:

'Football celebrates the hairdryer treatment. There's too little debate about the effect of that. Bullying is deeply ingrained in the game. Each case is subtly different, but what happens to a young player if he returns to a lonely room in digs after a day being subjected to aggressive behaviour? I've heard of so many stories from ex-pros suffering from depression, that's an obvious worry.'

He first registered his concerns with the academy manager in March 2016, and escalated them by contacting the head of the club's HR department in May. A member of the safeguarding team, approached in June, failed to follow up on promises to meet his son at home, where he felt safe to speak openly about the toxicity of the situation.

The father's initial letter to the safeguarding officer, which he signed 'sincerely, a very concerned parent', insisted 'we are not trouble makers'. A second amplified his worry that his son would 'fall victim to more prejudice and isolation after daring to stand up and complain'.

He contacted the Professional Footballers' Association, the Football Association and the Independent Football Ombudsman without satisfaction after what he thought was a cursory club investigation.

His son, meanwhile, had escaped an increasingly toxic situation. He was excelling on loan and had no plans to renew his contract, which was due to expire in the summer. His parent club were neglecting to pass on bonuses and appearance money to which he was entitled.

Football's child-protection practices have improved exponentially since the late nineties when a scandal at British Swimming, whose former chief coach Paul Hickson was sentenced to seventeen years' imprisonment for a fifteen-year sequence of attacks on teenaged girls, prompted a far-reaching review.

A change in legislation has shifted responsibility from the FA, as an umbrella body, to individual clubs. Those in the Premier League are 'expected to provide robust and consistent evidence' of their safeguarding provisions for 'vulnerable groups'; reports are collated and sense-checked on a quarterly basis by the NSPCC. Academy staff members are expected to follow a code of ethics and conduct in which relationships are 'based on openness, honesty, trust and respect'.

Yet the process of discovery, in areas other than sexual abuse, is damning. In the words of a highly respected administrator, 'some of the clubs historically kept their academies at arm's length. Now they've lifted up the rock and taken a look, they've been shocked by what's going on beneath.' Mental abuse, where boys are ostracised or shamed into submission, is common.

Younger coaches, in particular, are appalled, but have careers to protect in what remains a hierarchical industry. The vast majority of coaches and academy managers are diligent, socially conscious people who find the process of rejection upsetting, but a malevolent minority act as if they have a vested interest in a boy's sustained failure, since his success would encourage questioning of their wisdom.

One individual, described to me as 'the most hated man in football' by a peer who has known him for more than twenty years, is notorious for using his network of personal contacts to spread malicious gossip about certain players, or parents, in an attempt to prevent other clubs offering a chance of redemption.

The chasm between damaged children and heroic parents, enlightened coaches and hometown despots, must be bridged. Everyone in football talks about 'the journey'. No one has given me a better insight into its complexity, in a human sense, than Simon Edwards, a Harley Street-based behavioural specialist who works in senior football but has tangential experience of academy players through his work at MK Dons:

'We learn right from the word go. In the first year of life we learn to trust. We like consistency and security. Confidence builds because we are used to procedure. Over a lifetime hundreds of billions of little files are absorbed into the subconscious mind. All the way along the line there is unconditional love.

'In telling someone what not to do you are suppressing them. If we are suppressed we really become dependent on others. We can see a footballer becoming dependent on the coach, especially if they come from a non-sporting family, because there is no one to be a filter. If suppressed through criticism or control, we develop a sense of guilt.

'Think of the six-year-old who thinks he is a nuisance because he is being told off all the time. We feel we are getting the worst of those around us. We become followers and allow others to control us. That is very significant. If you have a bully as a father, coach or teacher, who is shouting and screaming, that is not helping at all.

'All kids really want to do is celebrate, jiggle and do their silly little dance by the corner flag. But between the age of six and puberty, a phase known as "industry and inferiority", that person is developing a sense of pride in their achievements, not necessarily from the ambitions of others for them. We start to dig deep. We start thinking of winning, not just being picked.

'If children are encouraged, they are more industrious, confidence builds. If discouraged, inferiority creeps in, and they doubt their ability. They only hear the negative. It is hard to move on. They are tropical fish in shark bay, vulnerable because they are just pleasing people. They are independent only if they are allowed to be so.

'We expect boys to be strong, but they might not be. One of the things that shocked me about footballers was some of them are tiny, smaller than you ever imagined. We know about the physiology because we can see it and measure it. Emotional intelligence, who knows? I look to measure what people want to do for themselves, not what they want to do for everyone else.

'The importance of being successful for somebody else is bigger than we think. That doesn't have to be a parent; it could be the coach, the gaffer, the crowd. Football has an intimacy that most young people wouldn't experience, but what you can't do is talk about your inner feelings. Everyone knows it is a transitory, superficial world. There may be camaraderie but there is no loyalty. You are blooded along the way, in a negative way.

'Bullying is everywhere in modern life. There are some fantastic people in football, but if coaches were in a legal firm in the city, or a regional supermarket manager, they wouldn't be able to say those things to their employees, or each other. Everyone in football has the caveat, "Well, it has always been like that." It's the dinosaur effect: "I was treated like that, so I am going to treat you like that."

'A youth coach is theoretically in a more responsible position than the first-team manager because you are preparing people for what's next. Is it living the dream, the ridiculous expectation that the young player is someday going to play for Real Madrid? Anticipatory feelings are very powerful. In therapy the most powerful negative is, what if?

'There is no reality in football because there is randomness going on. How can you promise someone it is going to be OK, that they are not going to have a terrible knee injury, or another misfortune? Those who speak negatively without offering encouragement will say, "We are showing them the real world." Well, you wouldn't send your children to a war zone or a ghetto. You wouldn't allow a five-year-old to play with scissors.

'An adolescent wants an identity. Yet in that phase of their lives, footballers are either being told they are rubbish, or amazing. That is not healthy. There is no consistency. They're all over the place emotionally. That's why you get lots of loners in groups. There are no real friendships because football is one-dimensional and ultra-competitive.

'They are the meat in the sandwich between over-the-top parents who are convinced their sons will be soon earning £50k a week and coaches who are saying, "Just listen to me because I am three times older than you." That is stunting because they are not being allowed to grow organically. Who are they? They don't really know. They've had part of their emotional growth taken away.

'What are their reference points? How are they developing as people? They are not. They are commodities either for the parents, the coach, or whoever has a commercial interest in them. Their emotional needs are probably enormous. Anyone close to them, parent, coach, agent or medical staff, has to be true and honest because that person is wide-eyed and believing.'

Innocence is a liability, a luxury when even captains of the football industry admit the view from the bridge is unedifying. One confided that he had no wish to expose his children to such a compromising environment. Poaching of young players is most prevalent in the delicate, academically sensitive phase in which scholarships are offered. The Premier League confirm they are dealing with 'ongoing reports and complaints involving multiple clubs and multiple players'.

Expedience – which prompted club chairmen to reach a so-called 'gentlemen's agreement', leading to an amnesty on poaching offences before the introduction of the Premier League's Five Step Process for transfers between Category One academies – remains a dominant factor. Several clubs in London and the North-west have come to an informal, mutually beneficial arrangement, in which they have pledged not to recruit from their respective academies.

The Five Step Process reinforces Premier League rule 299.1, which prohibits clubs from inducing, or attempting to induce, a player to join their academy by offering incentives of any type, whether in cash or in kind. Private investigators employed by the league have the power to seize phone records and bank statements from parents, or boys, in the search for illicit activity.

The process begins with a young player's new club submitting a signed registration form to the league, as usual. Exit interviews are conducted with the player, his parents, and both clubs involved in the transfer. Clubs and parents are required to sign a declaration that no financial or value-in-kind inducements, including contra deals, have been employed. A written assessment, together with recommendations, is presented to the Premier League board, which has the power to refer the case for review by an independent commission.

A Premier League executive acknowledged: 'This is going to take a bit of time, because you are shining a light on individuals, and a certain way of doing things. It would be naïve to think there are not a range of issues at play. The clubs, as a collective, all have their stories that "This boy was taken from us." But nobody was making any complaints, and nobody was saying, "Please hold this club to account."

'It all depends on what foot the shoe is on. Getting the Category One clubs to say, "We want to do something," is a big first step. Does it mean these murky practices will be eradicated overnight? Of course not. It is cops and robbers. You have to have the willingness of people who engage in what is a micro-society to say, "Actually we want to live under a different set of rules, and we want to abide by those rules."'

Good luck with that. Clubs and agents, concerned by the prospect of paying compensatory sums in excess of £1 million for sanctioned transfers between Category One academies, are already investigating the political and financial practicality of what could best be described as a 'foster club' scheme.

It demands the complicity of a young player's family, since, in theory, after being tempted away from his original academy, a boy would be housed, most probably for a season but maybe two, in a low-key league like Serie B before being signed by his original, secretive suitor in the Premier League. The pre arranged fee for that transfer would be moderate (£200,000 has been mentioned as being suitable for a recycled 18-year-old) and sweetened by the loan of further players to the foster club.

Club owners tend to speak about the iniquities of agents in splenetic terms, without appearing to draw breath, but many impulsively feed the multi-headed monster that threatens to devour them. There is widespread distaste for commercial activity around children, especially with the intrusiveness of the recruitment process, but punishments do not appear to fit the crime.

Danny Webber, who retired in June 2016 after a sixteen-year playing career that began at Manchester United, is developing a media career alongside his work for the Platinum One agency. He denied breaching FA Rule E1(b) by approaching a player 'in relation to intermediary activity before the 1st day in January of the year of that Player's sixteenth birthday', on November 17, 2016, and requested a personal hearing, at which he was found guilty on December 13. Webber was fined £1,000 and immediately banned 'from all intermediary activity' for twenty-eight days; the other fifty-six days of the sanction were suspended. The reputational damage, even for someone in the public eye, was relatively limited and the financial penalty was insubstantial.

Two more agents were disciplined for similar offences at around that time. Glen Tweneboah, found to have entered into a contract with a minor despite not being authorised to do so, was suspended for three months from November 18. Former Arsenal and Watford midfield player Paolo Vernazza was found guilty on December 4 of attempting to enter into a contract with two minors, despite not being cleared to work with children under the age of 18. His six-month suspension and £2,500 fine reflected the fact that one of the contracts had not been signed by the boy's parent or guardian.

Vernazza, who won two England under-21 caps, is Head of Football, UK, for the Platinum One Group, which bills itself as 'Britain's No. 1 Agency for Young Footballers'. His appeal was heard at Wembley Stadium on December 29 by a three-man panel led by Christopher Quinlan, QC. He argued that his errors were administrative in nature and stressed he retained the support of both boys' parents. However, his complaints about the severity of his punishment were dismissed. The episode received minimal publicity, despite written reasons for the decision being published on the FA website and the fact that one of the boys involved, Yosin Farah, is the cousin of multiple Olympic champion Sir Mo Farah. In a broader sense, such punishments pose few long-term problems to the transgressor, if any. A more substantial fine and a minimum of a year's suspension would have infinitely greater impact, especially if it were linked to a programme of re-education, most appropriately in a community coaching setting.

The football bubble is more of a shroud, since it is rarely transparent. Unanimity is even elusive when it comes to the deregulation of agents, a classic case of administrators abrogating their wider responsibilities to the game. When poachers and gamekeepers share the same world-weary caution there is little reason for optimism.

The Premier League executive is bleakly realistic: 'The activity of agents has been the big question facing football at many levels over a number of years. When they were regulated to within an inch of life, people thought, "Christ, that has sent everything under the table. Let's change to light-touch legislation so we can see what is going on."

'It is still an area of concern. Things are happening that shouldn't be happening, but how you stop them is a very difficult, very thorny issue. There is, at least, a mood that enough is enough. Will that effect a cultural shift? We will have to wait and see.'

The principal of a major agency, who claimed he had disciplined a junior member of staff who had contacted a 13-year-old player on Facebook, asking for his father's contact details, is more sanguine about the surge of newcomers to his profession, since he believes 'they are completely out of their depth'. He is, however, less confident of the black economy being broken:

'The system is as bad as it has been for years, but I don't think it has ever been right. Clubs were paying parents in the seventies. I can remember a captain of the England schoolboys' team getting £100k to sign around twenty years ago. No one questioned it, because everyone knew that was the sort of thing that happened. I can't see that changing. Relatives of players are getting involved in negotiations and they haven't got a clue.'

A League Two manager like Crawley Town's Dermot Drummy, a mediating force, understands both arguments: 'Loads of great work goes on in academies, getting the boys there, giving them food. People like Roy Massey and Steve Leonard at Arsenal have spent twenty years running up and down Camden Road, picking them up when their parents are at work. Neil Bath at Chelsea has a holistic care programme that helps lads on their way.

'When someone gets released at seventeen, eighteen, people tend to shut the door. Agents stop giving them a bell. They've had all these piranhas around them since they were fourteen. Money has always changed hands with parents, and I don't think it will ever stop. It is hard, on the breadline, to turn it down. There is money, but there is also failure. The player is not a commodity, but a person.'

Self-interest has been institutionalised by the Premier League's youth strategy, the Elite Player Performance Plan. Nearly £400 million has been invested over its first four years, a sum that will double by 2020. It represents a spectacular piece of empire-building by Ged Roddy, who has been promoted from his initial position, as the league's head of youth, to an overarching job as head of football development.

He has been a polarising figure since I first knew him in 2002, as a board member of the English Institute of Sport. He was obviously politically astute, but I found him glib and superficial. An interview, requested for this book, did not materialise, but officials argue that, although 'there will be bumps in the road', EPPP can only be judged fairly over a decade. In the words of one executive: 'No one says it is perfect. The idea is that it changes and develops. This is the most interventionist thing we have done. We are trying to effect an overall cultural shift and it will take time.'

Roddy suggested the rebranded Premier League 2, for under-23 teams, would make an 'immediate impact' when it was unveiled in July 2016; he was prescient, but perhaps not as he intended. It has been dismissed as 'crap' by Nicky Butt, director of Manchester United's academy, and 'a waste of time' by Gareth Southgate, the England manager.

The league plan to 'increase jeopardy' by promoting it more extensively on television, but the majority of matches are stripped of passion and pressure. Technical quality has undoubtedly improved, but tactical orthodoxy leaves most players with the improvisational instincts of the zombies amassing outside the pub in the film *Shaun of the Dead*. The top six clubs, increasingly operating in concert as a lobbying group, have been critical of several initiatives.

Despite the relationship between Richard Scudamore,

the Premier League's chief executive, and Dan Ashworth, the Football Association's technical director, being cordial and founded on mutual respect, football's version of the San Andreas Fault still runs from the league's powerbase in Gloucester Place, central London, to St George's Park, hub of a newly focused FA performance team.

There are positive, forward-thinking people within each organisation, but English football is defined by its predilection for trench warfare. It lacks a single, dominant body motivated solely by the good of the game. Each faction has a separate agenda, and the concentration on making money carries the danger of deflection from fundamental issues, such as a salary cap for young players and the overstocking of the system.

The next power shift is likely to involve coach education. Influential clubs are unhappy about the quality of the FA's work in this area, and there are wider concerns about the cost and availability of coaching courses. Under Roddy, the Premier League are close to setting up a mirror-image operation by offering 'Leadership Journey' coaching workshops and setting a so-called Coach Competency Framework.

Though his insistence that graduates 'will take the game to a whole new level' is hyperbolic, Roddy's pet project, the Elite Coach Apprenticeship Scheme, has much to commend it. An intensive two-year programme, broadened in 2015 to include six female and black, Asian and minority ethnic (BAME) coaches in each intake, it is similar to other schemes operated by UK Sport. Mentors are provided from business and other sports.

The initiative seeks to impart 'experiential learning' from such activities as cycling, dance and swimming. The performance principles of the Royal Shakespeare Company, which include advice on how to command an audience, are complemented by that traditional corporate gesture, an outward-bound course in the Brecon Beacons overseen by former members of the special forces.

Roddy retains Scudamore's support and, speaking in the more sanitised setting of the league's website, he felt confident enough to pronounce on the system's robustness: 'Do I think players are soft in this system? No way. These players are trying to create a career for themselves in the hardest league in the world. It's self-evident that our players have got to be among the best players in the world if they're going to play in it.

'We have got more talent pouring into the league than anywhere else on the planet. We had 67 debuts last year. The pipeline is still there. When we started out people would say there was no English talent, but now people say there is English talent but it needs an opportunity. That is a seismic shift from where we were only four seasons ago.'

For all its froth, the youth system magnifies the faults of the senior game, since the biggest clubs are using their economic and political power to amass huge stocks of promising players from the UK and further afield.

The resentment generated by such acquisitiveness was summarised by the tart observation of Karl-Heinz Rummenigge, chairman of Bayern Munich's executive board: 'We don't want to bring some ten- or eleven-year-old to Munich like the English do. You can almost speak of kidnapping with them and I would have moral reservations about that.'

Clubs like Chelsea and Manchester City produce outstanding under-18 teams, but there is no correlation between their potency and the pathway to the first team. Neil Bath, Chelsea's widely respected academy director, speaks of players 'crossing the road' into senior football when a more accurate analogy would involve crawling across an ice ladder, strung across a deadly deep crevasse in a Himalayan glacier field.

Some aspects of development, such as the seasonal disparity that leads to 73 per cent of academy players being born in the first half of the school year, are more easily addressed by bio-banding initiatives of the type led by Southampton. Minds have been concentrated by a study of 293 academy players at Manchester United, using skeletal development as a key criterion; late physical developers were twenty times less likely to be given a scholarship at 16. The bigger dilemma, captured by the presence of only one English player, Marcus Rashford, among the 100 most-used under twenties in Europe's leading leagues, can only be solved by a fundamental change in thinking.

Stockpiling forty or fifty players in an age group is insidious, since it inspires other clubs, like Manchester United, to embark on a frantic recruitment drive to equalise a competitive imbalance. Not for the first time, I find myself agreeing with Arsène Wenger: 'The whole system has to be questioned,' he told the *Guardian*'s Amy Lawrence. 'They organised a system where the best players finish at the biggest clubs. But they do not always have the best chance to play at the biggest clubs.'

Far-reaching debate is overdue because, as the powerful prevaricate, children are being compressed by parental pressure and coaches who mistrust freedom of expression. Wenger is concerned by the prevailing academy culture of isolation and intensity, and believes 'the longer you live a normal life the better'. Like the FA's Nick Levett, he worries about the wilful marginalisation of paediatricians who insist children should not specialise in a single sport until they are at least 15.

The mood of sober reflection generated by the sexual abuse scandal invites a reappraisal. In my view, no boy or girl should have a competitive affiliation with an academy until they are 14; a variation of Dave Parnaby's pioneering idea of a coaching registration, linking a young player to a particular club, could be introduced at the age of 11. The race to the bottom, in which 4-year-olds are being assessed, must cease.

Youth football is a parallel universe, and I often find myself recalling a meditative comment by Manchester

City's Grant Downie: 'I wish someone could invent a pair of glasses so that I could look through the eyes of a ten- or eleven-year-old, and the world changes.' Remove the contact lenses of adulthood, and it becomes clear children need room to breathe, to laugh, to love, to play on their own terms.

For all the talk about elitist exclusivity, the youth system is bloated, intoxicated by its wealth, and haphazard. Quotas are extremely difficult to enforce, but no club should be allowed to register more than twelve players in a year group; the obvious competitive issue, of fielding a team with sufficient numbers and diversity, could be tackled by merging age groups.

It is hard to envisage a weakening in resistance to the idea of lower-league feeder clubs, though my suspicion is that this will happen subtly, through the evolution and manipulation of the loan system. Manchester City's strategic link with NAC Breda, informed by Chelsea's pioneering partnership with Vitesse Arnhem, is a glimpse into a future shaped by Premier League paternalism and opportunism. Manchester United, monitoring potential feeder clubs in Belgium, the Netherlands and Portugal, are following their example.

It is too easy, amidst the fence-sitting and agenda-setting, to miss the point that football undervalues its basic ingredient. Although the phrase smacks of complacency and superficiality, it is a people business. Clubs and organisations are dependent on individuals, who form their molecular structure. I found good and bad working alongside each other; some clubs are casually demonised, because of jealousy generated by lavishly financed success, but others with considerably fewer scruples and infinitely less professionalism avoid censure.

Gareth Southgate understands that premature wealth complicates his search for humility in the young players he hopes to fashion as full internationals. That has a more serious connotation than throwaway lines about football's washbag culture, which surely reached its zenith when an alert cameraman spotted that the washbag of Georges-Kevin Nkoudou, Tottenham's £11 million summer signing from Marseille, was emblazoned with an image of his smiling face.

Despite the prudence of such clubs as Tottenham, Southampton and Liverpool, reward is too instant, too simple. Reputations are made and inflated even as hormones kick in and sycophants attach their suckers. It leads inevitably to tales that seep out from Mayfair nightclubs, in which players are buying £3,000 bottles of vodka, or standing £5,000 rounds, before their twenty-first birthday.

In such circumstances, the sport needs leaders of greater distinction than Gordon Taylor, the PFA chairman, who has given little external indication of justifying his 2015 pay increase, from £1.13 million a year to £3.37 million. He may promote worthwhile causes, and generate favourable headlines in a concussion-conscious age by suggesting the FA should consider banning players under 10 from heading the ball, but his organisation gives the impression of being loosely focused.

Although the principle of a salary cap is anathema to a trade union, the PFA's proactive support of reasonable limitation of a young player's initial earnings, linked to a structured trust fund, would signal overdue recognition of the greater good. The identity of prospective allies might surprise them, because Mark Allen, Manchester City's academy director, would welcome such a lead:

'We should be going down that road, without a shadow of a doubt. We've always said we'd love to be able to put in a player's contract, something like, "Your car limit is X." But we can't, by law. There is an exceptional circumstance around this industry, because at the moment, thankfully, the Premier League is the most global league in the world. The revenue it brings into not just Manchester City, but all the clubs, has a great effect on the economy. We do have a responsibility, but we need some legislative power to help fulfil that.'

Expecting the Premier League to stop flexing its financial muscle is as unrealistic as expecting a heavyweight champion boxer to pull a punch. The decision to ring-fence their funding of a head of coaching in all ninety-two clubs is, however, a portent of further opportunity. Instead of concentrating on academic minutiae, EPPP should service a centrally funded minimum wage for every full-time academy coach; an annual salary of £35,000 would incentivise those on half that who currently struggle to see a viable career pathway.

Think the unthinkable. Colchester United owner Robbie Cowling, a noted advocate of sensibly budgeted youth schemes who annually puts £3.5 million of his money where his mouth is, believes that the EPPP compensation system should be enhanced by a 5 per cent salary levy, imposed on Premier League clubs and recycled to those that originally developed their players.

Equally, there is nothing to stop the Premier League underpinning pastoral progress, beyond traditional community schemes; it might even reinforce a brand that already has access to 900 million homes in 229 'territories' around the world. Opportunity is hiding in plain sight; officials should revisit their reluctance to fund the Players' Trust, an independent organisation which judges its impact not on florid PR campaigns but on sound advice to confused parents and their vulnerable children. The Trust is gathering significant political support and is meeting a clearly defined need. An allocation, drawn from the £19 million the Premier League gives the PFA to find and facilitate benevolent support, would allow the new organisation to flourish.

Scudamore refers to virtual reality technology 'playing a huge part in the future exploitation of the Premier League', and yet the real thing is no less alluring. A price cannot be placed on the joyful discovery of a grassroots coach like Tony McCool, who, on a cold winter's night, recognised 'incredible' potential in a 13-year-old orphan refugee who had not played football three months previously.

In that sense, it was fitting my journey should end where it began, at the Brixton Recreation Centre. This is the place where magic can still happen. Zion Dixon, aged 12, was saying his farewells. He had signed for Derby County and his mother had resolved to build a better life, in a village setting far removed from the urban tension of south London. Ezra Tika-Lemba had grown three inches in a year and was excelling at Chelsea. Rinsola Babajide had joined Watford, and was preparing to represent England in the annual La Manga tournament.

Vontae Daley-Campbell was assuring his tearful mother, Anna Marie, that he would be able to cope when he moved away from home for the first time, to take up his scholarship at Arsenal, who had placed him in digs with two other top prospects. 'Are you really ready for this?' she asked. 'Yes, Mum. I am, because I am going to change your life.'

Nathan Mavila's football career might have turned full circle when he re-signed for Wealdstone following a brief flirtation with Soham Town Rangers, but his life is only just taking shape. He won the sports category in the Young Black Achievement awards, set up to counter negative stereotypes, to endorse a misrepresented community, and to generate hope through the portrayal of inspirational individuals.

His friend Leo Chambers could be found in the gym, pushing himself through three sessions a day with an easy disposition, to finally confirm his fitness. He had risen to the challenge of fatherhood; Millwall and Charlton Athletic were vying for his signature, but he was tempted by alternative offers to play in Europe.

Younger boys were wide-eyed when Josh Bohui returned to coach them after scoring for Manchester United in the semi-final and final of the Sparkasse & VGH Cup, a four-day, five-a-side under-19 tournament in Germany. They had seen, on their social networks, a seductive photograph of him stooping slightly to pose beside a tall, slender silver trophy. It was posted by his former school, the Evelyn Grace Academy, where the outreach work of Jay Jay Lodge continued.

Josh was a role model, a symbol of unfeasible possibility. To him, Steadman Scott was something more precious, a second father. A proud man, Scott had endured a difficult couple of months, during which his lack of mobility prevented his coaching. But the fire had been rekindled in those piercing eyes. Still the boys came in from the street. His ritual greeting, in that low lilt, was constant, as valuable now as it will ever be:

'What's your dream, son?'

Index